TOP FEDERAL TAX ISSUES FOR 2010
CPE COURSE

CCH Editorial Staff Publication

Contributors

Technical Reviewer.. George G. Jones, J.D., LL.M
Contributing Editors.. Torie D. Cole, J.D.
Hilary Goehausen, J.D.
Brant Goldwyn, J.D.
Sherri Morris, J.D, LL.M
George L. Yaksick, Jr., J.D.
Production Coordinator .... Gabriel E. Santana
Design/Layout...Laila Gaidulis
Production ....Lynn J. Brown

This publication is designed to provide accurate and authoritative information in regard to the subject matter covered. It is sold with the understanding that the publisher is not engaged in rendering legal, accounting, or other professional service. If legal advice or other expert assistance is required, the services of a competent professional person should be sought.

ISBN 978-0-8080-2162-9

© 2009, CCH INCORPORATED
4025 W. Peterson Ave.
Chicago, IL 60646-6085
1 800 248 3248
www.CCHGroup.com

TOP FEDERAL TAX ISSUES FOR 2010 CPE COURSE

Introduction

Each year, a handful of tax issues typically requires special attention by tax practitioners. The reasons vary, from a particularly complicated new provision in the Internal Revenue Code, to a planning technique opened up by a new regulation or ruling, or the availability of a significant tax benefit with a short window of opportunity. Sometimes a developing business need creates a new set of tax problems, or pressure exerted by Congress or the Administration puts more heat on some taxpayers while giving others more slack. All these share in creating a unique mix that in turn creates special opportunities and pitfalls in the coming year. The past year has seen more than its share of these developments.

CCH's *Top Federal Tax Issues for 2010 CPE Course* identifies the events of the past year that have developed into "hot" issues. These tax issues have been selected as particularly relevant to tax practice in 2010. They have been selected not only because of their impact on return preparation during the 2009 tax season but also because of the important role they play in developing effective tax strategies for 2010. Some issues are outgrowths of several years of developments; others have burst onto the tax scene unexpectedly. Among the latter are issues directly related to the recent economic downturn. Some have been emphasized in IRS publications and notices; others are too new or too controversial to be noted by the IRS either in depth or at all.

This course is designed to help reassure the tax practitioner that he or she is not missing out on advising clients about a hot, new tax opportunity or is not susceptible to being blindsided by a brewing controversy. In short, it is designed to give the tax practitioner a closer look into the opportunities and pitfalls presented by the changes. Among the topics examined in the *Top Federal Tax Issues for 2010 CPE Course* are:

- Tax Relief and Incentives for Individuals
- Tax Relief and Incentives for Businesses
- Preparer Restrictions and Other New Taxpayer Privacy Issues
- Working with Tax Losses
- Cancellation of Indebtedness Income: Rules and Exclusions
- Innocent Spouse Tax Issues
- Same-Sex Marriage/Domestic Partner Tax Issues
- Rebuilding Retirement Savings: Tax Strategies

Throughout the course you will find Study Questions to help you test your knowledge, and comments that are vital to understanding a particular strategy or idea. Answers to the Study Questions with feedback on both correct and incorrect responses are provided in a special section beginning on page 9.1.

To assist you in your later reference and research, a detailed topical index has been included for this course beginning on page 10.1.

This course is divided into three Modules. Take your time and review all course Modules. When you feel confident that you thoroughly understand the material, turn to the CPE Quizzer. Complete one, or all, Module Quizzers for continuing professional education credit. Further information is provided in the CPE Quizzer instructions on page 11.1.

October 2009

v

COURSE OBJECTIVES

This course was prepared to provide the participant with an overview of specific tax issues that impact 2009 tax return preparation and tax planning in 2010. These are the issues that "everyone is talking about;" each impacts a significant number of taxpayers in significant ways.

Upon course completion, you will be able to:

- Determine who gets the Making Work Pay Credit and how it is paid out through employer withholding;
- List the requirements for expanded net operating loss (NOL) carrybacks;
- Prepare a written and electronic use or disclosure consent that satisfies the requirements of the tax code and Treasury regulations;
- Explain when and how a deduction may be claimed from passive activities;
- Apply the deferral of income to the reacquisition of business debt;
- List the kinds of innocent spouse relief and their specific requirements;
- Identify ways that transfers of property between same-sex married people or domestic partners may create additional tax liability or tax savings; and
- Compare and contrast different retirement planning vehicles and their tax advantages.

CCH'S PLEDGE TO QUALITY

Thank you for choosing this CCH Continuing Education product. We will continue to produce high quality products that challenge your intellect and give you the best option for your Continuing Education requirements. Should you have a concern about this or any other CCH CPE product, please call our Customer Service Department at 1-800-248-3248.

NEW ONLINE GRADING gives you immediate 24/7 grading with instant results and no Express Grading Fee.

The **CCH Testing Center** website gives you and others in your firm easy, free access to CCH print courses and allows you to complete your CPE exams online for immediate results. Plus, the **My Courses** feature provides convenient storage for your CPE course certificates and completed exams.

Go to **www.cchtestingcenter.com** to complete your exam online.

One **complimentary copy** of this course is provided with certain CCH Federal Taxation publications. Additional copies of this course may be ordered for $33.00 each by calling 1-800-248-3248 (ask for product 0-0977-200).

TOP FEDERAL TAX ISSUES FOR 2010 CPE COURSE

Contents

5 Cancellation of Indebtedness Income: Rules and Exclusions

MODULE 3: NEW CHALLENGES FOR INDIVIDUALS

6 Innocent Spouse Tax Issues

7 Same-Sex Marriage/Domestic Partner Tax Issues

8 Rebuilding Retirement Savings: Tax Strategies1

MODULE 1: NEW LAWS/RULES — CHAPTER 1

Tax Relief and Incentives for Individuals

This chapter explores the many individual tax incentives in the *American Recovery and Reinvestment Act of 2009* (2009 Recovery Act). Congress passed, and President Obama signed, the massive 2009 Recovery Act in February 2009 to help jump start the U.S. economy out of recession. The 2009 Recovery Act provides tax breaks to working individuals, homeowners, new car and truck buyers, unemployed individuals, and other Americans.

LEARNING OBJECTIVES

Upon completion of this course, you will be able to:
- Identify recent tax acts passed by Congress;
- Describe the making work pay credit;
- Compare the 2008 and 2009 first-time homebuyer credits;
- Compute the temporary motor vehicle sales tax deduction;
- List the requirements of COBRA premium assistance;
- Describe enhancements to the health coverage tax credit;
- Identify energy tax incentives targeted to individuals;
- Explain the temporary suspension of required minimum distributions from retirement accounts; and
- Describe the CARS Act rules for trade-in autos and trucks and which types of vehicles qualify for new-vehicle vouchers.

INTRODUCTION

As the U.S. economy fell deeper into recession in early 2009, the new Obama Administration and Congress looked to the tax code to stimulate economic growth. The 2009 Recovery Act includes significant tax incentives to encourage consumer spending, especially in the areas of housing and transportation. Additionally, many wage earners have seen an increase in their take-home pay because of the making work pay credit (MWPC), one of the incentives in the 2009 Recovery Act. Like many recent tax laws, the incentives in the 2009 Recovery Act are temporary. Some, such as the MWPC, are new; others are extensions of previous tax breaks. Congress also imposed important income limitations on many of the incentives.

Three other recent acts offer relief to individuals. The *Worker, Retiree, and Employer Recovery Act of 2009* (WRERA) suspended required minimum distributions. Also, under "Michelle's Law," covered dependents who are full-time students and are at least 18 years old may maintain their parent's health insurance while the students take a medically necessary leave of absence from school. Finally, Congress also enacted a "cash-for-clunkers" law to encourage consumers to purchase new and more environmentally-friendly vehicles. As the economy starts to rebound, lawmakers must decide whether to extend these and other incentives.

AMERICAN RECOVERY AND REINVESTMENT ACT OF 2009

Making Work Pay Credit

The MWPC is the centerpiece of the tax title in the 2009 Recovery Act. The credit, which is targeted to lower- and middle-income taxpayers, is technically claimed by taxpayers when they file their 2009 (and 2010) returns. However, Congress wanted to accelerate the credit, so it is being delivered in small increments through reduced payroll withholding in 2009 and 2010. Like many other tax breaks, the MWPC is temporary and will expire after 2010 unless Congress extends it.

The MWPC is equal to the lesser of:

- 6.2 percent of the taxpayer's earned income; or
- $400 ($800 for married couples filing joint returns).

> **EXAMPLE**
>
> Nicole earns $56,000 a year at her job. She claims one withholding allowance and is paid weekly. The making work pay credit will generate approximately $10 more in Nicole's paycheck (or $400 based on a 40-week payout in 2009).

> **PLANNING POINTER**
>
> The MWPC is reduced by the amount of any economic recovery payment or government retiree credit (discussed later).

> **COMMENT**
>
> The $800 cap for married couples filing jointly applies whether or not both spouses have earned income for the year.

Income limitations. Higher-income individuals are generally ineligible for the credit. The MWPC is reduced (but not below zero) by 2 percent of a single individual's modified adjusted gross income (AGI) that exceeds $75,000. For married couples filing jointly, the threshold amount is $150,000. The MWPC phases out completely at modified AGI of

$95,000 for single individuals and at modified AGI of $190,000 for married couples filing jointly.

Earned income. The MWPC is limited to taxpayers who have earned income. Generally this means taxable compensation from employment, such as wages, salaries, and tips. Earned income does *not* include:
- Most nontaxable compensation;
- Amounts received as pension or annuity payments;
- Nonresident aliens' income that is not connected with U.S. businesses;
- Amounts earned for services provided by inmates at penal institutions; and
- Workfare payments that are subsidized under a state workfare program (such as Temporary Assistance for Needy Families (TANF)).

Net earnings from self-employment are considered earned income. However, earned income does not include net earnings from self-employment that are not taken into account in computing taxable income, such as an excludable parsonage allowance. Combat zone compensation, however, is counted.

The IRS issued revised withholding tables to reflect the MWPC in early 2009. The IRS instructed employers to start using the revised withholding tables no later than April 1, 2009.

COMMENT

The MWPC effectively eliminates the 6.2-percent employee share of Social Security tax on about the first $6,450 of a single worker's wages.

Eligible individuals. All individuals with earned income are eligible for the credit, except:
- Nonresident aliens;
- Individuals who can be claimed as another taxpayer's dependent for a tax year beginning in the calendar year in which the individual's tax year begins;
- Estates and trusts; or
- Taxpayers without valid Social Security numbers (SSNs) (or, on a joint return, an SSN for at least one of the spouses).

CAUTION

An individual cannot substitute an IRS-issued taxpayer identification number (TIN) for a valid SSN.

Special concerns. The MWPC may be problematic for individuals who have more than one job, because both employers will reduce withholding. Married taxpayers whose combined income places them in a higher tax bracket may also be negatively affected. Taxpayers in these situations may want to file a new Form W-4, *Employee's Withholding Allowance Certificate*, to adjust their withholding. Failure to adjust withholding could result in smaller refunds or may cause taxpayers to owe tax when they file their 2009 returns in 2010.

> **PLANNING POINTER**
>
> Employers are not required to determine an employee's eligibility for the MWPC.

> **EXAMPLE**
>
> Joshua earns $51,000 a year at his first job, claims one withholding allowance, and is paid weekly. The MWPC will generate approximately $10 more per paycheck (or $400 based on a 40-week payout in 2009) for his first job. Joshua earns $20,000 a year at his second job, claims one withholding allowance, and is paid weekly. The MWPC as reflected in the revised wage withholding tables will generate approximately $9 more per week in take-home pay for his second job (or $360 based on a 40-week payout in 2009). His total withholding of $760 will exceed the $400 maximum credit. James may want to adjust withholding at one employer.

> **EXAMPLE**
>
> Adam and Anne are married. Adam earns $44,000 a year, claims four withholding allowances, and is paid weekly. The MWPC will generate approximately $15 more per pay period for Adam. Anne earns $48,000 a year, claims four withholding allowances and is paid weekly. The MWPC credit will generate approximately $16 more per pay period for Anne. If Adam and Anne's modified AGI allows them to be eligible for the credit when they file their 2009 return, their credit would exceed the $800 maximum for married couples filing jointly based on a 40-week payout in 2009. Adam and Anne may want to adjust their withholding through their respective employers.

Pensioners. Pension payments are not considered earned income for purposes of the MWPC. Consequently, a pensioner having no earned income is ineligible for the credit and may not have enough tax withheld from his or her pension payment under the revised 2009 withholding tables. In

response, the IRS will allow plans to calculate optional additional withholding amounts for pension payments.

> ### COMMENT
>
> The income tax withholding method is optional. Pension plans do not have
> to use it; they may continue to use the revised withholding table.

Schedule M. The IRS has designed new Schedule M (Form 1040A or
1040), *Making Work Pay and Government Retiree Credits,* on its website.
Schedule M will be filed with taxpayers' 2009 Form 1040A or 1040.

Schedule M asks taxpayers to identify whether they have 2009 wages of more
than $6,451 ($12,903 if the taxpayer is married and filing a joint return). If the
individual/married couple meets these thresholds, the taxpayer is directed to
enter $400 ($800 if married filing jointly) on Schedule M. If not, the taxpayer
should enter his or her earned income in accordance with the instructions. Draft
Schedule M also applies the income phaseouts for the MWPC.

Economic recovery payments. In 2009, Social Security Administration,
Department of Veterans Affairs, and Railroad Retirement Board distributed
one-time economic recovery payments of $250 to qualified individuals.
Although the payments are not considered taxable income, the MWPC
must be reduced by the amount of any economic recovery payment individuals received.

Government retiree credit. Certain government retirees can claim a refundable $250 tax credit. The credit increases to $500 on a joint return
if both spouses are eligible. The government retiree must receive some
pension or annuity for service performed in the employ of the United
States or any state, or any instrumentality thereof, that is not considered
employment for purposes of the *Federal Insurance Contributions Act* (FICA)
tax. Government retirees will claim the credit when they file their 2009
(and 2010) returns.

The government retiree credit is coordinated with the MWPC. Taxpayers
who qualify for both must reduce the amount of their MWPC by the amount
of their government retiree credit.

First-Time Homebuyer Credit

The first-time homebuyer credit was originally enacted in 2008. Congress
extended and enhanced the credit in the 2009 Recovery Act. The enhanced
credit reaches 10 percent of the purchase price, with a cap of $8,000 ($4,000
for married couples filing separate returns). The $8,000 credit is available for
qualified home purchased after February 16, 2009, and before December

1, 2009. Eligibility for the first-time homebuyer credit is determined on the date of purchase.

> **CAUTION**
>
> The enhancements in the 2009 Recovery Act do not affect first-time homebuyers who purchased homes after April 8, 2008, and on or before December 31, 2008. For these taxpayers, the maximum credit remains $7,500 ($3,750 for married couples filing separately). Additionally, the credit for 2008 purchases generally must be repaid in equal installments over 15 years. For purchases in 2009 that take place before February 17, 2009, the credit is limited to $7,500 but the repayment rule does not apply.

Income limitations. Eligibility for the first-time homebuyer credit is restricted by income. The credit is subject to modified AGI phaseout ranging from $75,000 to $95,000 ($150,000 to $170,000 for joint filers) based on the tax-year return on which the credit is being claimed.

Claiming the credit. Shortly after Congress enhanced the credit, the IRS announced that individuals who qualify for the first-time homebuyer credit and purchase a home after December 31, 2008, and before December 1, 2009, may claim the credit on their 2008 or 2009 tax returns (IR-2009-14). The first-time homebuyer credit is claimed on Form 5405, *First-Time Homebuyer Credit*. Form 5405 is available on the IRS's website, **www.irs.gov.**

> **PLANNING POINTER**
>
> Taxpayers who filed a 2008 return and did not claim the credit for a 2009 purchase on the 2008 return should file Form 1040X with a completed and revised Form 5405. For taxpayers who have already filed Form 5405 for a 2009 purchase that claimed a $7,500 amount (either because the return was filed before the 2009 Recovery Act was enacted or because the taxpayer assumed that only a $7,500 credit could be claimed), an amended return Form 1040X for 2008 should be filed, along with another Form 5405, on which the taxpayer checks the box on Part I, line C to claim the additional $500 credit for homes purchased in 2009.

Qualified purchasers. A *first-time homebuyer* is any individual who has not held an ownership interest in any principal residence during the three-year period ending on the date of the purchase of the principal residence. Taxpayers who purchase a home from a close relative (spouse, parent, grandparent, child, or grandchild) cannot claim the credit. Nonresident aliens are also ineligible for the credit.

Qualified homes. To qualify for the first-time homebuyer credit, the home must be purchased and used as the taxpayer's primary residence. Vacation homes and rental property do not qualify for this credit.

New homes. The IRS has explained on its website that a new home constructed by the taxpayer is treated as purchased on the date the taxpayer first occupies the residence.

> **CAUTION**
>
> The first-time homebuyer credit is subject to the same offsets for debt (tax or other qualified debt) as any other refund.

Advance credit/monetization. The first-time homebuyer tax credit cannot be claimed in anticipation of a future purchase. The IRS has stated that taxpayers qualify for the credit when they finalize the purchase of their home, which for most purchasers occurs at the time of the closing. However, the U.S. Department of Housing and Urban Development (HUD) announced that it will allow taxpayers to monetize the first-time homebuyer credit. Under HUD's rules, taxpayers using FHA-approved lenders can apply the credit to their down payment in excess of the 3.5 percent of appraised value or their closing costs. FHA-lenders cannot monetize the credit to meet the required 3.5-percent minimum down payment. State housing agencies, on the other hand, can use the credit to advance 100 percent of the down payment.

> **COMMENT**
>
> The IRS has not commented on HUD's action other than to reiterate that the first-time homebuyer credit may not be claimed in advance. Taxpayers qualify for the credit when they finalize the purchase of their home. For a newly constructed home, the purchase date is the date the taxpayer first occupies the home. The credit does not preclude taxpayers from securing down payment assistance through legally available means, the IRS explained.

Allocation of the credit. Notice 2009-12 explained how to allocate the first-time homebuyer tax credit between two or more owners who are unmarried. Generally, the credit may be allocated according to the taxpayers' contributions to the purchase price, ownership interests in the residence, or "any other reasonable method."

STUDY QUESTIONS

---

1. Which of the following is considered earned income for purposes of qualifying to receive the MWPC?

    a. Income of nonresident aliens not arising from a connection with a U.S. business

    b. Net earnings from self-employment if they are taken into account in computing the individual's taxable income

    c. Annuity payments

2. Which of the following is a qualified purchaser eligible for the first-time homebuyer credit?

    a. A young adult who purchases her home from her grandparents

    b. An individual who has rented her only home since 2002

    c. A nonresident alien

New Vehicle Deduction

The 2009 Recovery Act created a temporary deduction to encourage taxpayers to purchase new cars, trucks, and motorcycles. State and local sales taxes on the purchase of a new motor vehicle may be deducted. The deduction is limited to the tax on up to $49,500 of the purchase price of an eligible motor vehicle. The new vehicle must be purchased after February 16, 2009, and before January 1, 2010, to qualify for the deduction. Both domestic and foreign-made vehicles qualify for the deduction.

> **PLANNING POINTER**
>
> The motor vehicle sales tax deduction's $49,500 purchase price limitation is imposed on a per vehicle basis. There is no limitation on the number of vehicles a taxpayer can purchase.

Qualified vehicles. The vehicle must be a passenger vehicle, light truck, or motorcycle. Motor homes also qualify for the deduction. Only new vehicles are eligible for the deduction.

Income phaseout. The deduction begins to phase out when an individual's modified AGI exceeds $125,000 ($250,000 for married couples filing joint returns). The deduction is reduced to zero when an individual's modified AGI reaches $135,000 ($260,000 for married couples filing joint returns).

Taking the deduction. The motor vehicle deduction can be taken regardless of whether the taxpayer itemizes other deductions on his or her tax return. As is the case with the limited real property tax deduction under Code Sec. 63(c)(1)(C) and the disaster loss deduction under Code Sec. 63(c)(1)(D), however, the motor vehicle sales tax deduction for taxpayers not itemizing is to be taken below that AGI line as an additional standard deduction.

> **CAUTION**
>
> Taxpayers who take the general sales tax itemized deduction in lieu of claiming the state income tax deduction cannot "double up" and also claim the new vehicle deduction for the same sales amount tax paid.

> **PLANNING POINTER**
>
> Several states do not impose state sales taxes. In these states qualified fees or taxes imposed by the state or local government may be deducted, the IRS explained in IR-2009-60. The fees or taxes must be assessed on the purchase of the vehicle and must be based on the vehicle's sales price or as a per unit fee.

> **COMMENT**
>
> Any "cash-for-clunkers" rebate will lower the purchase price of—and therefore the sales tax on—the vehicle for purposes of the new vehicle sales tax deduction.

Education Incentives

The 2009 Recovery Act significantly enhanced the HOPE scholarship credit and renamed it the American opportunity tax credit (AOTC). The AOTC has a higher maximum credit amount, is partially refundable, and has higher income phaseouts. The AOTC also is available for the first four years of post-secondary education. The AOTC is scheduled to expire after 2010 unless Congress extends it or makes it permanent, as the Obama Administration has proposed.

Amount of the credit. The AOTC is equal to 100 percent of the first $2,000 in qualified tuition and related expenses and 25 percent of the next $2,000 of qualified tuition and related expenses. This effectively results in a credit of $2,500 under the 2009 Recovery Act. The HOPE scholarship credit would otherwise have reached a maximum of $1,800 for 2009 as adjusted for inflation.

> **COMMENT**
>
> The 2009 Recovery Act expanded the definition of *related expenses* to include course materials.

Duration of the credit. An eligible taxpayer can claim the AOTC for each of the first four years of the student's post-secondary education. The taxpayer must be enrolled at least half-time in a qualified degree or certificate program. Many types of post-secondary programs qualify, such as institutions that offer an associate's degree, a bachelor's degree, or other recognized credential. However, graduate degree programs are not eligible for the AOTC.

> **COMMENT**
>
> The HOPE scholarship credit was limited to the first two years of a student's post-secondary education.

Refundable portion. Under the 2009 Recovery Act, 40 percent of the AOTC is refundable for qualified taxpayers. However, the AOTC is not refundable if the taxpayer claiming the credit is a child who has earned income subject to the "kiddie tax."

Income phaseouts. Eligibility for the AOTC phases out ratably for single individuals with modified AGI between $80,000 and $90,000 and for married couples filing joint returns with modified AGI between $160,000 and $180,000. Married couples who file as married filing separately returns cannot claim the AOTC. The income phaseouts for the HOPE scholarship credit were lower than the AOTC ($50,000 to $60,000 for single individuals, and $100,000 to $120,000 for married couples filing joint returns).

Child Tax Credit

Individuals who have dependent children younger than age 17 at the close of the tax year may be eligible for the child tax credit, one of the most popular incentives in the tax code. The child tax credit is $1,000 per child through 2010. The credit is reduced by $50 for each $1,000 (or fraction thereof) of modified AGI exceeding $75,000 for single individuals and $110,000 for married couples filing joint returns. If the credit exceeds the taxpayer's individual income tax liability, the taxpayer is eligible for a refundable credit equal to 15 percent of earned income in excess of a certain amount. This is known as the *additional child credit*.

The 2009 Recovery Act enhanced the child tax credit by increasing the refundable portion of the credit for 2009 and 2010. Eligibility for the refundable portion of the child tax credit previously required that an individual have earned income in excess of $12,550 in 2009. The 2009 Recovery Act substitutes $3,000 for $12,550 earned income minimum for 2009 and 2010.

EXAMPLE

In 2009, Lou and Debra have three children all under the age of six and have earned income of $25,000. They have no other income, no alternative minimum tax liability, and are not entitled to any nonrefundable personal credits other than the child tax credit. As joint filers, they are entitled to a standard deduction of $11,400. In addition, they are entitled to a personal exemption of $3,650 for each family member, or $18,250. This results in no taxable income and no federal tax liability. Their allowable nonrefundable child tax credit is equal to $3,000 ($1,000 per child). However, the nonrefundable credit is limited to the amount of tax liability, or $0. The refundable credit is equal to the lesser of either the unclaimed portion of the nonrefundable credit amount, $3,000 ($3,000 – $0), or 15 percent of the couple's earned income in excess of $3,000, or $3,300 (($25,000 – $3,000) × 0.15), because the additional credit for families having three or more children does not result in a greater refundable credit. Lou and Debra are entitled to a refundable credit of $3,000.

Earned Income Tax Credit

The earned income tax credit (EITC) is a refundable credit targeted to lower-income workers. The credit is based on earned income, which includes wages, salaries, and other employee compensation, plus earnings from self-employment. The amount of the EITC is determined by multiplying an individual's earned income by a credit percentage, subject to a various phaseout restrictions. The earned income and AGI limits and the phaseout thresholds applicable to the EITC vary according to whether the taxpayer has one qualifying child, two or more qualifying children, or no qualifying children.

The 2009 Recovery Act increased the EITC to 45 percent of a family's first $12,570 of earned income for families with three or more children. The 2009 Recovery Act also increased the beginning point of the phaseout range for all married couples filing a joint return, regardless of the number of children.

PLANNING POINTER

The Obama Administration has proposed eliminating the advanced EITC program as a program that is too underutilized to pay for its administrative costs. The advance EITC allows taxpayers who expect to qualify for the EITC and have at least one qualifying child to receive part of the credit in each paycheck during the year the taxpayer qualifies for the credit.

STUDY QUESTIONS

---

3. Which of the following individuals is ineligible for the AOTC?

  a. A full-time student pursuing a master's degree

  b. A full-time student in the third year of study toward a bachelor's degree

  c. A full-time student in a post-secondary program leading to an associate's degree

4. The motor vehicle sales tax deduction is allowed:

  a. On a per-vehicle basis

  b. On one qualified purchased before the deduction expires

  c. Only on vehicles manufactured in the United States

COBRA Premium Assistance

COBRA health insurance continuation coverage (named after the *Consolidated Omnibus Budget Reconciliation Act,* which was signed into law in 1986) gives workers who lose their jobs and thus their health benefits the right to purchase group health coverage. If the employer continues to offer a group health plan, the employee and his or her family can retain their group health coverage for up to 18 months by paying group rates. The COBRA premium may be higher than what the individual was paying while employed but generally the cost is lower than that for private, individual health insurance coverage. COBRA generally does not apply to plans sponsored by employers with fewer than 20 employees. However, many states have similar requirements for small plans providing benefits through an insurance company. These are known as "mini-COBRA" laws.

Under the 2009 Recovery Act, individuals involuntarily terminated from employment between September 1, 2008, and December 31, 2009, may qualify for nine months of COBRA premium assistance. The 2009 Recovery Act allows eligible individuals to pay 35 percent of the COBRA premium, and employers must treat that as full payment. Employers claim a credit for the other 65 percent of the premium on their payroll tax returns.

> **COMMENT**
>
> COBRA premium assistance is not available to self-employed individuals.

> **COMMENT**
>
> COBRA subsidy payments are not taxable income.

> **PLANNING POINTER**
>
> An individual may be eligible for COBRA continuation coverage and not be eligible for premium assistance. The qualifying event for COBRA premium assistance is involuntary termination of employment. Additionally, if an individual elects the health coverage tax credit (HCTC), he or she cannot double dip and claim COBRA premium assistance as well.

> **EXAMPLE**
>
> When Alice is divorced from Clay in December 2008, she loses health plan coverage. Alice is eligible for and timely elects COBRA continuation coverage. After the divorce, and before December 31, 2009, Alice's ex-husband Clay is involuntarily terminated from employment and loses health coverage. Clay elects COBRA continuation coverage that begins before December 31, 2009. Alice is not eligible for COBRA premium assistance because the qualifying event with respect to her COBRA continuation coverage is not an involuntary termination. Clay is eligible for COBRA premium assistance because he was involuntarily terminated from employment.

Coverage period. COBRA premium assistance applies as of the first period of coverage beginning on or after February 17, 2009. For most plans, this was March 1, 2009. The nine-month subsidy period ends earlier if the individual becomes eligible for Medicare or another group health plan (for example, a plan sponsored by a new employer) or the individual reaches the end of the maximum COBRA coverage period. Additionally, COBRA premium assistance is not retroactive. For example, if an individual has been enrolled in COBRA coverage since December 2008, he or she will not receive a refund of 65 percent of premiums paid before February 17, 2009.

> **COMMENT**
>
> COBRA premium assistance is not optional. Employers maintaining a group health plan subject to federal COBRA continuation coverage require-ments must make the 65 percent payment if they receive a 35 percent payment from an eligible individual.

Payroll tax credit. Employers recover their 65 percent share of COBRA premium assistance through a payroll tax credit. The COBRA payroll tax credit may exceed payroll tax liabilities and the IRS will issue a refund. If the employer has unpaid payroll tax liabilities, the IRS will use the COBRA payroll tax credit to offset the unpaid taxes against the balance due before refunding any balance to the employer. Employers will be notified of any offset. The IRS is not requiring employers to report the COBRA subsidy on the recipient's Form W-2 or on a Form 1099.

The IRS has also updated Form 941-X, *Adjusted Employer's Quarterly Federal Tax Return or Claim for Refund,* to reflect the employer's credit for temporary COBRA premium assistance.

Generally, employers claim the credit. However, when coverage is pro-vided by a multiemployer plan, the multiemployer plan claims the credit. In the case of fully insured coverage subject to state continuation coverage requirements, the insurer providing coverage under the group health plan takes the credit.

> **PLANNING POINTER**
>
> Some employers continue to provide heath coverage to former employees after involuntary termination from employment. If the employer treats the provision of health coverage as deferring the loss of coverage, the loss of coverage occurs when the employer's provision of coverage ends.

Involuntary termination. An *involuntary termination,* according to the IRS, is a severance from employment due to the employer's unilateral author-ity to terminate the employment. Involuntary termination can also occur when an employer:

- Declines to renew an employee's contract;
- Tells an employee to "resign or be fired;"
- Furloughs an employee;
- Reduces the employee's hours to zero;
- Moves its office or plant and the employee declines to relocate; or
- Locks out its employees.

The IRS will accept an employer's determination of involuntary termination as long as it is consistent with a reasonable interpretation of the statutory language and guidance, and adequate supporting documentation is present. Supporting documentation for an insurer or multiemployer plan must include a statement from the employee or the employee's former employer that the employee was involuntarily terminated and that the termination occurred between September 1, 2008, and December 31, 2009.

Income limitations. COBRA premium assistance is excluded from gross income. However, the subsidy phases out for higher-income individuals. Individuals with modified AGI between $125,000 and $145,000 ($250,000 and $290,000 married couples filing jointly) must repay a portion of the subsidy to the IRS. If a taxpayer's modified AGI exceeds $145,000 ($290,000 for married couples filing jointly), the full amount of the subsidy will be repaid as an additional tax.

Premium calculation. An individual's 35 percent premium is based on the cost that would be charged to him or her for COBRA continuation coverage. Generally, the maximum COBRA premium is 102 percent of the applicable premium for continuation coverage. If the premium is less than the maximum, the reduced amount is the base for calculating the individual's 35 percent share.

Seasonal workers. The end of employment for a seasonal worker may be treated as an involuntary termination, the IRS advised. If an individual is willing and able to continue employment but ends employment because the employer does not have additional work, an involuntary termination has occurred.

Multiemployer plans. Under some multiemployer plans, an individual's eligibility for health coverage is based on a minimum number of hours of covered employment. The IRS will deem an individual to have been involuntarily terminated if a reduction in his or her total hours of covered employment causes the individual to lose regular coverage and become eligible for COBRA plan coverage.

Health Coverage Tax Credit

Congress created the HCTC as part of the *Trade Adjustment Act of 2002* (TAA) to enable trade-displaced workers to continue health care coverage. Individuals ages 55 to 64 receiving benefits from the Pension Benefit Guaranty Corporation (PBGC) may also be eligible for the HCTC. Additionally, to claim the HCTC individuals must be enrolled in a qualified health plan.

Individuals can receive the HCTC either monthly as their premium becomes due or yearly as a credit on their federal tax return. Individuals electing a monthly credit receive an invoice from the IRS each month. Individuals claiming COBRA premium assistance under the 2009 Recovery Act are ineligible for the HCTC during the same month.

> **COMMENT**
>
> A qualified health plan may be COBRA continuation coverage, a state-qualified plan, spousal coverage, or a nongroup/individual plan. Medicare is not a qualified health plan for purposes of the HCTC. Individuals taking advantage of COBRA premium assistance under the 2009 Recovery Act are ineligible to receive the HCTC during the same month.

Prior to passage of the 2009 Recovery Act, individuals paid 35 percent of their health insurance premiums and the HCTC program paid 65 percent. The 2009 Recovery Act raised the government-paid portion from 65 percent to 80 percent.

STUDY QUESTIONS

> **5.** The triggering event for COBRA premium assistance is involuntary termination of employment. *True or False?*
>
> **6.** Employers recover their 65 percent share of COBRA premium assistance through:
>
>   **a.** A payroll tax credit
>   **b.** A one-time refund to be distributed in 2011
>   **c.** Employers do not recover their 65 percent share of COBRA premium assistance
>
> **7.** The 2009 Recovery act increased the government-paid portion of the HCTC to:
>
>   **a.** 35 percent
>   **b.** 80 percent
>   **c.** 100 percent

Unemployment Benefits Exclusion

When Congress was debating the scope of the 2009 Recovery Act, some lawmakers proposed to exclude all unemployment benefits from the recipient's taxable income. Lawmakers compromised and voted to exclude the first $2,400 of unemployment benefits from the recipient's taxable income for

2009. The exclusion is temporary and is available only for unemployment compensation received in 2009.

> **PLANNING POINTER**
>
> For a married couple, the exclusion applies to each spouse, separately. If both spouses receive unemployment benefits during 2009, each may exclude from income the first $2,400 of benefits they receive.

Individuals can elect to have income tax withheld from their unemployment benefit payments. Withholding on these payments is voluntary. Individuals who choose this option will have a flat 10 percent tax withheld from their benefits.

Unemployed individuals who expect to receive more than $2,400 in benefits in 2009 may want to consider having tax withheld from their benefit payments in excess of that amount.

Transportation Fringe Benefits

Qualified transportation fringe benefits are excluded from an employee's gross income for income tax purposes and from an employee's wages for payroll tax purposes. The transportation benefits must be offered by the employer; they cannot be established unilaterally by an employee. The benefits may be funded through employer contributions that are excluded from income. Alternatively, benefits may be funded through pretax salary reduction contributions provided by the employee through the employer or the employer's third-party vendor.

Qualified transportation fringe benefits are:

- Van pooling;
- Transit passes;
- Qualified parking; and
- Bicycle commuting.

An employer can provide an employee with any combination of the first three benefits simultaneously. However, an employer cannot offer a qualified bicycle commuting reimbursement to an employee in any month during which a van pooling, transit pass, or qualified parking subsidy or reimbursement is used. The benefit for commuting using a bicycle is a maximum of $20 per month.

Higher exclusion amounts. Under the 2009 Recovery Act, employees can exclude up to $230 per month for van pooling, transit passes and qualified parking. Previously, the exclusion amounts for van pooling and transit passes were $120 per month. The $230 level for parking remains the same. The higher $230 amount for van pooling and transit passes is available from March 2009 through the end of 2010, with an adjustment for inflation for 2010. The 2009 Recovery Act also allows employers to combine the van pooling and transit pass exclusion with the parking exclusion, for a maximum of $460 per month.

EXAMPLE

Dean's employer provides Dean and his co-workers with a subway pass worth $235 every month between April 2009 and December 2009. The exclusion for transit passes is $230 per month. Dean can exclude $230 of the $235 from income but must include in income $5 each month, for a total of $45 for nine months of 2009 (April through December).

COMMENT

Employers have a choice of either paying for the transportation fringe benefit outright or offering it to employees on a pretax basis taken from their salaries.

Energy Tax Incentives

The 2009 Recovery Act made some valuable enhancements to energy tax incentives for individuals who make energy-efficient improvements to their homes. These incentives are temporary and will expire after 2010.

Code Sec. 25C credit. Individuals installing insulation, exterior windows and doors, and heating and air conditioning systems may be eligible for a credit of 30 percent of the cost of qualifying improvements under Code Sec. 25C. The limit on the amount that can be claimed for improvements placed in service during 2009 and 2010 is $1,500 combined for both years. Additionally, the 2009 Recovery Act revised the energy-efficiency standards for insulation, exterior windows and doors, and certain heating and cooling systems placed in service after February 17, 2009. The Code Sec. 25C credit is a nonrefundable personal credit.

EXAMPLE

Theresa installed energy-efficient windows in her home in April 2009 at a cost of $3,500. Theresa also replaced her gas furnace with an energy-efficient model at a cost of $4,000 in June 2009. Theresa's Code Sec. 25C credit would be $1,500 (($3,500 + $4,000) × 0.30 = $2,250, but limited to $1,500 maximum).

COMMENT

Before the 2009 Recovery Act, certain improvements had set credit amounts (for example, there was a $150 for any qualified natural gas, propane, or oil furnace or hot water boiler). All credit limitations applicable to specific property have been removed for qualifying expenditures in 2009 and 2010.

PLANNING POINTER

Homeowners investing in energy-efficient windows, doors, and other items can rely on existing manufacturers' certifications that the products are eligible for the energy tax credit under Code Sec. 25C, the IRS advised. The IRS anticipates issuing updated certification guidelines later this year.

Code Sec. 25D credit. The Code Sec. 25D residential energy efficient property credit is a separate credit from the Code Sec. 25C credit. The Code Sec. 25D credit rewards taxpayers for installing solar water heaters, geothermal heat pumps, and small wind turbines in their homes. The credit reaches 30 percent of the cost of qualified property generally without limitation. The Code Sec. 25D credit is a nonrefundable personal credit and is available at the higher 2009 Recovery Act levels through 2016.

EXAMPLE

Rory purchased a qualified heat pump for his home in January 2009 at a cost of $9,500. Rory may claim a Code Sec. 25D credit of $2,850 ($9,500 × 0.30 = $2,850).

COMMENT

In Notice 2009-41, the IRS explained the certification process for property eligible for the credit. Manufacturers may provide a certification statement by including a written copy of the statement with the property, in printable form on their websites, or in any other manner that permits the taxpayer to keep the certification for tax recordkeeping purposes. Taxpayers do not have to attach the certification to their tax returns.

Plug-in electric vehicles. The 2009 Recovery Act modified the plug-in hybrid electric vehicle credit. Generally, the minimum amount of the credit for qualified plug-in electric drive vehicles is $2,500. The IRS has indicated it will issue more guidance about plug-in electric vehicles.

STUDY QUESTION

> **8.** Unemployment benefits received in 2009 may be excluded from a recipient's taxable income up to a maximum of:
>
> **a.** $2,400
> **b.** $12,500
> **c.** All unemployment benefits are excluded from 2009 taxable income

WORKER, RETIREE, AND EMPLOYER RECOVERY ACT OF 2008

In December 2008 Congress passed, and President Bush signed, the *Worker, Retiree, and Employer Recovery Act of 2008* (WRERA). Most of the provisions in the law are targeted to pension funds, especially underfunded plans. Congress also included some provisions pertinent to individuals in WRERA.

Required Minimum Distributions

WRERA suspends mandatory required minimum distributions (RMDs) for 2009. The RMD rules limit the time period that funds may remain tax-deferred in qualified retirement plans after an individual reaches retirement age. Generally, individuals must receive the entire balance of their IRA or similar arrangement or start receiving periodic distributions from it by April 1 of the year following the year in which they reach age 70½. Individuals who turned 70½ in 2008 had until April 1, 2009, to take their 2008 distribution. However, individuals who reached age 70½ before 2008 had to take their RMDs by December 31, 2008. Otherwise, individuals risk a 50-percent excise tax.

For IRAs and defined contribution plans, the RMD for each year generally is determined by dividing the account balance as of the end of the prior year by a distribution period determined using the uniform lifetime table in IRS regulations. The table is based on joint life expectancies of the individual and a hypothetical beneficiary 10 years younger than the individual.

> **CAUTION**
>
> WRERA suspended RMDs for 2009. However, to avoid penalty an individual who turned age 70½ in 2008 must have taken an RMD by April 1, 2009.

> ### EXAMPLE
> Eleanor has a traditional IRA account with a balance of $500,000 as of January 1, 2008. Eleanor turned 76 in 2008 and her RMD for 2008 was $22,727 Under WRERA, Eleanor is not required to withdraw any amounts under the minimum distribution rules for 2009.

> ### PLANNING POINTER
> The RMD suspension will not help an individual who needs the cash flow to live on. He or she will still have to sell a portion of his or her retirement assets and pay tax in 2009 on any distributions that are actually made.

Public Safety Employees

The *Pension Protection Act of 2009* (PPA) gave retired public safety employees (law enforcement personnel, fire fighters, emergency medical technicians, and others) a special tax break to help pay for health insurance coverage. Eligible taxpayers can exclude from income up to $3,000 annually in distributions from government retirement plans. The funds must be used to pay for health insurance for the taxpayer and spouse/dependents. After Congress passed the PPA, there was some uncertainty about whether the exclusion applied to premiums paid to a self-insured plan. WRERA clarified that the exclusion does apply to premiums paid to a self-insured plan.

MICHELLE'S LAW

Background

In October 2008, President Bush signed a bill known as "Michelle's Law" (P.L. 110-381). This law allows full-time students to maintain their parents' health insurance if the students take a medically necessary leave of absence from college or any post-secondary school. The law is named after Michelle Morse, a college student who carried a full course load to qualify as a dependent under her parents' health insurance while undergoing cancer treatment. If Morse had fallen below full-time status, she would no longer have been covered by her parents' plan.

Covered Individuals

Michelle's Law covers students who are dependents of participants or beneficiaries of a group health plan. The dependent generally must be 18 years of age or older and enrolled in the plan. For calendar-year group health plans, Michelle's Law is effective as of January 1, 2010.

> **COMMENT**
>
> Questions have arisen about how Michelle's Law interacts with COBRA continuation coverage. COBRA generally allows individuals to purchase group health coverage after they experience a job loss or other qualifying event. The individuals, and in some cases their family, can retain their group health coverage for up to 18 months. Additionally, the individual may be eligible for COBRA premium assistance under the 2009 Recovery Act. The IRS has indicated it will issue guidance but has not specified when.

CARS ACT

In the *Consumer Assistance to Recycle and Save Act of 2009* (CARS Act), Congress created a temporary "cash for clunkers" program for cars and trucks. In exchange for trading in an old gas guzzler, a consumer may qualify for a voucher of $3,500 or $4,500 toward the purchase of a new fuel-efficient vehicle. The dealer must be registered for the program with the federal government. Leased vehicles are also eligible. The minimum lease period for a vehicle is five years. Used vehicles, regardless of their fuel economy ratings, are ineligible for the program. Both domestic and foreign-made vehicles qualify if they meet the CARS Act standards.

> **COMMENT**
>
> The cash-for-clunkers vouchers will not be treated as income to consumers but are income to auto/truck dealers, according to the IRS. In a special "Automotive Alert" issued in July 2009, the IRS explained that a dealer's gross receipts include the full selling price of the vehicle, regardless of the form of the customer's payment. The voucher is included in the dealer's gross receipts from the sale in the year the vehicle is sold. Any scrap value for the trade-in is also included in the dealer's income.

> **CAUTION**
>
> The National Highway Traffic Safety Administration (NHTSA), which is administering the cash-for-clunkers program, often refers to the vouchers as "credits," leading some consumers to equate them with tax credits. The vouchers are not tax credits. The benefit is a reduction in purchase price.

Trade-In Vehicles

The CARS Act establishes certain basic eligibility qualifications for the trade-in vehicle. For passenger cars, the vehicle must;

- Have been manufactured more recently than 25 years before the trade-in date;
- Have a combined city/highway fuel economy of 18 miles per gallon or less;
- Be in drivable condition; and
- Be continuously insured and registered to the same owner for the full year preceding the trade-in.

The criteria for trucks—including SUVs and work trucks—are similar, with differences for fuel economy. There are also some special rules for work trucks.

> **COMMENT**
>
> The month and year of manufacture generally appear on the safety certification on the frame or edge of the driver's door in most vehicles.

Four Groups of Vehicles

The CARS Act divides motor vehicles into four groups: Passenger automobiles and three categories of trucks:

- Category 1 trucks are nonpassenger automobiles and include SUVs and small/medium pickup trucks and small/medium vans;
- Category 2 trucks are, in most cases, large pickup trucks or van based on the length of the wheelbase (more than 115 inches for pickup trucks and more than 124 inches for vans); and
- Category 3 trucks are work trucks and rated between 8,500 and 10,000 pounds gross vehicle weight. This category includes very large pickup trucks (having cargo beds 72 inches or more in length) and very large cargo vans.

New Vehicle Fuel Economy Standards

The new vehicle must have a manufacturer's suggested retail price of not more than $45,000 and meet certain fuel-efficiency standards.

Passenger automobiles. For passenger automobiles, the new vehicle must have a combined fuel economy value of at least 22 mpg.

Category 1 trucks. The combined fuel economy value for a new category 1 truck is 18 mpg or more.

Category 2 trucks. For category 2 trucks, the new vehicle must have a combined fuel economy of at least 15 mpg.

Category 3 (work) trucks. Category 3 (work) trucks have no minimum fuel economy requirements.

Vouchers

Taxpayers may qualify for vouchers of either $3,500 or $4,500, depending on the difference between the fuel economy of the trade-in vehicle and the fuel economy of the new vehicle.

Passenger automobiles. The value of the voucher for the purchase or lease of a new passenger car depends upon the difference between the combined fuel economy of the vehicle that is traded in and that of the new vehicle that is purchased or leased:

- If the new vehicle has a combined fuel economy that is at least 4 mpg but less than 10 mpg higher than the traded-in vehicle, the credit is $3,500; and
- If the new vehicle has a combined fuel economy value that is at least 10 mpg higher than the traded-in vehicle, the credit is $4,500.

Trucks. The value of the voucher for the purchase or lease of a category 1 or 2 truck generally depends on the difference between the combined fuel economy of the vehicle that is traded in and that of the new vehicle that is purchased or leased:

- If the new vehicle is a category 1 truck that has a combined fuel economy value that is at least 2 mpg but less than 5 mpg higher than the traded-in vehicle, the credit is $3,500;
- If the new category 1 truck has a combined fuel economy value that is at least 5 mpg higher than the traded-in vehicle, the credit is $4,500;
- If both the new vehicle and the traded-in vehicle are category 2 trucks and the combined fuel economy value of the new vehicle is at least 1 mpg but less than 2 mpg higher than the combined fuel economy value of the traded in vehicle, the credit is $3,500;
- If both the new vehicle and the traded-in vehicle are category 2 trucks and the combined fuel economy of the new vehicle is at least 2 mpg higher than that of the traded-in vehicle, the credit is $4,500; and
- A $3,500 credit applies to the purchase or lease of a category 2 truck if the trade-in vehicle is a category 3 (work) truck that was manufactured not later than model year 2001, but not earlier than 25 years before the date of the trade-in.

Consumers will not receive a paper voucher. Rather, dealers will apply the amount of the voucher against the purchase/lease price. Dealers will be reimbursed by the NHTSA. Reimbursements will occur roughly 10 days after the sale or lease of the new vehicle, the NHTSA explained.

STUDY QUESTIONS

---

9. Under the CARS Act, a passenger car that is traded-in for a new fuel efficient vehicle must have been manufactured ___ years before the trade-in date.

   a. Less than 10
   b. Less than 25
   c. 26 or more

10. Under the CARS Act, a voucher toward the purchase of a new vehicle is worth _____ if the new passenger automobile has a combined fuel economy that is at least 4 mpg (but less than 10 mpg) higher than the trade-in vehicle.

   a. $1,000
   b. $3,500
   c. $4,500

CONCLUSION

At the time this CPE course was published, Congress was beginning debate about many other pieces of tax legislation that affect individual taxpayers. Waiting for Congressional action are healthcare reform, the fate of lower individual marginal income tax rates enacted in 2001 but set to expire after 2010, estate tax reform, proposals to overhaul the international tax rules, and numerous incentives for businesses. Congress also may extend some of the temporary incentives in the 2009 Recovery Act, WRERA, the CARS Act, and other laws. With all of these issues pending in Congress, undoubtedly the remainder of 2009 and 2010 will be active years for tax law developments.

Tax Relief and Incentives for Businesses

This chapter explores the businesses tax incentives in the *American Recovery and Reinvestment Act of 2009* (2009 Recovery Act) and pending tax legislation. Congress passed, and President Obama signed, the massive 2009 Recovery Act in February 2009 to help jump-start the U.S. economy out of recession. The 2009 Recovery Act provides tax breaks intended to encourage business spending, the hiring of veterans and disconnected youth, the development and production of alternative energy, and more. The 2009 Recovery Act also provides temporary COBRA premium assistance to individuals and gives employers a payroll tax credit in return.

LEARNING OBJECTIVES

Upon completion of this course, you will be able to:
- Identify recent tax acts passed by Congress that impact business;
- List the requirements for expanded net operating loss (NOL) carrybacks
- Describe bonus depreciation;
- Explain small business expensing;
- Describe temporary cancellation of debt (COD) income provisions;
- Explain the enhanced work opportunity tax credit (WOTC);
- Describe COBRA premium assistance;
- Identify energy tax incentives for businesses;
- Explain the new markets tax credit, Build America Bonds, and other financing tools; and
- Explain the Obama Administration's international tax reform proposals.

INTRODUCTION

The year 2009 began with Congress passing one of the largest stimulus and tax incentive bills in recent sessions. The 2009 Recovery Act included nearly $300 billion in tax relief. Many of the provisions are targeted to individuals to encourage consumer spending on homes, cars, energy, and other goods. Congress also included some direct tax breaks for businesses in the form of both extensions of tax incentives enacted in 2008 and other incentives to help struggling Americans to get back on their feet. The 2009 Recovery Act passed the House by a vote of 246 to 183 and the Senate by a vote of 60 to 38. President Barack Obama signed the bill into law on February 17, 2009. Many of the tax incentives are temporary and will expire either near or at the end of 2009 or at the end of 2010.

AMERICAN RECOVERY AND REINVESTMENT ACT OF 2009

Net Operating Losses

Because of the economic downturn, many businesses are in a loss position. The tax code generally allows eligible taxpayers to carry back net operating losses (NOLs) two years with some exceptions. Corporations and other businesses that are now running at a loss but had been making profits in recent years can generate a current tax refund by using an NOL carryback. The idea is that a business that operates at a loss can use that loss to offset profits from a previous year. This, in effect, averages the business gains and losses over prior years and provides a refund of the taxes paid on the prior year's profits, which can be used to help with current operating expenses. The 2009 Recovery Act extends the carryback period to five years for small businesses (which the new law defines as businesses with average gross receipts of $15 million or less). The treatment is temporary, applying only to 2008 NOLs. Taxpayers on a calendar year must have elected the extended carryback by October 15, 2009, but they have the normal deadline for filing the refund claim.

PLANNING POINTER

Taxpayers do not have to carry back the NOL for the full five-year period. Taxpayers can elect to carry back the NOL for any number of years from three to five. Alternatively, taxpayers can elect to waive the carryback period and carry the NOL forward for 20 years. Taxpayers on a fiscal year may elect to carry back the NOL for either fiscal year 2008 or 2009, but not for both years.

COMMENT

Before the 2009 Recovery Act, taxpayer generally could carry back the NOL 2 years from the year that the NOL is incurred. If the NOL is not used fully, the taxpayer can carry forward the NOL up to 20 years from the year of the loss.

EXAMPLE

ABC Corp. is an eligible small business whose fiscal year ends on September 30. ABC has suffered losses for the past 18 months and it expects the losses to continue for one more year. ABC's applicable 2008 NOL is its NOL for the tax year that began on October 1, 2007, and ended on September 30, 2008. Alternatively, it could elect to treat its NOL for the tax year that began on October 1, 2008, and will end on September 30, 2009, as its NOL.

COMMENT

The *Emergency Economic Stabilization Act of 2008* (EESA) previously created a temporary five-year carryback period election for NOLs attributable to federally declared disasters. This is different from the 2009 Recovery Act's small business NOL relief. This special treatment is available for federal disasters occurring after December 31, 2007, and before January 1, 2010.

Claiming NOLs. Corporations and individuals can apply for an NOL refund in two ways. The quickest method is to file an *Application for Tentative Refund,* Form 1139, for a corporation, and Form 1045 for an individual, trust, or estate. The other method is to file an amended income tax return, Form 1120-X for a corporation or Form 1040-X for an individual. Forms 1045 and 1139 should be filed separately from the taxpayer's income tax return for the year of the loss.

Corporations. A corporation must file Form 1139 within 12 months following the end of the year in which the NOL was incurred (the "loss year"), whereas an amended return can be filed up to three years from the due date of the return for the loss year. Corporations must include the first two pages of Form 1120 with their Form 1139. The IRS must respond to Form 1139 (but not Form 1120-X) within 90 days of the later of the filing or the due date (including extensions) for filing the return for the loss year. The IRS owes interest if it does not respond within 45 days of the applicable date. The IRS can deny the refund on Form 1139 if there is a material omission or error in computation.

Waiver. Under Code Sec. 172(b)(3), a taxpayer may make an irrevocable election to relinquish the two-year carryback period with respect to an NOL for any tax year. The 2009 Recovery Act allowed taxpayers to revoke a previous election relinquishing the two-year carryback period and to make a new election to take advantage of the extended carryback period.

> ### PLANNING POINTER
>
> A waiver may be useful for several reasons:
> - The taxpayer can claim tax credits on income in the prior years;
> - Income may be taxed at a higher rate in a later year;
> - The taxpayer generally may want to retain the NOL to use in a future year; or
> - The NOL, by reducing an individual's income, may diminish the allowable individual retirement account contribution or itemized deductions.
>
> Conversely, using the NOL could benefit the individual by reducing the adjusted gross income floor and increasing the itemized medical deduction, for example.

The IRS explained how to revoke a previous election to take advantage of the extended net operating loss (NOL) carryback in the 2009 Recovery Act in Rev. Proc. 2009-19. However, the IRS discovered that many taxpayers were confused by Rev. Proc. 2009-19 and streamlined the procedures in Rev. Proc. 2009-26.

Under Rev. Proc. 2009-26, an electing small business may elect a three, four, or five-year carryback period to carry back 2008 NOLs by filing:
- Form 1045, *Application for Tentative Refund;*
- Form 1139, *Corporation Application for Tentative Refund;* or
- An amended return.

Gross receipts. To qualify for the NOL carryback, a small business must have an average of $15 million or less in gross receipts over a three-year period ending with the year giving rise to the loss, the IRS explained. A small business is a corporation or partnership that meets the gross receipts test for the tax year in which the loss arose or, in the case of a sole proprietorship, would meet the test if the proprietorship was a corporation.

> ### COMMENT
>
> Individuals generally claim an NOL as the result of Form 1040 Schedule C losses or from passthrough losses received as a partner or an S corporation shareholder.

Bonus Depreciation

Congress has used bonus depreciation many times in recent years to stimulate the economy. The 2009 Recovery Act allows a business to depreciate 50 percent of the adjusted basis of qualified property during the year it is placed in service.

The 2009 Recovery Act extended bonus depreciation deduction one year to apply to property placed in service before January 1, 2010 (January 1, 2011, in the case of qualifying property with a longer production period and certain noncommercial aircraft). Bonus depreciation can be claimed for both regular and alternative minimum tax (AMT) liability unless the taxpayer makes an election out. Once made, an election out cannot be revoked without IRS consent.

PLANNING POINTER

There is no limit on the total amount of bonus depreciation that may be claimed in any given tax year. Nor is there a limit to the size of the business claiming it.

Property. Bonus depreciation is available for every item of tangible personal property except inventory. Bonus depreciation, as is the case for regular depreciation, is not available for intangible property except for certain computer software. Additionally, bonus depreciation cannot be taken for tangible personal property used outside the United States or for property depreciated under the alternative depreciation system.

The taxpayer must place the property in service during 2009 with additional time for certain property, such as transportation property (property used to transport people or cargo), and for certain aircraft.

EXAMPLE

ABC Co. purchases new depreciable property in 2009 and places it in service in the same year. The property costs $100,000 and is five-year property subject to a half-year regular depreciation convention. ABC Co. can take 50-percent bonus depreciation of $50,000 in the first year. This reduces the property's basis to $50,000. The taxpayer can also take one-half of a full-year's depreciation ($10,000) for the first year. Thus, for 2009, the taxpayer can deduct depreciation of $60,000; in this case, 60 percent of the property's basis. The remaining $40,000 is deducted throughout the remaining four years (into the fifth year due to the half-year convention)of the property's term, using either the general depreciation schedule under MACRS or the alternative depreciation schedule (straight-line depreciation).

> **CAUTION**
>
> In 2008, Code Sec. 168 was amended to provide a 15-year recovery period for *qualified retail improvement property* placed in service in 2009, and to expand the definition of *qualified restaurant property,* for property placed in service in 2009. Some of this property would previously have been classified as qualified leasehold improvement property, which is eligible for bonus depreciation. The 2008 amendments specified, however, that qualified retail improvement property and qualified restaurant property placed in service in 2009 cannot be qualified property eligible for the 50-percent bonus depreciation deduction.

> **PLANNING POINTER**
>
> Bonus depreciation operates independently of Code Sec. 179 expensing, so qualifying taxpayers can find themselves with an overall greater tax benefit for the sum of all property purchased. Note, however, that bonus depreciation applies to property placed in service during calendar year 2009, whereas Code Sec. 179 expensing ends at the end of the taxpayer's tax year that began in 2009, which is later for fiscal year taxpayers.

Luxury Car Depreciation Cap

Code Sec. 280F imposes dollar limitations, also referred to as *luxury auto limits,* on the depreciation deduction for the year that a business vehicle is placed into service by the taxpayer and each succeeding year. The 2009 Recovery Act increased the bonus depreciation allowed under Code Sec. 280F(a)(1)(A) by $8,000 for a business vehicles acquired before January 1, 2010, and placed into service during 2009 to which the 50-percent additional first year depreciation deduction would otherwise apply.

STUDY QUESTIONS

1. The 2009 Recovery Act changes NOL carryover treatment for small businesses by:
   a. Providing an election to carry forward losses for up to 10 years
   b. Extending the carryback period for to up to five years
   c. Enabling businesses to apply the temporary extended NOL carryover treatment to returns for the 2008, 2009, and 2010 tax years.

---

2. Bonus depreciation of 50 percent of adjusted basis was extended by the 2009 Recovery Act for most types of business property:
   a. Placed in service before January 1, 2010
   b. Placed in service before filing the corporate return for 2010
   c. Purchased between January 1, 2009, and December 31, 2011

Increased AMT and Research Credits

Because bonus depreciation is not useful to businesses operating at a loss, 2009 Recovery Act allows taxpayers (primarily corporations) to claim refundable credits instead of bonus depreciation. The amount of additional research credit and/or AMT credit that a corporation may claim if it elects to forgo bonus depreciation is determined by increasing the Code Sec. 38(c) business credit and Code Sec. 53(c) AMT credit limitations by the bonus depreciation amount for the tax year.

Minimum tax credit. Under Code Sec. 53, a corporation required to pay AMT for one year can claim a minimum tax credit in any later tax year in which it has no AMT liability. A corporation's minimum tax credit for any tax year is the excess of the adjusted net minimum tax imposed for all prior tax years beginning after 1986 over the amount allowed as a minimum tax credit for all such prior years. The minimum tax credit that may be claimed in any tax year is limited to the excess of the corporation's regular tax liability over its tentative minimum tax liability.

Research credit. The Code Sec. 41 research credit is part of the general business credit, which, for a tax year, is the sum of:
- Business credit carryforwards;
- The current year business credit; and
- Business credit carrybacks.

When the general business credit exceeds the tax liability limitation in any year, the excess or unused amount may be carried back one year and forward 20 years. Unused general business credits are treated as used on a first-in, first-out (FIFO) basis by offsetting the earliest-earned credits first. Credits applied in any tax year are, first, the carryforwards to that year (the earliest carryforwards first—FIFO), followed by the general business credit earned in that year, and finally, any carryback to that year.

In Rev. Proc. 2009-33, the IRS issued guidance on the election to claim refundable credits instead of bonus depreciation for 2009. The guidance indicates what property is eligible for the election, when and how to make elections, and how to compute and allocate the refundable credits.

Code Sec. 179 Expensing

The 2009 Recovery Act extended Code Sec. 179 expensing (also known as *small business expensing*). Under Code Sec. 179, taxpayers can elect to recover all or part of the cost of qualifying property, up to a limit, by deducting it in the year it is placed in service. The Code Sec. 179 small business expensing deduction enables many businesses to deduct the entire cost of their depreciable property during the tax year in which it is purchased and placed in service.

Dollar limits. The 2009 Recovery Act extended for 2009 the $250,000 dollar limit that had been temporarily increased for 2008 by the EESA. Unless Congress extends the higher amount, the dollar limit will fall to $125,000 ($134,000 as indexed for inflation) for 2010.

> **COMMENT**
>
> The higher expensing limit applies to property placed in service in tax years beginning in 2009. Therefore, noncalendar fiscal year taxpayers have until their tax year's end in 2010 to take advantage of this election.

Expensing phaseout. The Code Sec. 179 deduction is reduced on a dollar-for-dollar basis if the cost of qualifying assets placed in service by the taxpayer exceeds $800,000 for tax years beginning in 2009. For example, taxpayers placing qualifying property in excess of $1,050,000 in service during a tax year beginning in 2009 may not elect to expense directly any part of the cost ($1,050,000 − $800,000 = $250,000 annual limit for 2009).

> **COMMENT**
>
> The Code Sec. 179 deduction is limited to the taxable income derived from the taxpayer's active conduct of the trade or business. This limit prevents the generation of an NOL based on expensing that would otherwise be able to be carried back for a refund. Any unused portion, however, may be carried forward indefinitely into future years.

Property. The property must be purchased for use in a trade or business. The property cannot be held for investment or the production of income. Additionally, property that is purchased for personal use and subsequently converted to business use does not qualify for Code Sec. 179 expensing.

> **COMMENT**
>
> Code Sec. 179 is treated like depreciation for many purposes. Thus, it is subject to recapture as depreciation. In addition, it is subject to recapture if the taxpayer no longer used in a trade or business.

Cancellation of Debt Income

The 2009 Recovery Act created Code Sec. 108(i), allowing businesses to delay recognition of cancellation of debt (COD) income in certain situations. The COD income entitled to this special relief must result from the taxpayer's reacquisition of an applicable debt instrument in 2009 and 2010. Taxpayers making this special election can report the deferred COD income throughout a specific period: 2014 through 2018. For a reacquisition occurring in 2009, the COD income is reportable as income starting in the fifth tax year following the tax year in which the debt is repurchased. For a reacquisition occurring in 2010, the COD income is reportable ratably over five tax years starting in the fourth tax year following the reacquisition year (2014–2018).

> **COMMENT**
>
> The 2009 Recovery Act broadly defined *applicable debt instrument* to include a bond, debenture, note, certificate, or any other indebtedness issued in connection with the conduct of a trade or business. The IRS is expected to issue guidance with more precise definitions.

If new debt is issued with original issue discount (OID), the deduction for OID must be deferred. The 2009 Recovery Act also provides for a special acceleration rule if the taxpayer liquidates, seeks bankruptcy protection, or goes out of business.

Election. The election must be made on a debt instrument by debt instrument basis. The 2009 Recovery Act provides that the election is irrevocable. For passthrough entities, such as a partnership or S corporation, the election is made at the entity level. A taxpayer makes an election with respect to a debt instrument by including with its return for the tax year in which the reacquisition of the debt instrument occurs a statement that:

- Clearly identifies the debt instrument; and
- Includes the amount of deferred income under this provision.

> **COMMENT**
>
> When it issues regulations, the IRS may add further requirements to the procedure for making the election.

PLANNING POINTER

The exclusions for discharge under a Chapter 11 bankruptcy, when the taxpayer is insolvent, qualified farm indebtedness, and qualified real property business indebtedness do not apply if the taxpayer elects the special treatment in the 2009 Recovery Act. Unlike use of one of the Code Sec. 108 exclusions of cancellation of indebtedness, use of the COD income deferral does not require any reduction of tax attributes in return.

CAUTION

Under Code Sec. 108(d)(6), the general COD income exclusion and tax attribute reduction rules are applied at the partner level. The 2009 Recovery Act provides that the special COD income deferral election rule is made and applied at the partnership level. The IRS is expected to clarify this relationship when it issues regulations.

COMMENT

In a related development, the 2009 Recovery Act temporarily suspended rules for OID on certain high-yield discount obligations, referred to as "applicable high-yield discount obligations" (AHYDOs).

Work Opportunity Tax Credit

The work opportunity tax credit (WOTC) rewards employers that hire individuals from targeted groups. The credit generally equals 40 percent of first-year wages up to $6,000 ($3,000 for summer youth employees, and $12,000 for qualified veterans). For long-term family aid recipients, the credit also includes 50 percent of qualified second-year wages. Generally, the individual must begin work before September 1, 2011. The 2009 Recovery Act expanded the WOTC to cover two new targeted groups: unemployed veterans and disconnected youth.

CAUTION

The targeted group of "unemployed veterans" is separate from the targeted group of "veterans." The latter group reaches veterans who are members of a family that receives federal food stamp assistance and who served on active duty. For individuals who begin work for an employer after May 25, 2007, the targeted veterans group also includes veterans with service-connected disabilities.

Unemployed veterans. An *unemployed veteran* for purposes of the WOTC is any veteran who is certified by the designated local agency as:

- Having been discharged or released from active duty in the U.S. Armed Forces at any time during the five-year period ending on the hiring date; and
- Receiving unemployment compensation for not less than four weeks during the one-year period ending on the hiring date.

Disconnected youth. A disconnected youth for purposes of the WOTC is any individual who is certified by the designated local agency as:

- Having attained age 16 but not age 25 on the hire date;
- Not regularly attending any secondary, technical, or post-secondary school during the six-month period preceding the hiring date;
- Not regularly employed during the six-month period; and
- Not readily employable by reason of lacking a sufficient number of basic skills.

The disconnected youth must state in writing he or she has not attended a secondary, technical, or post-secondary school for more than an average of 10 hours per week. This does not count periods during which the school is closed for scheduled vacations.

STUDY QUESTIONS

3. If a business places in service qualifying property exceeding _____ in the 2009 tax year, the business may not expense any part of the purchase under Code Sec. 179.

   a. $800,000
   b. $1,050,000
   c. $15 million

4. The WOTC generally provides a credit of _____ to employers of first-year wages to targeted groups such as unemployed veterans and disconnected youth.

   a. 20 percent of wages up to $5,000 ($2,500 for summer youth employees)
   b. 40 percent of wages up to $6,000 ($3,000 for summer youth employees)
   c. 50 percent of wages up to $8,000 ($4,500 for summer youth employees)

S Corporation Built-In Gains Period

If a taxable corporation converts into an S corporation, the conversion is not a taxable event. However, following the conversion, an S corporation must hold its assets for 10 years to avoid a tax on any net recognized built-in gains that existed at the time of the conversion under Code Sec. 1374. The *net recognized built-in gain* is, for any tax year in the recognition period, the lesser of:

- The amount that would be the taxable income of the S corporation for the tax year if (before reduction by NOL carryforwards from C years) only recognized built-in gains and built-in losses were taken into account; or
- The corporation's taxable income for the tax year.

> **EXAMPLE**
>
> ABC, an S corporation, would have $200,000 of taxable income in a tax year if it were still a C corporation. That amount reflects a $40,000 NOL carryover and a dividends-received deduction of $10,000. In determining taxable income for purposes of the built-in gains computation, the NOL and the dividends-received deduction are restored. As a result, ABC has taxable income for that year of $250,000 for built-in gain purposes.

> **COMMENT**
>
> The built-in gains tax was enacted to prevent a C corporation from electing S corporation status to avoid a corporate-level tax on gain from unrealized appreciation of C corporation assets or gain from C corporation assets on which depreciation deductions had been taken. To avoid the built-in gains tax, the S corporation must not sell the assets during the recognition period applicable to the assets. The built-in gains tax does not apply if the assets are sold after the recognition period.

The 2009 Recovery Act temporarily reduces the holding period from 10 to 7 years for sales occurring in 2009 and 2010. Effectively, no built-in gains tax will be imposed on gains recognized in 2009 and 2010 if the seventh tax year in the recognition period preceded the 2009 or 2010 tax year.

> **EXAMPLE**
>
> ABC Corp. elected S corporation status for its tax year beginning on January 1, 2002. Under the 2009 Recovery Act, ABC can sell appreciated assets it held on that date during 2009 (and 2010) without being subject to tax under Code Sec. 1374.

COMMENT

The purpose of the shortened built-in gain period under the 2009 Recovery Act is to enable businesses under these times of economic distress to more freely dispose of assets that may not be as productive to the business as had been hoped for when the assets were acquired. In either the 7- or 10-year holding period, the amount subject to built-in gains tax is determined under a "cliff" rule. There is no pro-rata exclusion for time that has elapsed within the 7- or 10-year period.

COMMENT

The special recognition rule for 2009 and 2010 does not apply to distributions to shareholders relating to pre-1988 bad debt reserves of thrift and former thrift institutions that became S corporations.

Individual Estimated Tax Payments

Individuals generally must base their estimated tax payments on one of three calculations. The 2009 Recovery Act decreases estimated tax payments required from individuals whose incomes primarily come from a small business in 2009.

A taxpayer qualifies for this treatment if:

- The adjusted gross income (AGI) shown on the individual's return for the preceding tax year is less than $500,000; and
- More than 50 percent of the gross income shown on the return for the preceding tax year is from a business that employed fewer than 500 employees on average during the calendar year that ends with or within the preceding tax year of the individual.

COMMENT

The individual must certify that more than 50 percent of the gross income shown on the return for the preceding tax year was "income from a small business."

PLANNING POINTER

The IRS is expected to issue regulations on the form of the certification and the time/manner of filing.

COBRA Premium Assistance

The *Consolidated Omnibus Budget Reconciliation Act* (COBRA) provides continuation of employer-sponsored group health coverage that otherwise might be terminated when an employee leaves his or her employment. COBRA generally applies to group health plans maintained by employers having 20 or more employees in the prior year. The 2009 Recovery Act provides a temporary enhancement to COBRA. Individuals involuntarily terminated from employment between September 1, 2008, and December 31, 2009, may qualify for nine months of COBRA premium assistance.

Under the 2009 Recovery Act, individuals pay 35 percent of the COBRA premium and employers must treat that as full payment. There is no option not to treat the 35 percent payment as full payment, the IRS has cautioned. The 2009 Recovery Act allows employers claim a credit for the other 65 percent of the premium on their payroll tax returns.

> **COMMENT**
>
> COBRA premium assistance applies as of the first period of coverage beginning on or after February 17, 2009. For most plans, this was March 1, 2009.

Involuntary termination. An individual must be involuntarily terminated from employment to qualify for COBRA premium assistance. The 2009 Recovery Act did not define *involuntary termination*. The House Ways and Means Committee, when it was debating the 2009 Recovery Act, explained that *involuntary termination* takes place when an employer directs an employee to leave and not return to work. After Congress passed the 2009 Recovery Act, the IRS issued guidance defining *involuntary termination*.

In Notice 2009-27, the IRS explained that an involuntary termination is a severance from employment due to the employer's unilateral authority to terminate the employment. Involuntary termination can also occur when an employer:

- Declines to renew an employee's contract;
- Tells an employee, "Resign or be fired;"
- Furloughs an employee;
- Reduces the employee's hours to zero;
- Moves its office or plant and the employee declines to relocate; or
- Locks out its employees.

Some events are not an involuntary termination for purposes of COBRA premium assistance. For example, a reduction in hours that is not a reduction to zero hours is not an involuntary termination. If the employee voluntarily quits rather than work reduced hours, this may be deemed an involuntary termination, according to the IRS.

Seasonal workers. The IRS has addressed the end of employment for a seasonal worker, which may be treated as an involuntary termination. If an individual is willing and able to continue employment but ends employment because the employer does not have additional work, an involuntary termination has occurred, the IRS advised.

Severance packages. Some employers continue to provide health coverage to former employees after their involuntary termination from employment. If the employer treats the provision of health coverage as deferring the loss of coverage, the loss of coverage occurs when the employer's provision of coverage ends.

> **PLANNING POINTER**
>
> The IRS will accept an employer's determination of involuntary termination as long as it is consistent with a reasonable interpretation of the statutory language and guidance, and adequate supporting documentation is present. Supporting documentation for an insurer or multiemployer plan must include a statement from the employee or the employee's former employer that the employee was involuntarily terminated and that the termination occurred between September 1, 2008, and December 31, 2009.

Payroll tax credit. Employers claim the COBRA premium assistance payroll as a tax credit. If the employer's COBRA premium assistance credit exceeds its payroll tax liabilities, the IRS will generally refund the excess. However, the IRS will apply the excess to any unpaid tax liabilities.

> **COMMENT**
>
> Generally, employers claim the credit. However, when coverage is provided by a multiemployer plan, the multiemployer plan claims the credit. In the case of fully insured coverage subject to state continuation coverage requirements, the insurer providing coverage under the group health plan takes the premium credit.

> **PLANNING POINTER**
>
> An employer can claim the credit only after it has received the 35 percent premium payment from the individual.

The COBRA premium assistance credit is claimed on Line 12a of revised Form 941. Filers also need to report the number of individuals provided COBRA premium assistance on Line 12b. The IRS has posted revised Form 941 on its website. Additionally, the revised form was sent to employers.

Employers do not have to report COBRA premium assistance on the recipient's Form W-2 or on a Form 1099.

No additional information relating to the subsidy has to be submitted with Form 941. However, employers must maintain supporting documentation, such as proof of eligibility for COBRA coverage and receipt of the employee's 35 percent share of the premium.

> **PLANNING POINTER**
>
> The IRS has also revised Form 941-X, *Adjusted Employer's Quarterly Federal Tax Return or Claim for Refund,* to reflect the employer's credit for temporary COBRA premium assistance. Revised Form 941-X and its Instructions have been posted on the IRS website. Any errors on a previously filed Form 941 relating to COBRA premium assistance should be reported on Form 941-X, the IRS advised. Form 941-X. Taxpayers should use line 17a on Form 941-X to report the correct total of COBRA premium assistance payments originally reported on line 12a of Form 941. Taxpayers should enter the total number of individuals provided COBRA premium assistance on line 17b on Form 941-X.

Appeals. Individuals who believe that their former employer has improperly denied them COBRA premium assistance may appeal to the U.S. Department of Labor (DOL) or the U.S. Department of Health and Human Services (HHS), if their coverage is provided through a federal, state, or local government plan or under state insurance law. The DOL has created an electronic appeals process on its website (**www.dol.gov/ebsa**). The DOL allows individuals to print its online appeals form and send it to the DOL by mail or fax.

> **COMMENT**
>
> Many appeals are expected to arise from an employer's decision not to treat an individual's separation from employment as an involuntary termination. The DOL and HHS will allow employers to explain why they denied COBRA premium assistance to an individual.

STUDY QUESTIONS

> **5.** For purposes of COBRA premium assistance, involuntary termination of employment includes:
>
> **a.** End of employment of a seasonal worker willing and able to continue employment
> **b.** A reduction in work hours to an amount greater than zero
> **c.** An involuntary termination occurring during the first quarter of 2012

> **6.** Employers claim the tax credit for their percentage of the COBRA premium assistance:
>
> **a.** On their 2009 tax year federal returns (Form 1065, 1120, etc.)
> **b.** On their quarterly tax return, Form 941-X
> **c.** On their supporting statement to correct information, Form 941c

Energy Tax Incentives

The 2009 Recovery Act expanded and extended a number of energy tax incentives for businesses. Many of them are designed to encourage the production of renewable energy.

Renewable energy production tax credit. The 2009 Recovery Act extended the placed-in-service date for wind facilities for three years, through December 31, 2012. The 2009 Recovery Act also extended the placed-in-service date for closed-loop biomass, open-loop biomass, geothermal, small irrigation, hydropower, landfill gas, waste-to-energy, and marine renewable facilities for three years, through December 31, 2013.

Election to claim the investment tax credit. Facilities that produce electricity from wind, closed-loop biomass, open-loop biomass, geothermal, small irrigation, hydropower, landfill gas, waste-to-energy, and marine renewable energy are eligible for the Code Sec. 45 production credit. Under the 2009 Recovery Act, taxpayers that place in service wind property in 2009 through 2012, and other renewable energy property placed in service in 2009 through 2013, can elect to claim the investment tax credit in lieu of the production tax credit.

In Notice 2009-52, the IRS provided the requirements for electing the investment tax credit in lieu of the energy production credit for property that is an integral part of a renewable electric energy facility. The election is available for property placed in service after December 31, 2008.

The election is irrevocable and must be made on Form 3468, *Investment Credit*, with a timely return (including extensions) filed for the year the property is placed in service. Taxpayers must make a separate election for each qualified facility. They must also attach a statement to Form 3468, under penalties of perjury, containing the following:

- A detailed technical description of the facility and the energy property placed in service that is an integral part of the facility;
- The date the property was placed in service;
- A statement that the taxpayer will not obtain a grant for the property; and
- An accounting of the taxpayer's basis and a depreciation schedule for the remaining basis after claiming the credit.

PLANNING POINTER

The basis in the property must be reduced by 50 percent of the investment tax credit claimed. Also, any bonus depreciation can be taken only after the basis reduction.

CAUTION

Taxpayers cannot claim both credits for the same facility.

Subsidized energy financing limitation. The 2009 Recovery Act repealed the subsidized energy financing limitation on the investment tax credit even if such property is financed with industrial development bonds or through any other subsidized energy financing. This provision is in effect for periods after December 31, 2008.

New clean renewable energy bonds. The 2009 Recovery Act increased the amount of funds available to issue new clean renewable energy bonds from the one-time national limit of $800 million to $2.4 billion. These qualified tax credit bonds can be issued by qualified nonprofit electricity producers to finance certain types of facilities that generate electricity from renewable sources (for example, wind and solar).

Repeal of limits on business credits for renewable energy property. The 2009 Recovery Act repealed the $4,000 limit on the 30 percent tax credit for small wind energy property and the limitation on property financed by subsidized energy financing. The repeal applies to property placed in service after December 31, 2008.

Renewable energy grants. Business taxpayers can apply for a federal grant instead of claiming either the energy investment tax credit or the renewable energy production tax credit for property placed in service in 2009 or 2010. In some cases, if construction begins in 2009 or 2010, the grant can be claimed for energy investment credit property placed in service through 2016, and for qualified renewable energy facilities, the grant is 30 percent of the investment in the facility and the property must be placed in service before 2014 (2013 for wind facilities).

Alternative fuel vehicle refueling property. The 2009 Recovery Act modified the credit rate and limit amounts for property placed in service in 2009 and 2010. Qualified property (other than property relating to hydrogen) is now eligible for a 50-percent credit, and the per-location limit increases to $50,000 for business property (increases to $2,000 for other/residential locations). Property relating to hydrogen keeps the 30-percent rate as before, but the per-business location limit rises to $200,000.

Plug-in electric vehicles. Congress created tax incentives for the purchase of plug-in electric vehicles in the *Emergency Economic Stabilization Act of 2008* (EESA) and revised them in the 2009 Recovery Act. The Code Sec. 30 credit in the 2009 Recovery Act is for a low-speed vehicle propelled to a significant extent by a rechargeable battery with a capacity of at least four kilowatt hours. The credit also applies to a two- or three-wheeled vehicle propelled to a significant extent by a rechargeable battery with a capacity of at least 2.5 kilowatt hours. Original use of the vehicle must begin with the taxpayer that purchases or leases the vehicle for use and not resale. The vehicle also must be used predominately in the United States.

The qualified vehicle must be purchased after February 17, 2009, and before January 1, 2012. The amount of the credit is 10 percent of the cost of the vehicle, up to a maximum credit of $2,500. In addition, a 10-percent credit of up to $4,000 is available for the conversion of existing vehicles to plug-in electric vehicles before 2012.

PLANNING POINTER

A similar but separate credit applies to qualified electric drive motor vehicles under Code Sec. 30D. A vehicle may qualify for both the Code Sec. 30 credit and the Code Sec. 30D credit. However, taxpayers cannot claim both credits for the same vehicle.

COMMENT

Credits for plug-in electric vehicles may be claimed whether placed in service for business or personal use. If used in a trade or business, the amount of the credit is treated as a business credit. Otherwise, it is treated as a nonrefundable personal credit. In either case, the amount of the credit reduces the taxpayer's basis in the vehicle.

Manufacturers may certify to purchasers that a plug-in electric vehicle satisfies all of the requirements for the Code Sec. 30 credit. Manufacturers (and U.S. distributors of foreign manufacturers) must certify that the plug-in vehicle is propelled to a significant extent by an electric motor drawing power from a battery. The battery must be capable of being recharged from an external source of energy. A low-speed vehicle generally must not exceed speeds of 25 miles-per-hour.

The IRS will review a manufacturer's certification and issue an acknowledgement letter to the manufacturer. The acknowledgement letter will advise if purchasers can rely on the manufacturer's certification. If the IRS subsequently withdraws a manufacturer's certification, taxpayers may not rely on it.

Code Sec. 382

When a corporation undergoes an ownership change, Code Sec. 382 may apply to limit the use of the corporation's prechange net operating losses (NOLs), certain built-in losses, and certain deductions attributable to the prechange period. Congress intended to prevent the trafficking of losses through acquisitions. A Code Sec. 382 ownership change generally occurs if the percentage of the stock owned by any one or more "5-percent shareholders" has increased by more than 50 percentage points over the lowest percentage owned by these shareholders at any time during the preceding three years.

In 2008, the IRS issued Notice 2008-83 to provide incentives for the acquisition of struggling banks by exempting banks' built-in losses from the Code Sec. 382 limitation following an ownership change. For purposes of Code Sec. 382(h), any deduction properly allowed after an ownership change of a bank with respect to losses on loans or bad debts, including any deduction for a reasonable addition to a reserve for bad debts, would not be treated as a built-in loss or a deduction attributable to periods before the change date. Many members of Congress were unhappy with Notice 2008-83, believing that the IRS had overstepped its authority.

The 2009 Recovery Act repealed Notice 2008-83 effective January 16, 2009 for most prospective transactions. However, Notice 2008-83 would remain effective for ownership changes on or before January 16, 2009. Notice 2008-83 will also apply with respect to any ownership change occurring after January 16, 2009, if the ownership change is:

- Under a written binding contract entered into on or before that date; or
- Under a written agreement entered into on or before that date and that was described on or before that date in a public announcement or in an SEC filing.

STUDY QUESTIONS

> **7.** Under the 2009 Recovery Act, business taxpayers can apply for a federal grant instead of claiming either the investment tax credit or the renewable energy production tax credit for property placed in service in 2009 or 2010. *True or False?*

---

8. The 2009 Recovery Act repealed Notice 2008-83 (which provided incentives for the acquisition of struggling banks by exempting banks' built-in losses from the Code Sec. 382 limitation following an ownership change) effective for most prospective transactions:

   a. January 1, 2009
   b. January 16, 2009
   c. February 17, 2009

Government Withholding

Delayed implementation of withholding on payments. In the *Tax Increase Prevention and Reconciliation Act of 2005* (TIPRA), Congress ordered that the federal government and every state and local government withhold tax at the rate of 3 percent on certain payments to persons providing any property or services. The withholding requirement applies even if the government entity making the payment is not the recipient of the property or services.

The 2009 Recovery Act delayed by one year the withholding requirement. The withholding and reporting requirements under Code Sec. 3402(t) will now apply to payments made after December 31, 2011.

Proposed regulations. The IRS issued proposed regulations on government withholding in 2008. Among other things, the proposed regulations provide rules regarding which government entities are required to withhold, which payments are subject to withholding, when withholding is required, and how government entities pay and report tax to the IRS.

Under proposed regulations, federal entities subject to these rules include the federal legislative, judicial, and executive branches, including all departments and agencies. State entities subject to these rules would include the District of Columbia, but not Indian tribal governments. There also would be a small entities exception for political subdivisions and instrumentalities making less than $100 million in payments for property or services annually. Additionally, the withholding requirements would not apply to any payment of less than $10,000. Certain payments, such as unemployment compensation and Social Security compensation, would continue to be excluded from mandatory withholding.

New Markets Tax Credit

Under the new markets tax credit (NMTC) program, taxpayers receive a credit against federal income taxes for making qualified equity investments in designated community development entities (CDEs). The CDE must use substantially all of its cash to make qualified low-income community investments, and maintain accountability to residents of low-income communities. Except for certain small business investment companies and financial institutions, CDEs must be certified by the IRS.

The NMTC totals 39 percent of the cost of the investment and is claimed over a seven-year credit allowance period. In each of the first three years, the investor receives a credit equal to 5 percent of the total amount paid for the stock or capital interest at the time of purchase. For the final four years, the value of the credit is 6 percent annually. Investors may not redeem their investments in CDEs before the end of the seven-year period.

The 2009 Recovery Act increased the maximum amount of qualified equity investments in CDEs by $1.5 billion for 2008 and 2009. However, the 2009 Recovery Act did not extend the NMTC beyond 2009. The NMTC is set to expire after 2009 unless Congress extends it.

> **COMMENT**
>
> In May 2009, the Treasury Department announced $1.5 billion in NMTC awards for 32 organizations—including renewable energy projects, charter schools, healthcare facilities, and retail centers—in 33 states, the District of Columbia, and Puerto Rico.

New Bonds

The 2009 Recovery Act authorized new Build America Bonds (BABs) and Qualified School Construction Bonds (QSCBs) to jump-start the sluggish bond market and encourage construction projects. States, municipalities, and school districts will be able to issue bonds at lower borrowing costs. BABs are designed to offer a higher interest rate than taxable bonds offered by private companies. QSCBs are tax-credit bonds that provide a tax credit instead of tax-free interest income to investors.

> **COMMENT**
>
> The 2009 Recovery Act also enhanced Qualified Zone Academy Bonds (QZABs). QZABs are used for renovating schools, purchasing equipment, and developing curricula. Private business must contribute equipment, technical assistance, employee volunteers, or other assistance worth at least 10 percent of the QZAB. For 2008, there is a cap of $400 million for QZABs issued after October 3, 2008; for 2009 and 2010, a $1.4 billion cap applies to each year.

Build America Bonds. There are three types of BABs. The first provides a subsidy through a refundable tax credit to the issuer, equal to 35 percent of interest. Under the second type, the federal government provides a tax credit to the investor, rather than to the issuer. The tax credit is equal to 35 percent of the interest payable by the issuer. The third type of BABs is Recovery Zone Economic Development Bonds, which have a refundable subsidy of 45 percent of the interest owed to investors. These bonds have a cap of $10 billion.

The IRS issued Notice 2009-26 to provide guidance on BABs. Among the highlights are:

- Issuers should apply for reimbursement from the IRS on new Form 8038-CP, *Return for Credit Payments to Issuers of Qualified Bonds,* filed at least 45 days before the interest payment date;
- Issuers that want to participate in the program should make an election on their books and records on or before the date of issue of the bonds; and
- The bonds should be reported on modified IRS Form 8038-G, *Information Return for Tax-Exempt Governmental Obligations.*

QSCBs. In Notice 2009-35, the IRS allocated to states and local governments the authority for 2009 to issue $11 billion in QSCBs. QSCBs must be used for school construction, rehabilitation, repair, and equipment. The $11 billion cap applies for 2009 (after February 17, 2009) and 2010. The allocation includes $6.6 billion for the states and $4.4 billion for the 100 largest school districts, based on levels of federal funding.

CORPORATE ESTIMATED TAX SHIFT ACT OF 2009

The *Tax Increase Prevention and Reconciliation Act of 2005* (TIPRA) and subsequent legislation increased corporate estimated tax payments due in July, August, or September 2013 to 100.25 percent. On July 28, 2009, President Obama signed into law the *Corporate Estimated Tax Shift Act of 2009.* The 2009 act impacts estimated tax payments large corporations will make in 2014.

The act revokes all the TIPRA and related provisions. The act increases estimated tax payments for corporations in the $1 billion-plus category to 100.25 percent for estimated payments due in July, August, or September of 2014.

INTERNATIONAL BUSINESS TAX REFORM

At the time this course went to press, Congress had many tax bills pending on its agenda. One of the most far-reaching for businesses would be proposed changes to the taxation of global corporate earnings and new measures to combat offshore tax evasion. President Obama has proposed limits on the tax-deferral rules, use of foreign tax credits, and the check-the-box rules. According to the Obama Administration, the proposals, which require approval by Congress, will "level the playing field" and raise nearly $200 billion in revenue.

> **COMMENT**
>
> President Obama did not call for complete removal of the deferral rules as many observers had predicted. The proposals are more tailored. "The proposals would limit the ability of a U.S. taxpayer to take deductions for offshore expenses against U.S. income."

Deferral

Generally, the foreign income of a foreign corporation is not subject to U.S. taxation even if the foreign corporation is organized by a U.S. taxpayer subject to U.S. taxation on foreign income earned by it directly. A U.S. taxpayer may organize a foreign corporation and defer U.S. taxation on foreign income until that income is repatriated. Additionally, taxpayers may be able to deduct some of the expenses that support their overseas operations before they repatriate profits.

According to the Obama Administration, this treatment shelters overseas profits from taxation and encourages U.S. taxpayers not to invest in domestic operations. Under the administration's proposal, taxpayers would generally be required to defer deductions—such as interest expenses associated with untaxed overseas investment—until the taxpayer repatriates its earnings. However, the proposal would allow a deduction for research and experimentation expenses.

> **COMMENT**
>
> President Obama did not call for complete removal of the deferral rules, as many observers had predicted. The proposals are more tailored. He summarized in May 2009, "The proposals would limit the ability of a U.S. taxpayer to take deductions for offshore expenses against U.S. income."

Foreign Tax Credit

The foreign tax credit allows U.S. taxpayers to reduce U.S. tax paid on foreign income by the amount of foreign taxes paid on the income. According to the Obama Administration, some taxpayers claim foreign tax credits for taxes paid on foreign income that is not subject to current U.S. taxation. Under the president's proposal, a taxpayer's foreign tax credit would be determined based on the amount of total foreign tax the taxpayer actually pays on its total foreign earnings. Additionally, a foreign tax credit would no longer be allowed for foreign taxes paid on income not subject to U.S. tax.

Check-the-Box

The check-the-box regulations automatically classify certain organizations as corporations and allow taxpayers to elect the federal tax classification of other business entities. According to the Obama Administration, some taxpayers have abused the check-the-box rules to evade U.S. taxation. Under the president's proposal, U.S. businesses that establish certain corporations overseas would be required to report them as corporations on their U.S. tax returns.

Research Credit

The research tax credit rewards taxpayers that invest in research and development activities. The credit is temporary and is set to sunset after 2009. The administration has asked Congress to make the research credit permanent.

Congressional Action

Congress has not yet scheduled hearings on the Obama Administration's international tax reform proposals. Some lawmakers have strongly endorsed them; others have been less enthusiastic. Some concerns include the possible negative impact of the proposals on job creation. At the same time, the proposals would generate large amounts of revenue during a time of large federal government budget deficits.

STUDY QUESTIONS

9. Qualified School Construction Bonds (QSCBs):
   a. Offer a higher interest rate than private bonds to jump-start construction projects
   b. Provide a tax credit rather than tax-free interest to investors
   c. May be used for renovating schools and developing curricula

10. The Obama Administration has proposed to Congress:
   a. To accelerate the expiration of the research tax credit to December 31, 2009
   b. To make the research credit permanent
   c. To extend the research credit one more year, through December 31, 2010

CONCLUSION

One of the chief goals of the 2009 Recovery Act was to stimulate the economy. Although many of the incentives benefit individuals, businesses were not left out. Bonus depreciation, Code Sec. 179 expensing, and the extended NOL carryback are three popular incentives that can help businesses during the current economic slowdown. It is likely that Congress may extend these incentives into 2010. Other business tax incentives in the 2009 Recovery Act may also be extended. The uncertainty over the fate of these business provisions complicates short-term tax planning; however, Congress is not expected to convert them from temporary to permanent incentives.

MODULE 1: NEW LAWS/RULES — CHAPTER 3

Preparer Restrictions and Other New Taxpayer Privacy Issues

LEARNING OBJECTIVES

Upon completion of this chapter, the student will be able to:

- Understand the restrictions on disclosure and use of tax return information, and the civil and criminal penalties for not adhering to such restrictions;

- Understand the exceptions to the prior consent requirement for disclosing return information;

- Determine the special data protection safeguards that apply to disclosures of Social Security numbers to preparers located outside the United States;

- Prepare a written and electronic use or disclosure consent that satisfies the requirements of the tax code and Treasury regulations;

- Determine the practice obligations imposed on preparers and the accountability of preparers under Circular 230 and how violations of such obligations are handled;

- Assess the appropriate standard imposed on preparers for disclosed return positions, undisclosed positions, and tax shelter positions, and the requirements for satisfying such standards; and

- Analyze the applicability of the attorney–client privilege, work product doctrine, and tax practitioner privilege to communications and documents.

INTRODUCTION

The increasing federal budget deficit, the widening "tax gap" (the difference between what taxpayers should pay and what is collected), and the increasing incidence of identity theft all present serious threats to economic security. IRS statistics indicate that more than 80 percent of taxpayers use either a paid-preparer or third-party software to prepare their annual tax returns. It should not be surprising, therefore, that Congress and the IRS have recently focused attention on tax return preparers, who are entrusted with considerable confidential taxpayer information and are often the decision-makers concerning the extent to which such information is presented on their clients' returns.

CONFIDENTIALITY OF TAX RETURN INFORMATION

The information that a taxpayer supplies to a preparer in connection with having a return prepared is expected to remain confidential. Thus, preparers are prohibited from disclosing or using tax return information other than for the specific purpose of preparing, assisting in preparing, or obtaining or providing services in connection with the preparation of, any tax return of the taxpayer (Code Secs. 6713 and 7216(a)). Civil and criminal penalties apply to an unauthorized use or disclosure of such information by a preparer. Preparers may, however, use or disclose certain information with the prior written consent of the taxpayer.

Although restrictions on preparers' disclosure and use of return information has been a part of the tax code since 1971, for returns prepared on or after January 1, 2009, more stringent requirements are being imposed on preparers concerning the use and disclosure of such information. These new restrictions are set forth in final Code Sec. 7216 regulations regarding the disclosure and use of return information by preparers.

If a tax return preparer knowingly or recklessly makes an unauthorized use or disclosure of tax return information, the preparer can be charged with a misdemeanor bearing a fine of up to $1,000 and up to one year of imprisonment per violation, together with having to pay the costs of prosecution (Code Sec. 7216).

> **CAUTION**
>
> A violation of Code Sec. 7216 is deemed to be a violation of Circular 230, which means that the violations will also involve the Office of Professional Responsibility (OPR).

Code Sec. 6713 imposes a civil penalty of $250 on any person who prepares returns for compensation and discloses any information furnished for, or in connection with, the preparation of any such return, or who uses any such information for any purpose other than to prepare or assist in preparing any such return.

> **COMMENT**
>
> Imposition of the civil penalty under Code Sec. 6713, unlike the criminal penalty under Code Sec. 7216, does not require that the disclosure be knowing or reckless. Independent of any penalties assessed by the IRS, the taxpayer is, of course, able to pursue a civil cause of action against the preparer for any damages resulting from an unauthorized disclosure of confidential information.

DEFINITION OF A TAX RETURN PREPARER

General Definition

For most purposes under the tax code (but not for purposes of Code Sec. 6713 or 7216, as discussed below), a *tax return preparer* is defined as any person who prepares for compensation all or a substantial part of any return or claim for refund under the income tax, estate and gift tax, employment tax, excise tax, and exempt organization provisions of the tax code (Code Sec. 7701(a)(36)).

The performance of any of the following acts will not, however, classify a person as a preparer:

- Preparation of a return for a friend, relative or neighbor free of charge even if the person completing the return receives a gift of gratitude from the taxpayer;
- The furnishing of typing, reproducing, or other mechanical assistance in preparing a return;
- Preparation by an employee (not an independent contractor) of a return or claim for refund for his or her employer, for an officer of the employer, or for another employee if he or she is regularly and continuously employed by that employer;
- Preparation as a fiduciary of a return or claim for refund for any person; or
- Preparation of a tax refund claim filed as the result of an IRS audit under certain circumstances.

Preparer for Confidentiality/Privacy Rules (Code Sec. 6713 and 7216 Definitions)

There is no single, uniform definition of a tax preparer for purposes of Code Secs. 6713 and 7216. Under Code 6713, which imposes a civil penalty for unauthorized use or disclosure of return information, a preparer is someone:

- Who is engaged in the business of preparing income tax returns;
- Who provides services in connection with the preparation of tax returns; or
- Who prepares returns for a taxpayer for compensation (Code Sec. 6713(a)).

For purposes of the imposition of criminal penalties under Code Sec. 7216 for a knowing or reckless use or disclosure of return information, the definition of *tax return preparer* uses neither the Code Sec. 6713 definition nor the general definition contained in Code Sec. 7701(a)(36). Instead, the regulations under Code Sec. 7216 cast a broader net, stating that a tax return preparer is any person who:

- Is engaged in the business of preparing, or assisting in the preparing, of tax returns;
- Is engaged in the business of providing auxiliary services in connection with the preparation of tax returns;
- Is remunerated for preparing, or assisting in preparing, a tax return for any other person; or
- As part of his or her duties or employment with any of the above individuals, performs services that assist in the preparation of, or assist in providing auxiliary services in connection with, the preparation of, a tax return.

The scope of Code Sec. 7216 for a tax return preparer includes all persons engaged in the business of preparing returns or providing auxiliary services, and individuals whose duties include performing such services. It includes not only individuals who hold themselves out as professional return preparers but also those who prepare tax returns for others without charging a fee. The definition includes individuals who perform such services full-time, as well as those who do so only on a part-time or incidental basis.

COMMENT

Tax return preparers under Code Sec. 7216 would therefore include volunteers with the Volunteer Income Tax Assistance (VITA) and Tax Counseling for the Elderly (TCE) programs.

For this purpose, a tax return includes any income tax return or amended income tax return or any declaration or amended declaration of estimated tax. For returns prepared after May 25, 2007, returns include estate and gift tax, employment tax, excise tax, and exempt organization returns. Auxiliary services include any service designed to aid a preparer in the preparation of a return. For example, a person who runs a business that provides computerized tax return processing services based on tax return information furnished by another person is a tax return preparer.

A person does not become a preparer, however, merely by leasing office space to a preparer, furnishing credit to a taxpayer whose tax return is prepared by a preparer, or otherwise performing a service that only incidentally relates to the preparation of tax returns.

EXAMPLE

Perry Preparer contracts with the FashionCo department store for the rental of space in the store. FashionCo advertises that taxpayers who use Perry Preparer's tax return preparation service may charge their tax preparation fees to their FashionCo charge account. FashionCo would not be considered a tax return preparer.

Tax return information. Tax return information protected under the confidentiality provisions of Code Secs. 6713 and 7216 is broadly defined to include the taxpayer's name, address, or identifying number. It includes information that the taxpayer furnishes to a preparer and information furnished to the preparer by a third party. Third parties include any person required under Code Sec. 6012 to make a return for such taxpayer, such as a:

- Guardian for a minor;
- Duly authorized agent for a principal;
- Fiduciary for an estate or trust; or
- Receiver, trustee in bankruptcy, or assignee for a corporation.

Tax return information also includes information the preparer derives or generates in connection with the preparation of a taxpayer's return. It therefore includes all computations, worksheets, and printouts the preparer creates in the process of preparing the return, as well as correspondence from IRS during the preparation, filing, and correction of a return, statistical compilations of tax return information, and tax return preparation software registration information. It also includes information received by the preparer from the IRS in connection with the processing of a tax return, including an acknowledgment of acceptance or notice of rejection of an electronically filed return. It also includes statistical compilations of tax return information, even in a form that cannot be associated with a particular taxpayer.

Tax return information does not, however, include any information that is identical to return information previously furnished to a preparer if the identical information was obtained other than in connection with the preparation of a tax return.

Use and disclosure of tax return information. *Use of tax return information* that is governed by Code Secs. 6713 and 7216 includes any circumstance in which a preparer refers to, or relies upon, return information as the basis to take an action.

> **EXAMPLE**
>
> In the course of preparing Chloe Client's 2009 federal income tax return, PrepCo., a return preparer, determines that Chloe is due a refund. An employee of PrepCo asks Chloe whether she would like a refund anticipation loan. PrepCo. does not ask this question of clients not due a refund. PrepCo. is using return information when it asks whether Chloe is interested in obtaining a refund anticipation loan because PrepCo. is basing the inquiry on Chloe's entitlement to a refund.

Disclosure means the act of making return information known to any person in any manner whatever. Hyperlink transfers are, for example, disclosures. To the extent that a taxpayer's use of a hyperlink results in the transmission of return information, this transmission of return is a disclosure by the preparer. For this purpose, a *hyperlink* is a device used to transfer an individual using tax preparation software from a preparer's webpage to a webpage operated by another person without the individual having to separately enter the web address of the destination page.

Exceptions to nondisclosure or use. Although the scope of Code Sec. 7216 is broad, there are three statutory exceptions to the penalty for using or disclosing return information The penalty does not apply to:

- Disclosures that are authorized by the tax code or made under court order;
- The use of furnished information to prepare state and local tax returns or declarations of estimated tax; or
- Disclosure or uses of information permitted by the regulations.

The 2008 final regulations identify 18 instances (analyzed in greater detail below) in which a disclosure or use of return information may be made by a preparer without the taxpayer's prior consent:

- Disclosures pursuant to other provisions of the tax code;
- Disclosures to the IRS;
- Disclosures or uses for preparation of a taxpayer's return;
- Disclosures to other tax return preparers;
- Disclosures or use of information in the case of related taxpayers;
- Disclosures pursuant to certain court or administrative orders, demands, requests, summonses, or subpoenas;
- Disclosures for use in securing legal advice, Treasury investigations, or court proceedings;
- Certain disclosures by attorneys and accountants;
- Uses by corporate fiduciaries;
- Disclosures to a taxpayer's fiduciary;
- Disclosures or use in preparation or audit of state or local tax returns, or assisting a taxpayer with foreign tax obligations;
- Disclosures and uses in connection with receiving payments for tax preparation services;
- Retention of records;
- Lists for solicitation of tax return business;
- Producing statistical information in connection with tax return preparation business;
- Disclosures or use of information for quality or peer reviews;
- Disclosures to report the commission of a crime; and
- Disclosures due to a preparer's incapacity or death.

STUDY QUESTIONS

---

1. Violations of the confidentiality provisions for tax return information under Code Sec. 6713:

   a. Incur a $250 IRS penalty and possibly being named in a civil action by the taxpayer

   b. Also are in violation of Circular 230 provisions for professional practice

   c. May result from volunteer services in programs such as Tax Counseling for the Elderly

2. Which of the following instances of use or disclosure of tax return information is subject to penalties under Code Sec. 7216 if the preparer does not obtain the client's consent?

   a. Disclosures to the IRS

   b. Disclosures for purposes of creating statistical compilations of tax return information

   c. Disclosures to a taxpayer's fiduciary

DISCLOSURE RULES

Certain Permitted Uses and Disclosures

A preparer does not need the taxpayer's consent to disclose return information made pursuant to any other provision of the tax code or regulations, or to make a disclosure to an officer or employee of the IRS (Treas. Reg. §301.7216-2(a) and (b)). In the former case, disclosure is appropriate because another tax code or regulation provision requires it, whereas disclosures to the IRS are "protected" because the IRS is itself bound to keep the information confidential under threat of penalty pursuant to Code Sec. 6103 (discussed below).

The preparer may also retain the taxpayer's return information, including an electronic or paper copy of the return, and use the information in the course of preparing other returns for the taxpayer, or in any subsequent audit or litigation relating to the return (Treas. Reg. §301.7216-2(m)). A preparer also does not need prior consent to use a taxpayer's federal return information in the course of preparing, or handling the audit of, the taxpayer's state or local returns. Similarly, the preparer may use such information in assisting the taxpayer in satisfying its foreign tax obligations (Treas. Reg. §301.7216-2(k)).

If a preparer provides software to a taxpayer that is used in connection with preparing or filing the taxpayer's return, the preparer is permitted, without obtaining the taxpayer's consent, to use the taxpayer's return information to update the taxpayer's software. It may also be used for purposes of addressing changes in IRS forms, e-file specifications, and administrative, regulatory, and legislative guidance or to test and ensure the software's technical capabilities (Treas. Reg. §301.7216-2(c)(1)).

> **EXAMPLE**
>
> Prepco, a preparer, provides tax preparation software to Acme, Inc, for use in the preparation of Acme's 2009 federal income tax return. Prepco wants to update Acme's tax preparation software to reflect last minute changes to the tax laws, that will require use of Acme's return information furnished while registering for the software. Prepco does not need Acme's consent to update the software.

Disclosures to Other Firm Officers, Employees, or Members

Preparer's location a factor. An officer, employee, or member of a preparer's firm located in the United States (including its territories and possessions) may use return information, and disclose return information to another officer, employee, or member of the same firm, if connected with the preparation of the taxpayer's federal, state, local, or foreign return. This exception does not apply if the disclosure is made to someone outside the United States even if connected with the same firm (Treas. Reg. §301.7216-2(c)(2)). If, however, the taxpayer initially provided return information to a preparer located outside of the United States, then an officer, employee, or member of the preparer may, without the need for consent, use the taxpayer's return information, and disclose such information to other officers, employees, and members of the same firm in connection preparation of the return (Treas. Reg. §301.7216-2(c)(3)).

> **EXAMPLE**
>
> Tula Johnston is a client of ReturnCo, a U.S. tax return preparer. Tula discloses return information to Ed Gray who works for ReturnCo in New Jersey. In connection with the preparation of Tula's return Ed discloses the information to Faina who works for ReturnCo in Michigan. Also in connection with the preparation of Tula's return, Ed discloses return information to Guy who works for ReturnCo in France. The disclosure of Tula's return information to Faina Singleton in Michigan would not require Tula's written or electronic consent, whereas the disclosure to Guy Lebarre in France would.

Exceptions for certain practitioners. Two related exceptions cover disclosures made by accounting and attorney preparers. First, such preparers are permitted to disclose return information to other officers, employees, or members of the same firm (not including related or affiliated firms) in the course of providing other legal or accounting services to the taxpayer, such as estate planning, or the preparation of books and records or accounting statements (Treas. Reg. §301.7216-2(h)(1)).

> **COMMENT**
>
> The prohibition on disclosing return information to related or affiliated firms is designed to prevent separate entities that may have a legal relationship, but that the taxpayer would probably not understand were related, from receiving the taxpayer's return information.

In addition, attorney and accountant preparers may take the return information into account as relevant and necessary in representing other clients, or disclose such information to other officers, members, and employees of their firm for the same purpose, but this exception does not extend to disclosing such information to anyone else (Treas. Reg. §301.7216-2(h)(2)).

> **EXAMPLE**
>
> Alita Accountant, who is a member of AccuCount, an accounting firm, renders an opinion in connection with Mistax, Inc.'s financial statements filed with a Securities and Exchange Commission (SEC) registration statement. Before the registration statement becomes effective, another member of AccuCount, Bert Badnews, prepares a return for Notright, Inc, a corporation that does business with Mistax. Bert advises Alita about certain information Bert discovered in the course of preparing the statements, and that is contained in, Notright's return. The information materially impacts the accuracy of Mistax's financial statement. Alita does not disclose Notright's return information to either Mistax or the SEC, but advises both that amended financial statements need to be filed. Such disclosure by Bert, and use by Alita, does not require Notright's prior consent.

Disclosures to Other Preparers Outside the Firm

The previous discussions address use and disclosure within the preparer's same firm, although in different locations, but there is a separate exception to the need for taxpayer disclosure when a preparer discloses return information to another preparer located in the United States who is not an officer, employee, or member of the same firm. Such disclosure is permitted without the need for the taxpayer's written or electronic consent, provided such disclosure is made in connection with the preparation of the taxpayer's federal, state, local, or foreign return, and the services of the second preparer do not involve substantive determinations or advice (i.e., analysis, interpretation, or application of the law). This exception is designed to cover situations such as a preparer providing return information to a second preparer so that the latter may provide return processing services such as transferring the information to, and computing the liability, on the return (Treas. Reg. §301.7216-2(d)(1)).

Disclosures to Contractors, and Related Party Use and Disclosures

Prior consent is also not needed for disclosures to a contractor of the preparer in connection with the programming, maintenance, repair, testing, or procurement of tax preparation equipment or software, but only to the extent necessary to obtain such services, and only if the preparer provides such contractors written notice about the applicability, requirements, and penalties of Code Secs. 6713 and 7215. These contractors will themselves be deemed preparers because they are providing auxiliary services in connection with the preparation of returns (Treas. Reg. §301.7216-2(d)(2)).

In preparing returns for two related taxpayers, a preparer may use and disclose to the second taxpayer any return information that the preparer obtained from a first taxpayer if the first taxpayer's tax interest in the information is not adverse to the second taxpayer's tax interest in the information; and the first taxpayer has not expressly prohibited the disclosure or use. A taxpayer is considered related to another taxpayer if they have any one of the following relationships:

- Husband and wife;
- Child and parent;
- Grandchild and grandparent,;
- Partner and partnership;
- Trust or estate and beneficiary;
- Trust or estate and fiduciary;
- Corporation and shareholder or members of a controlled group of corporations as defined under Code Sec. 1563 (Treas. Reg. §301.7216-2(e)).

EXAMPLE

Tom and Theresa Taxpayer, a married couple, arrange to have their 2009 federal income tax returns prepared by Peggy Preparer, using married filing separately status. In the course of preparing Tom's separate return, he sends Peggy his 2009 Form W-2. Neither Tom nor Theresa has prohibited Peggy from disclosing their return information to the other. In the course of meeting with Tom and Theresa's financial planner, Theresa contacts Peggy and inquires about how much Tom contributed to his 401(k) plan account in 2009. Peggy may disclose the information to Theresa without the need to obtain Tom's consent.

Disclosures Pursuant to Court or Administrative Order

Disclosures made pursuant to certain court or administrative orders also do not require the taxpayer's consent. Such disclosures may be made in response to:

- An order of any federal, state or local court;
- A federal or state grand jury subpoena;
- Congressional subpoena; or
- An order, demand, summons, or subpoena of any federal agency or any state agency, body, or commission that oversees the licensing, registration, or regulation of preparers.

The regulations also include disclosures in response to a written request from an ethics committee or board investigating the conduct of a preparer, inquiries by the Public Company Accounting Oversight Board in connection with certain inspections under Section 104, or investigations under Section 105, of the Sarbanes-Oxley Act of 2002, 15 U.S.C. 7215 (Treas. Reg. §301.7216-2(f)).

COMMENT

If a summons is served on a preparer that requires the production of records pertaining to a taxpayer, the IRS is required to notify the taxpayer within 3 days after service of the summons on the preparer and at least 23 days before the date fixed in the summons for examination of the summoned records (Code Sec. 7609(a)(2); Treas. Reg. §301.7609-2(a)(2)). The taxpayer then has the right to institute a proceeding to quash the summons within 20 days thereafter. In order to do so the taxpayer must:

1. File a petition to quash in the district court having jurisdiction;
2. Notify the IRS by sending a copy of that petition by registered or certified mail; and
3. Notify the preparer by sending a copy of the petition by registered or certified mail.

If a taxpayer fails to institute a proceeding to quash, the IRS may examine the records summoned on the 24th day after the notice was served on or mailed to the taxpayer. If the taxpayer fails to institute such proceedings, the IRS may also notify the preparer of that fact and provide a certificate that confirms this (Code Sec. 7609(i)(3)). After receiving this certificate the preparer may release the records to the IRS and will not be liable to the taxpayer for releasing the records.

Disclosures Made in Obtaining Legal Advice

Another category of exception to the taxpayer consent requirement applies when the preparer discloses return information:

- In order to obtain legal advice from an attorney;

- In connection with IRS or Treasury Department investigations of the preparer; or
- In connection with any court or grand jury proceedings involving either the preparer to the taxpayer (Treas. Reg. §301.7216-2(g)).

Disclosures Made for Reporting Criminal Violations

A preparer is also permitted to disclose return information to federal, state, or local law enforcement agents to report, or assist in the investigation of, a crime. This latter exception applies if the preparer has a bona fide belief that such criminal violation has occurred, even if it turns out that such belief was incorrect (Treas. Reg. §301.7216-2(q)).

COMMENT

A *whistleblower* is someone who reports to the IRS instances of violations of the Internal Revenue Code by one or more third parties. The IRS Whistleblower Office analyzes such information and, if the office determines that it needs the assistance of the whistleblower (or the whistleblower's legal representative), the office may disclose return information to the whistleblower under a written contract to render assistance. Such disclosures are only to be made to the extent the IRS deems it necessary for tax administration, and must be limited to only the parts or portions of return information needed by the whistleblower in aiding the Whistleblower Office. The whistleblower must agree not to disclose or otherwise use the disclosed return information for any other purpose and must generally agree in writing, before any disclosure of return information is made, to permit an inspection of his or her premises by the IRS relative to the maintenance of the disclosed information (Temp. Reg. §301.6103(n)-2T).

STUDY QUESTIONS

3. A preparer may not disclose return information in connection with any court or grand jury hearing involving the preparer or taxpayer without the taxpayer's prior consent. *True or False?*

4. The IRS Whistleblower Office may disclose return information regarding a third party to a whistleblower:

  a. If the whistleblower is under a written contract to render assistance and agrees to inspection requirements

  b. In order to determine whether the office requires the whistleblower's assistance in investigating the third party

  c. Only in cases of actual criminal violations

Fiduciary Uses and Disclosures

There are two exceptions to the consent requirement for use and disclosures by, and disclosures to, fiduciaries:

- A trust company, bank trust department, or other corporate fiduciary that prepares a return for its client may, unless the client has specified otherwise, use such information in the course of providing fiduciary, investment, or other custodial or management services to the client, and also supply return information to the client's attorney, accountant, and/or investment advisor (Treas. Reg. §301.7216-2(i)); and
- If a preparer's client dies, becomes incompetent, insolvent, or bankrupt, or is the subject of a conservatorship or receivership, the preparer may disclose return information to a duly appointed fiduciary of the taxpayer or the taxpayer's estate, or such fiduciary's agent (Treas. Reg. §301.7216-2(j)).

Use and Disclosures for Statistical Compilations

A preparer is also permitted to disclose and use certain statistical compilations of anonymous tax return information in support of the preparer's tax return preparation business (Treas. Reg. §301.7216-2(o)). The purpose and use of the statistical compilation must relate directly to the internal management or support of the preparer's business.

The IRS has provided interim guidance concerning this exception. Marketing and advertising are considered in direct support of the preparer's business, so long as they are not false, misleading, or unduly influential. Fundraising activities conducted by Volunteer Income Tax Assistance programs and other Code Sec. 501(c) organizations in direct support of their tax return preparation services are also not considered marketing and advertising under the interim guidance (*Notice 2009-13*, 2009-6 I.R.B. 447).

However, the disclosure of anonymous statistical compilations of average refund, credit, or rebate amounts, or any part thereof, is prohibited. Moreover, any disclosure of a statistical compilation must be in a form that cannot be associated with, or otherwise identify (directly or indirectly) a particular taxpayer. To protect anonymity, the disclosure must not disclose Excel or similar digitized cells containing data from fewer than 25 tax returns. The preparer also may not sell or exchange for value the compilation except in conjunction with a sale or other disposition of the preparer's tax return preparation business.

Practice-Related Disclosures

There are four exceptions to the consent requirement that address using and disclosing return information in connection with the operation of the preparer's practice.

Payment Information. The preparer is permitted to use and disclose information provided by the taxpayer in paying for the preparation of the return (Treas. Reg. §301.7216-2(l)).

> **EXAMPLE**
>
> In the course of paying to have his return prepared by Philipa Preparer, Tony Taxpayer provides Philipa with his Visa card number and expiration date. Philipa may disclose to the Visa credit card company Tony's name, credit card information, and the amount due for the preparation services in order to process the payment.

Contact list. The preparer is permitted to compile a list containing solely the names, addresses, e-mail addresses, and phone numbers of its clients, and use the list to contact such clients to provide tax information or offer additional tax preparation services. The preparer may not transfer any part of the list except in conjunction with a sale or other disposition of the preparer's tax return preparation business. In the event of such sale or disposition, the purchaser/transferee will be bound by the same restrictions set forth in this paragraph (Treas. Reg. §301.7216-2(n)).

Peer review. The preparer may disclose the information in connection with a peer review of the preparer by attorneys, CPAs, enrolled agents, and/or enrolled actuaries eligible to practice before the IRS. The preparer may provide the information to the reviewer, or to the reviewer's administrative or support personnel (Treas. Reg. §301.7216-2(p)).

Continuation of preparer's practice. In the event the preparer dies or becomes incapacitated, disclosure may be made to allow the preparer, his legal representative, or representative of the estate, as applicable, to operate the business. Any of these individuals receiving a return will also be considered a preparer for purposes of Code Secs. 7216 and 6713 (Treas. Reg. §301.7216-2(r)).

> **COMMENT**
>
> Although this exception to the consent requirement covers death and disability of an individual preparer, it does not cover the bankruptcy or receivership of an individual or entity preparer.

Special Rules for Social Security Numbers

In December 2008 the IRS issued final, temporary, and proposed regulations that modify the rule prohibiting disclosure of the taxpayer's Social Security number (SSN) occurring on or after January 1, 2009, and on or before January 1, 2012 (T.D. 9437). The regulations apply to disclosures in connection with a return in the Form 1040 Series returns (Form 1040, Form 1040NR, Form 1040A, and Form 1040EZ).

If the preparer obtains consent from a taxpayer to disclose return information to a preparer located outside of the United States (other than temporarily), the preparer must redact or otherwise mask the taxpayer's SSN before the return information is disclosed. However, if a preparer located within the United States initially received or obtained the taxpayer's SSN from another preparer located outside of the United States, the preparer within the United States may, without consent, retransmit the taxpayer's SSN to the preparer located outside the United States that initially provided the SSN to the U.S.-based preparer.

A preparer located within the United States (including any of its territories or possessions) may obtain consent to disclose the taxpayer's SSN to a preparer located outside of the United States if the preparer uses an adequate data protection safeguard as described in Rev. Proc. 2008-35, I.R.B. 2008-29, 162, issued concurrently with the regulations.

Rev. Proc. 2008-35 defines an *adequate data protection safeguard* as a security program, policy, and practice approved by management and implemented to include administrative, technical, and physical safeguards in protection of tax return information from misuse or unauthorized access or disclosure. The safeguard must meet or conform to one of the following privacy or data security frameworks:

- The United States Department of Commerce safe harbor framework for data protection (or successor program);
- A foreign law data protection safeguard that includes a security component, e.g., the European Commission's Directive on Data Protection;
- A framework that complies with the requirements of a financial or similar industry-specific standard that is generally accepted as best practices for technology and security related to that industry, e.g., the BITS (Financial Services Roundtable) Financial Institution Shared Assessment Program;
- The requirements of the AICPA/CICA Privacy Framework;
- The requirements of the most recent version of IRS Publication 1075, *Tax Information Security Guidelines for Federal, State and Local Agencies and Entities;* or
- Any other data security framework that provides the same level of privacy protection as contemplated by one or more of the frameworks previously listed here.

STUDY QUESTIONS

5. Disclosure of anonymous statistical compilations of average refund, credit, or rebate amounts:
   a. Is prohibited
   b. Is permissible only for averages for three or more successive tax years
   c. Is permissible only when returns from multiple offices or branches of the preparer's firm are included

6. Under the regulations for Social Security numbers on returns effective January 1, 2009, a preparer located in the United States:
   a. May not disclose the SSN to a preparer located outside of the United States without the taxpayer's consent
   b. Must mask the taxpayer's SSN to disclose return information to a preparer located outside of the United States, even with the prior consent to do so from the taxpayer
   c. Is prohibited from transmitting or retransmit a taxpayer's SSN to a preparer located outside of the United States

Form Used to Obtain Consent and Timing of Consent

The requirements applied when a preparer obtains a valid consent from a taxpayer/client are elaborate and strict. A consent to disclose or use tax return information with respect to a taxpayer not filing a return in the Form 1040 series may be in any format, including an engagement letter to a client, as long as the consent includes the following:

- The name of the tax return preparer and the name of the taxpayer;
- The identity of the intended purpose of the disclosure, the specific recipient, and the particular use authorized; and
- A specification of the tax return information to be disclosed or used by the return preparer.

For consents not involving a return in the Form 1040 series, a single written consent may authorize both use and disclosure of return information. The consent must be obtained prior to any disclosure if a preparer to whom the tax return information is to be disclosed is located outside of the United States. The taxpayer must sign and date the consent (Treas. Reg. §301.7216-3)).

EXAMPLE

TaxPrep, Inc. sends its corporate client, Client, Inc., an engagement letter. That letter also requests the consent of Client to TaxPrep's disclosure of Client's Form 1120 tax return information to an investment banking firm to assist the investment banking firm in securing long term financing Client. The engagement letter includes TaxPrep Inc.'s name, Client's name, and a signature and date line for Client. The engagement letter also includes a statement that "Client authorizes TaxPrep to disclose the portions of Client's 2009 Form 1120 tax return information to the firm retained by Client as necessary for the purposes of assisting Client secure long-term financing." The engagement letter satisfies the requirements of the regulations for disclosing the information provided therein for the specific purpose stated.

For the Form 1040 series of returns (Form 1040, Form 1040NR, Form 1040A, and Form 1040EZ) the IRS issued Rev. Proc. 2008-35, I.R.B. 2008-29, 162, in connection with the final Code Sec. 7216 regulations, which provides guidance concerning the requirements for the consent form.

The consent form must specifically identify each disclosure or use of return information to which the taxpayer is consenting. Although a single consent form may cover more than one disclosure or use of tax return information, the taxpayer must affirmatively select those disclosures or uses to which he or she is consenting. Disclosure of information on a joint return requires the consent of both taxpayers. Moreover, a single consent form cannot authorize both use and disclosure of tax return information. One document must be used to authorize use(s) and a separate document must be used to authorize disclosure(s).

COMMENT

An exception to dual forms applies to taxpayers not filing returns in the Form 1040 series. Those taxpayers may authorize both uses and disclosures in a single written consent (Treas. Reg. §301.7216-3(a)(3)(iii)).

The consent form must be in 12-point type on 8½-by-11-inch paper (unless generated electronically, as described below) and must include:

- The preparer's name and the taxpayer's name;
- The nature of the disclosure(s);
- The identity of those to whom the disclosures will be made;
- Details on the information being disclosed;
- The particular use authorized; and
- The product or service for which the tax return information will be used.

If the taxpayer consents to use of tax return information, the consent must describe the particular use authorized. For example, if a preparer intends to use return information to generate solicitations for products or services other than tax return preparation (such as financial planning, balance-due loans, mortgage loans, or life insurance), the consent must identify each specific type of product or service for which the preparer may solicit use of the return information.

The consent must inform the taxpayer that signing the consent is not required, and granting the consent must be both knowing and voluntary. Conditioning the provision of any services on the taxpayer's furnishing consent will cause the consent to be deemed involuntary, unless the condition is disclosure of the taxpayer's return information to another preparer for the purpose of performing services that assist in the preparation of, or provide auxiliary services in connection with the preparation of, the tax return (Treas. Reg. §301.7216-3(a)(1)).

> **EXAMPLE**
>
> Paul Preparer works for PCA, Inc., a tax preparation firm located in the United States. PCA is retained by Acme, Inc. to provide tax return preparation services for Acme's employees. Eddie Employee works for Acme in Germany. To provide tax return preparation services for Eddie, Paul requires the assistance of, and needs to disclose Eddie's return information to, a preparer who works for PCA's affiliate located in Germany. PCA may condition its provision of tax return preparation services upon Eddie consenting to the disclosure of Eddie's return information to the preparer in Germany.

The consent must advise the taxpayer that in signing the consent the taxpayer may specify a time period for the duration of the consent. If no time period is specified, the consent will be effective for a period of one year from the date of the taxpayer's signature on the consent. It must also inform the taxpayer that if the taxpayer believes return information has been disclosed without consent or used improperly, the taxpayer may report such disclosure to the Treasury Inspector General for Tax Administration.

The consent must contain the taxpayer's affirmative consent to the use or disclosure. Thus, a consent would not be valid if it advised that taxpayer that consent would be presumed unless the taxpayer "opts out" by returning the form. It must also be signed and dated by the taxpayer. The taxpayer must also receive a copy of the executed consent at the time of execution.

The client cannot retroactively consent to the use or disclosure after the preparer uses or discloses return information. Instead, the consent must be obtained by the preparer *before* any use or disclosure is made.

If the preparer requests the client's consent to use or disclose information, and the client initially refuses such consent, the preparer may not make repeated subsequent requests to try to get the client to change his or her mind. However, this does not prohibit the preparer from responding to a subsequent inquiry from the taxpayer independently asking about, or requesting, the disclosure or use of return information.

> **EXAMPLE**
>
> In July 2009 Carmella Client, who has not previously signed a consent to disclose return information, contacts her preparer, Petra Preparer, and asks Petra to forward certain gross income and adjusted gross income information from Carmella's 2009 Form 1040 to Murray Mortgagebroker, who is assisting Carmella in obtaining financing for a residence Carmella is purchasing. Until Petra obtains a signed consent from Carmella, which conforms to the new requirements of Treas. Reg. §301.7216 and Rev. Proc. 2008-35, Petra may not forward the information to Murray.

If a taxpayer furnishes consent to disclose or use tax return information electronically, the taxpayer must furnish the tax return preparer with an electronic signature that will verify that the taxpayer made an affirmative, knowing, and voluntary consent to each disclosure or use. A tax return preparer seeking to obtain a taxpayer's consent to the disclosure or use of tax return information electronically must obtain the taxpayer's signature on the consent in one of the following manners:

- Assign a personal identification number (PIN) that is at least five characters long to the taxpayer (the PIN may be preassigned but may not be automatically furnished by the software);
- Have the taxpayer type in the taxpayer's name in full and then press the Enter key to authorize the consent; or
- Any other manner in which the taxpayer affirmatively enters five or more characters that are unique to that taxpayer that are used by the tax return preparer to verify the taxpayer's identity. (*Rev. Proc. 2008-35,* I.R.B. 2008-29, July 1, 2008).

> **EXAMPLE**
>
> Peter Preparer offers tax preparation services over the Internet. Candy Client accesses Peter's website, where she finds the following "Privacy Statement":
>
> > Your privacy is very important to us. During the course of providing our services to you, we may offer you various other services that may be of interest to you based on our determination of your needs through analysis of your data. Your use of the services we offer constitutes a consent to our disclosure of tax information to the service providers. If at any time you wish to limit your receipt of promotional offers based upon information you provide, you may call us.
>
> Beneath the Privacy Statement, Candy finds the following acknowledgment line next to "yes" and "no" button images reads, "I have read the Privacy Statement and agree to it by clicking here." If Candy clicks "no," a message appears on the screen informing her that Peter will not proceed with preparation of her return. Peter has failed to comply with the requirements for obtaining Candy's consent to disclosure. Peter has made the use of the program contingent on Candy's consent disclosure and use of her tax return information for purposes other than tax preparation He has also failed to identify the return information that he will disclose or use, to identify the purposes of the disclosures and uses, and has not advised Candy that she has the ability to request a more limited disclosure of return information as she may direct. The single document attempts to have Candy consent to both disclosures and uses. It does not contain the required mandatory statements. The consent is not also considered signed by Candy because Peter has not provided a means for Candy to electronically sign the consent in the required manner. Finally, the consent is not dated.

Code Secs. 6103 and 7431(b). Code Sec. 6103(a)(3) imposes a penalty against improper disclosure of return information by any person who receives returns in the course of public business, such as employees of the IRS, state employees to whom the IRS makes authorized disclosures, and private persons who obtain return information from the IRS with restrictions attached. Under Code Sec. 7431(b) a taxpayer has the right to bring a private cause of action for damages for an improper disclosure of the taxpayer's return information.

Code Sec. 6103 applies mainly to IRS personnel. It does not apply to private tax preparers (*Pinero v. Jackson Hewitt Tax Service Inc*, E.D. LA, 2009-1 USTC ¶50,162, 594 FSupp2d 710, motion to reconsider den'd 2009-1 USTC ¶50,410). Commercial preparers are, as discussed above, forbidden from making improper disclosures under Code Sec. 7216.

> **COMMENT**
>
> A taxpayer may also bring a civil action for damages against the U.S. government if an IRS employee offers the taxpayer's accountant, attorney, or other tax professional favorable tax treatment in exchange for information about the taxpayer (Code Sec. 7435). This provision is intended to deter IRS employees from enticing tax professionals to breach their fiduciary responsibilities and divulge information about their clients.

Circular 230. The rules governing practice before the IRS for attorneys, CPAs, enrolled agents, and enrolled retirement plan agents are contained in the provisions of Treasury Circular No. 230, which is codified in the Code of Federal Regulations (31 C.F.R. Part 10). Practice before the IRS includes all matters connected with presentations to the IRS, including:

- The preparation and filing of necessary documents;
- Correspondence with and communications to the IRS; and
- The representation of a client at conferences, hearings, and meetings.

> **COMMENT**
>
> Unenrolled preparers are not governed by Circular 230; they are regulated by the compliance center of the applicable IRS operating division (either Wage and Investment Operating Division or the Small Business/Self-Employed Operating Division).

Circular 230 sets forth "best practices" for rendering almost all tax advice (which includes communication with the client, evaluating the reasonableness of any assumptions, and acting with fairness and integrity in practicing before the IRS). The following are some of the significant duties and restrictions imposed on preparers under Circular 230:

- A practitioner who acts on behalf of a taxpayer and knows that the taxpayer has not complied with the law, or has made an error or omission on a return, must promptly inform the client of the fact, along with the consequences of the noncompliance, error, or omission;
- A practitioner is required to exercise due diligence in preparing, approving, and filing tax returns. A practitioner is deemed to have exercised due diligence in relying upon the work product of another reasonably trained and supervised person, except with respect to advise in preparing returns, covered opinions, or other written advice; and
- A practitioner who prepares tax returns is prohibited from endorsing or otherwise negotiating any check issued to a client by the government with respect to a federal tax liability.

> **CAUTION**
>
> The IRS has indicated on its website that under the due diligence provisions of Circular 230 (§10.22) preparers also have an obligation to make inquiry and document such inquiry concerning the filing of the Report of Foreign Bank and Financial Accounts (FBAR) form (TD F 90-22.1).

Enforcing Circular 230. The Office of Professional Responsibility is organized into three branches:
- Case Development and Licensure;
- Enforcement I (attorneys, CPAs, and enrolled agents); and
- Enforcement II (enrolled actuaries, enrolled retirement plan agents, and appraisers).

The OPR has the ability of:
- Issuing a private reprimand (by sending a letter to the practitioner indicating that there was a violation of Circular 230);
- Issuing a *censure* (a letter of reprimand where the fact of the censure is released to the public through the Internal Revenue Bulletin);
- Imposing monetary sanctions on firms that knew or should have known of violations by its employees; or
- Suspending (for a term of months up to five years), or disbarring the practitioner from practicing before the IRS.

Once disbarred, a practitioner may only seek reinstatement after five years, upon proof of good behavior.

STUDY QUESTIONS

7. The penalty imposed on IRS personnel who improperly disclose return information is authorized under:
   a. Code Sec. 6103(a)(3)
   b. The applicable compliance center within an IRS operating division
   c. Circular 230

8. The Office of Professional Responsibility is authorized for all of the following actions against preparer practitioners who violate Circular 230 rules *except:*
   a. Censure
   b. Criminal proceedings
   c. Disbarment

Privilege Defenses to Disclosure

The IRS has asserted that "there is no tax preparer privilege." Information disclosed by a taxpayer to a preparer in the course of and in furtherance of the preparation of the taxpayer's return is not privileged information that cannot otherwise be reached by an IRS or court-ordered summons. However, just because an individual is a preparer does not necessarily mean that he or she wears an entirely different hat—that of either "attorney" or "federal tax practitioner"—in connection with certain information. In those latter cases, the client may assert either an attorney–client or a federal tax practitioner privilege to prevent disclosure of that information.

> **COMMENT**
>
> The privilege defense against disclosure belongs to the client, although the practitioner invokes the privilege on the taxpayer/client's behalf any time the practitioner is asked to reveal such information. The tax practitioner must assume that the client will raise these defenses. Waiver of the privilege by the client should be in writing to protect the practitioner. Ignorance on the part of the practitioner about availability of a privilege defense cannot protect the practitioner against a claim by the client unless the practitioner also can show a reasonable basis for his or her assumptions.

Attorney–client privilege. If the professional engaged by the taxpayer is an attorney, the attorney–client privilege applies to all private communications between the taxpayer and an attorney. In order for the privilege to apply, the communication between the taxpayer and the attorney must not have been disclosed to third parties unconnected with representing the client in the matter. If, for example, the information is communicated by the taxpayer to an attorney for inclusion in a tax return (including an amended return), such information is not privileged because it is communicated for the purpose of disclosure (***Evergreen Trading***, 2008-1 USTC ¶50,109 , 80 FedCl 122).

If an attorney engages an accountant for the purpose of assisting the attorney in representing the client, the attorney–client privilege extends to communications among the attorney, the client, and the accountant concerning the scope of the representation. For example, an accountant who assists an attorney in communicating effectively with the attorney's client does not serve to waive any attorney–client privilege that would otherwise apply to privileged information that was disclosed to the accountant (***United States v. Kovel***, 2nd Cir., 62-1 USTC ¶9111, 296 F.2d 918).

Work-product protection. The attorney—client privilege covers communication; there is a separate protection for an attorney's "work product." *Work products* include the documents and tangible objects produced by an attorney or other representative in anticipation of litigation or in preparation for trial (Federal Rule of Civil Procedure 23(b)(3)).

The purpose of the work-product doctrine is to prevent an opponent in litigation from being able to gain access to, and make use of, the fruits of the labors of counsel for the other side. In the absence of the protection, practitioners would be reluctant to put their thoughts and strategies in writing.

This is an area of considerable ongoing controversy, primarily surrounding the issue of whether tax accrual workpapers—prepared prior to any audit of the taxpayer but that evaluate the risks of a particular tax issue—have been prepared in anticipation of litigation. The IRS, in Announcement 2002-63, took the position that such workpapers are not generated in connection with seeking legal or tax advice, but instead are developed to evaluate a taxpayer's deferred or contingent tax liabilities in connection with its disclosure to third parties of its financial condition. The IRS also stated in the announcement that tax accrual workpapers are not protected by either the attorney—client privilege or the tax practitioner privilege.

The First Circuit Court of Appeals has held that the tax accrual workpapers of a publicly traded corporation suspected of engaging in prohibited tax shelter activity documents were not protected by the work-product doctrine (*U.S .v. Textron*, 2009-2 USTC ¶50,574). Rather than being prepared in anticipation of litigation, the court reasoned that tax accrual workpapers are generally prepared in the ordinary course of business and, therefore, are not protected by the work-product doctrine from IRS summonses.

Federal tax practitioner privilege. Under Code Sec. 7525, added to the tax code in 1998, there is also a limited privilege attached to certain communications between a taxpayer and a federally authorized tax practitioner. The privilege only applies in noncriminal tax matters before the IRS, and in noncriminal tax proceedings in federal court brought by or against the United States. The privilege applies to the same extent that communication would be considered a privileged communication if it were between a taxpayer and an attorney.

The privilege only extends to advice with respect to matters within the scope of the authority to practice as a federally authorized tax practitioner. *Most significantly, this privilege does not include communications regarding tax return preparation.* This is because a return is meant to be disclosed to the IRS; therefore, anything reflected on the return was never intended to remain confidential (*U.S. v. BDO Seidman*, 7th Cir., 2003-2 USTC ¶50,582, 337 F.3d 802, 810). The privilege also does not apply to the extent the advice concerns only foreign tax, and not US federal tax, obligations (*Valero Energy Corp. v. US*, DC Ill., 2008-2 USTC ¶50,482).

The privilege also does not apply to any written communication by a tax practitioner in connection with the promotion of a direct or indirect participation of such corporation in a tax shelter. *Tax shelter* is defined under Code Sec. 6662(d)(2)(C)(iii) and therefore has the same definition used for purposes of the preparer penalty under Code Sec. 6694 discussed above. This definition encompasses any partnership or other entity, any investment plan or arrangement, or any other plan or arrangement, if a significant purpose of such partnership, entity, plan, or arrangement is the avoidance or evasion of federal income tax.

> **COMMENT**
>
> Whether a practitioner will be deemed to be "promoting" a tax shelter may depend on the context in which the preparer alerts the client to the planning opportunity. If, for example, the practitioner has a long and close relationship with the taxpayers, including preparing returns, assisting with tax planning, and responding to federal and state tax officials on their behalf, then advising the taxpayers with respect to a transaction that constitutes a tax shelter may not be deemed "promoting" the shelter (*Countryside Limited Partnership*, 132 TC No. 17, Dec. 57,846).

Code Sec. 6694 Preparer Penalty for Nondisclosure

As discussed above, preparers are subject to civil and criminal penalties for improperly disclosing or using tax return information. These penalties are designed to keep return information confidential. On the flip side, there are affirmative obligations imposed on preparers either to have adequate support for the reporting positions they take, or to ensure that their client discloses information to the IRS about the position at the time the return or claim for refund is filed.

Legislative background of tax position standards. The standards to which preparers are held for positions taken on a return have been the subject of several recent legislative changes. The *Small Business and Work Opportunity Tax Act of 2007* (P.L. 110-28) intended that preparers be held to a higher standard than their taxpayer clients with respect to undisclosed positions taken on a return. For undisclosed positions, a preparer had to have "reasonable belief" that the position would "more likely than not be sustained on its merits." This standard was higher than the "substantial authority" standard imposed on taxpayers under the Code Sec 6662 accuracy-related penalty. For undisclosed positions, a preparer had to have reasonable belief that the position would "more likely than not be sustained on its merits."

The *Emergency Economic Stabilization Act of 2008* (P.L. 110-343) simplified Code Sec. 6694 by replacing the "more likely than not" standard for undisclosed tax positions with a "substantial authority" standard, which is the same standard applied to penalties imposed on taxpayers for purposes of the accuracy penalty under Code Sec. 6662. The IRS also issued final regulations in December 2008 (T.D. 9436), along with interim guidance concerning the penalty.

> **COMMENT**
>
> The IRS has clarified that the definitions of a *tax preparer* under Code Sec. 6694 means "a person who for compensation prepares all or a substantial portion of a [listed] tax return, or a claim for refund with respect to any such tax return." It also provided a comprehensive list of the types of tax returns and refund claims for which the preparer penalty may be imposed (Rev. Proc. 2009-11, IRB 2009-3, December 15, 2008). Thus, unlike the confidentiality provisions of Code Sec. 7216, individuals who prepare a return for free are not subject to the Code Sec. 6694 penalty.

> **COMMENT**
>
> The final regulations provide that an individual is a preparer if he or she is primarily responsible for the position on the return or claim for refund giving rise to the understatement. Only one person within a firm will be considered primarily responsible for each position giving rise to an understatement and, therefore, be subject to the penalty. If there is no signing preparer for the return or claim for refund, or if the signing preparer is not primarily responsible for the position, the nonsigning preparer within the firm having overall supervisory responsibility for the position giving rise to the understatement will generally be considered responsible for the position. If the evidence shows that both the signing preparer and a nonsigning preparer within a firm are primarily responsible for the position(s) giving rise to the understatement, the IRS may, depending on the evidence presented, assess the penalty against either one of them (not both), as the primarily responsible preparer. The signing or supervisory nonsigning preparer is able to avoid the penalty by showing that another person within the firm was responsible for the position giving rise to the understatement.

For disclosed positions, the preparer must have a "reasonable basis" for the position. *Reasonable basis* means that there must be at least a 15 percent probability that the position would be sustained in an administrative proceeding or in litigation if challenged.

For undisclosed position (other than for tax shelters and reportable avoidance transactions), the standard for preparers is the "substantial authority" standard if a tax position has not been disclosed on a return. Generally, substantial authority exists for the tax treatment of an item if the weight of the authorities supporting the treatment is substantial in relation to the weight of authorities supporting contrary treatment. Substantial authority generally means that the preparer believes that there is at least a 40 percent probability that the reporting position would be sustained in an administrative proceeding or in litigation if challenged by the IRS.

> **COMMENT**
>
> The phrase has the same meaning and uses the same analysis as in the accuracy-related penalty regulations (Treas. Reg. §§1.6662-4(d)(2) and (d)(3)(i) through (ii)). The kinds of authorities described in those regulations are considered in determining whether there is substantial authority for a position (Treas. Reg. §1.6662-4(d)(3)(iii)).

For positions taken for tax shelters and reportable avoidance transactions, nondisclosure of a position is not an option. Furthermore, the tax position taken on a return prepared for tax years beginning after October 3, 2008, must be at least reasonable enough for the preparer to believe that the tax position would "more likely than not" be sustained in an administrative proceeding or in litigation if challenged. This means that there would be a greater than 50 percent likelihood of being sustained if challenged (Treas. Reg. 1.6694-2(b)(1)).

> **COMMENT**
>
> Although the scope of the preparer penalty was expanded in 2007 to include not only income tax return preparers but also preparers of all tax returns including estate, excise, and employment tax returns, the more likely than not standard for tax shelters only covers transactions with a significant avoidance of federal *income* tax. This arises from the definition of *tax shelter* for purposes of Code Sec. 6694, which relies on how that term is defined under Code Sec. 6662(d)(2)(C). The latter only includes transactions with a significant purposes of avoiding of federal *income* tax.
>
> Reportable avoidance transactions are any listed transactions or any reportable transactions with a significant tax avoidance purpose. A *reportable transaction* is any transaction with respect to which information must be included with the taxpayer's return because the IRS has determined that the transaction is of the type that has the potential for tax avoidance or evasion. A *listed transaction* is a reportable transaction that is the same as or substantially similar to a transaction that has been specifically identified by the IRS as a tax avoidance transaction.

> **COMMENT**
>
> Listed transactions have been identified in Notices 2004-67, 2004-2 CB 600 and Notice 2009-59, I.R.B. 2009-31).

For purposes of the Code Sec. 6694 disclosure penalty, a preparer may rely on advice furnished by another advisor, another preparer, or other party, even if the other advisor or preparer is within the preparer's same firm. However, preparer must meet the diligence standards in order to rely properly on information and advice provided by taxpayers or other individuals.

Aiding and abetting penalty. As an alternative to the Code Sec. 6694 preparer penalty, the IRS may seek to impose a penalty under Code Sec. 6701 for aiding and abetting the understatement of a tax liability. The preparer may incur a $1,000 penalty ($10,000 with respect to corporate tax returns and documents). The IRS may not impose *both* the preparer penalty and the aiding and abetting penalty, but choose one or the other.

STUDY QUESTIONS

9. The attorney–client privilege applies to information from the taxpayer:
   a. Provided for inclusion on the tax return only
   b. Communicated to an accountant engaged by the attorney to assist in representing the client
   c. Disclosed to third parties unconnected with representing the client in matters associated with the return

10. The "more likely than not" standard for tax positions taken by the preparer is _____ than the "substantial authority" standard imposed on taxpayers.
    a. Higher than
    b. Essentially the same as
    c. Lower than

CONCLUSION

Recent changes in the tax code and regulations has resulted in heightened obligations on preparers with respect to return information confidentiality, reaching a particular confidence level with respect to a position taken on a tax return, and meeting affirmative obligations under Circular 230 to ensure integrity and fairness in practicing before the IRS. At the same time, practitioners have certain privileges that protect taxpayer information from disclosure by the IRS in controversy proceedings. An understanding of these confidentiality, disclosure, and practice obligations is critical for practitioners to remain compliant with the law while serving the best interest of their clients.

CPE NOTE: When you have completed your study and review of chapters 1-3, which comprise Module 1, you may wish to take the Quizzer for this Module.

For your convenience, you can also take this Quizzer online at **www.cchtestingcenter.com.**

Working with Tax Losses

The unfortunate reality is that individuals and businesses sometimes lose money. Especially in times of a down economy, it is important for taxpayers to take advantage of those losses from a tax perspective. Not all tax losses are treated the same, however, with certain losses only allowed to be netted against similar gains—first in the same tax year and then in some, but not all instances, either as a carryback or carryforward loss into a different tax year. Taxpayers should be advised regarding these rules so that losses do not go unused or underused, or incorrect assumptions do not linger about their effect on a particular tax liability.

LEARNING OBJECTIVES

Upon completion of this course, you will be able to:

- Recount the timing rules for claiming a net operating loss deduction;
- Describe limitations on claiming passive activity and at-risk loss deductions;
- Identify tax benefits from loss in value of stock, theft of property, disaster losses, bad debt, and abandonment of property;
- Explain when and how a deduction may be claimed from gambling losses;
- Describe when an activity does not produce deductible losses because it is considered a hobby; and
- Understand when involuntarily converted property produces a loss deduction for the taxpayer.

INTRODUCTION

This chapter explores the special rules for computing, carrying forward, and carrying back net operating losses (NOLs). The chapter also looks at the limitations on deductions for losses due to taxpayers' passive participation in a trade or business, lack of capital at risk in the enterprise, or lack of profit-seeking motive. The special rules for claiming loss deductions from sales of stock, theft, abandonment, and wagering are outlined. Also covered are special rules for reporting loss deductions related to exchanges or involuntary conversions of property used in a trade or business.

PUTTING LOSSES TO WORK

This chapter discusses 11 different types of losses requiring special treatment under the tax code:

- Net operating losses;
- Passive activity losses;
- At-risk loss limitations;
- Stock losses;
- Theft losses;
- Casualty losses;
- Bad debt losses;
- Abandonment losses;
- Wagering losses;
- Hobby losses; and
- Code Sec. 1231 losses.

Code Sec. 165(a) is the principal Internal Revenue Code provision that allows loss deductions. It generally enables taxpayers to claim deductions for losses. However, there is a specific definition of what qualifies as a loss that uses those activities from which particular losses are realized as the point of reference. Code Sec. 165(c)(1) limits the types of losses that can be deducted against gross income to ones arising from:

- A trade or business (i.e. business losses);
- Activities engaged in for profit;
- Sales and exchanges of capital assets;
- Destruction of property by fire, storm, or shipwreck (casualty losses); and
- Theft of property.

The type of loss affects its deductibility in several ways. A taxpayer may be able to use an *ordinary loss* to offset other unrelated sources of income. However, a taxpayer may find that application of the loss is limited to offsetting gains specific to the activity. In this latter case, taxpayers might also be forced to recognize a net loss in a "carryover" tax year or may forfeit putting the loss to work entirely if a particular deadline has passed or if simply no loss carryover is allowed.

STUDY QUESTION

1. A loss that occurs when property is damaged by hurricanes is known as:
   a. A casualty loss
   b. An extraordinary loss
   c. An activity-specific loss

NET OPERATING LOSSES

Certain categories of losses, when they exceed gain, may combine and generate what the Internal Revenue Code categorizes as NOLs. Taxpayers have an NOL when their income tax deductions exceed their gross income for the year. Such a loss generally applies to income earned from a trade or business.

> **COMMENT**
>
> The term *net operating loss* is somewhat of a misnomer. When taxpayers use NOLs, the resulting deduction may not actually include an economic loss, but rather tax benefits, such as depreciation (although bonus depreciation cannot be included in computation of an NOL). It is important to understand how to retain these tax benefits until taxpayers may properly claim deductions for them.

Once a taxpayer's potential tax deductions for the year have equaled the amount of the taxpayer's gross income for that tax year, the deductions surrender their current benefit. Tax deductions reduce gross income; in that they differ from *refundable tax credits,* which give refunds to taxpayers even when they have a zero income tax liability. The question for taxpayers having excess deductions then becomes: How can NOLs provide the most benefit?

NOLs may present a strategic tax advantage during a sharp transition from economic boom to economic bust. Code Sec. 172(a) allows taxpayers to deduct against a tax year's income those NOLs both carried over to the tax year from previous tax years and carried back from later tax years. As a result, taxpayers have the ability to spread their NOLs across tax years and significantly—often retroactively--decrease their tax liabilities from years that they had net income. Taxpayers who had high incomes when the economy was growing and paid a substantial amount of tax as a result may be able to allocate their NOL deductions to these years, thus reducing their reported taxable income for the year.

> **EXAMPLE**
>
> During 2008, Williams Corporation had net income of $30,000 and paid taxes on this amount. During 2010, the company had a net loss of $20,000. Williams may file an amended return with the IRS to carry back the $20,000 loss to 2008. This would allow the company to claim a refund for that year equal to the income tax it paid on $20,000.

Taxpayers generally are allowed to carry back an NOL up to 2 tax years and carry it forward up to 20 tax years. Longer carryback periods in certain situations:

- 3 years for NOLs from casualty, theft, or presidentially declared disasters;
- 5 years for a farming loss; and
- 10 years for losses from product liabilities, workplace liabilities, and environmental remediation.

Under Code Sec. 172(b)(2), taxpayers using carrybacks are required to apply the NOL to the earliest year allowed. They must apply the NOL to the income earned during that prior tax year until there is no outstanding tax liability. After offsetting their taxable income for that particular year, they then can carry any remaining NOL to the subsequent year.

> **COMMENT**
>
> Despite this rule, however, taxpayers are not required to always carryback an NOL before they are allowed to carry it forward. Rather, under Code Sec. 172(b)(3), taxpayers may opt to waive their ability to carry the NOL back and carry their NOLs forward within the 20-year limit. To complete this carryforward, taxpayers must attach a statement to their original return for the tax year in which the NOL was accumulated, stating their intention to waive their carryback of the NOL.

> **EXAMPLE**
>
> Williams Company had net income of $30,000 in 2009, net income of $10,000 in 2010, and then a net operating loss of $20,000 in 2011. Although Williams is allowed to carry back the net operating loss incurred in 2011, the company must first apply the loss against the income in 2009 before applying the loss against its 2010 income. As a result, Williams may apply for a refund of tax paid on $20,000 in 2009. Or Williams could waive its right to carryback the 2011 NOL and instead carry it forward to a future tax year occurring before 2031.

> **COMMENT**
>
> For 2008 NOLs, *qualified small businesses* (those having average annual gross receipts of $15 million or less) were entitled to carry back NOLs for a three-, four-, or five-year period. Congress will consider whether to extend this relief to later years and to larger businesses.

NOL Calculation

An NOL starts with taxable income. For there to be any NOL at all, this must be a negative number. Certain deductions, called "modifications," are added back to the negative number to arrive at a new amount. The resulting number, if negative, becomes the NOL for that year.

The modifications for an individual first ignore any NOL deductions from other years. Then, they add back:

- Certain capital losses (generally, no more than the maximum $3,000 capital loss deduction; other net capital losses are carried forward for future netting with capital gain independent of and in place of any NOL treatment);
- Nonbusiness deductions in excess of nonbusiness income;
- The domestic production Code Sec. 199 deduction; and
- The personal exemptions.

A corporation's NOL is generally the same as the negative taxable income reported on its return. However, the Code Sec. 199 deduction is not allowed and it may be necessary to modify the dividends-received deduction. Flow-through entities (S corporations and Partnerships) do not have NOLs as such. A limited liability company may have an NOL if it elected to be taxed as a C corporation.

Individuals

Partners and shareholders. Individuals as well as corporations may incur NOLs. NOLs may not pass from a C corporation to its shareholders (or vice versa). However, when a partnership or S corporation incurs an NOL, it passes through to the individual partners or shareholders, who may carry back or carry forward the loss. Disregarded entities and sole proprietorships also impart the NOL benefit to their individual owner.

Divorce. Circumstances may arise in which an individual has NOLs and then becomes divorced. The U.S. Court of Appeals for the Tenth Circuit has restricted the carryback of NOLs for married taxpayers filing a joint income tax return (*A.E. Calvin, 354 F.2d 202*). If the NOL is incurred in a year before the couple was married, the court has stated that the NOL deduction may only be applied against income specific to the spouse who actually generated the loss.

> **EXAMPLE**
>
> Charles and Janet Knight, a married couple filing a joint income tax return, married in 2010. Before the couple married, Charles recognized an NOL from his landscaping business during 2009. To carry forward his 2009 net loss to the 2010 tax year, when the couple had net income, Charles would have to calculate his individual portion of the net income the couple experienced in 2010. Then, Charles could only claim a refund for tax paid on his portion of the couple's 2010 net gain. If Charles had income in 2010 and Janet had a loss, Charles could not apply the NOL on their 2010 return.

If taxpayers are divorced and one of them incurs an NOL after the divorce, a similar rule applies when the NOL is carried back to a year that the couple was married. The NOL may only offset the income that the taxpayer would have reported if the couple had filed separate returns (that is, the loss may not offset the other spouse's income).

> **EXAMPLE**
>
> Charles and Janet run the landscaping business together and have net income for 2010. The couple divorce in 2011. In 2011, Charles experienced a net loss from his business. To carry back his 2011 net loss, Charles would have to calculate his individual portion of the couple's net income for 2010 and file an amended return claiming a refund for 2010 tax paid on his portion of the income.

S Corporations

A C corporation that converts or has converted from Subchapter S corporation status may not carry forward or carry back its NOLs to years when it is an S corp. And, the reverse is true as well. An S corp may not carry back or carry forward NOLs to tax years when it was a C corporation.

However, it is noteworthy that the allowable time period for NOL carryovers does not disappear when a C corporation changes its status. If a C corporation temporarily changes to an S corporation and subsequently decides against this option, the company's NOLs are preserved until it returns to C corporation status. The law simply treats the company's taxable income as zero during the years the business was an S corporation.

EXAMPLE

Miller, Inc., was a C corporation during 2009 earning $50,000 in net income. Miller converted to a Subchapter S corporation for 2010, when it recognized a $20,000 NOL. However, not satisfied with its S corp status, Miller converted back to C corporation status for 2011, when it experienced an NOL of $30,000. Miller may not carry back the 2010 NOL, incurred when the company was an S corp, to the 2009 return, when the business was a C corporation. However, the company may carry back the C corporation's $30,000 NOL for 2011 to its 2009 return and claim a refund for the income tax paid on that amount.

STUDY QUESTION

2. The NOLs of a Subchapter S corporation:
   a. May carry forward to 10 subsequent tax years when it converts to a C corporation
   b. Pass through to its shareholders
   c. May be applied to gains from prior years when it was a C corporation

Limitations on NOL Carryforwards

Acquired businesses. A significant rule limits the amount of NOL carryforwards a corporation may claim after it has been acquired. Under Code Sec. 382, a corporation that undergoes a change in ownership and also has NOLs to carry forward from a previous year is limited in the amount it may deduct for the NOLs. This rule is intended to prevent *trafficking of NOLs* by corporate buyers who would acquire a target corporation so that they could use the company's NOLs to offset their own income. To prevent abuse of this tactic, the Internal Revenue Code limits the corporation's NOL carryforwards during the year of the company's acquisition to the value of the corporation's stock before the change in ownership, multiplied by the long-term tax-exempt rate.

EXAMPLE

Parker Corporation, a company with assets valued at $5 million, has accumulated NOLs of $1 million from the previous two tax years. Parker is acquired by Burrox Company during 2010. Burrox would like to use Parker's NOLs to offset some of its own 2010 income. Assuming the tax-exempt rate for 2010 is 5 percent, Burrox may only carry over $250,000 ($5 million × 5 percent) of Parker's NOLs from the previous two years to 2010.

If the NOLs allowable under the Code Sec. 382 limitation exceed the combined corporation's taxable income for the year after the ownership change, the corporation is allowed to carry over the remaining amount allowed by the limitation to subsequent years.

> **EXAMPLE**
>
> If Burrox had net income of $100,000 for 2010, it may claim an NOL carryforward of $100,000 for 2010. Burrox may, however, carry forward the remaining $150,000 of NOLs into 2011 if it recognizes net gain for that year.

Government relief programs. In 2008, the IRS provided an exception to the Code Sec. 382 limitations for private acquisitions of troubled banks. Under this relief, there is no limitation of NOL carryovers of the acquired banks after the change in ownership. In the *American Recovery and Reinvestment Act of 2009* (*2009 Recovery Act*), Congress allowed this relief to stand for acquisitions on or before January 16, 2009, but repealed the relief for ownership changes after that date.

However, a separate provision of the *2009 Recovery Act* provided relief from the Code Sec. 382 limitation in response to the government's "bailout" of several high-profile banks and acquisition of their stock. Certain restructuring agreements—required under the government's Troubled Asset Relief Program (TARP) in exchange for loans from the Treasury Department--produced a change in ownership that would normally fall within the scope of Code Sec. 382 restrictions. Some of these banks had NOL carryforwards or incurred NOLs during the year in which they entered into restructuring agreements with the government. Under the new law, there is no NOL carryover limitation on these taxpayers merely because of the government's acquisition of stock.

Continuity of business. Finally, to deduct even the amount allowed under the Code Sec. 382 limitation, the corporation must continue the business enterprise of the old corporation for a two-year period after the change in ownership occurs.

> **EXAMPLE**
>
> Before its acquisition, Parker was a publishing company. After acquiring Parker Corporation, Burrox Company sells off the assets of Parker and begins a new business in 2011, under the Parker business name, of environmental consulting. Because it did not continue Parker's original business enterprise, Burrox may not carry forward any of Parker's NOLs after the year of acquisition.

STUDY QUESTIONS

3. NOL carryforwards for the year in which a corporation is acquired:

   a. May not be applied to the acquirer's future tax liabilities

   b. May not exceed value of the acquired corporation's stock times the long-term tax-exempt rate

   c. May be applied to up to five prior tax years' gains by the acquiring corporation but no current year income

4. Under the *2009 Recovery Act* provisions for Troubled Asset Relief Program (TARP) restructuring agreements with the government, banks that received bailouts:

   a. Have no limitation on NOL carryovers because the government acquired the banks' stock

   b. Are subject to the Code Sec. 382 limitations for the 2008 and 2009 tax years

   c. May not apply NOLs against future income until bailout funds are repaid

PASSIVE LOSSES

Several loss limitations have been written into the tax code to restrict the ability of certain categories of losses to offset income associated with another category. One of the more prominent among them is the limitation on passive activity losses.

Under Code Sec. 469, taxpayers may not claim deductions for passive activity losses against nonpassive income. A *passive activity* is a trade or business in which the taxpayer does not materially participate during the year.

> **COMMENT**
>
> The rules for deducting passive losses first assume that a trade or business for profit exists. Sometimes the IRS questions that underlying assumption under the hobby loss rules.

Use of passive loss deductions is limited to netting against the taxpayer's income from passive activities. If passive deductions exceed passive income, the enterprise has incurred passive activity losses for the taxpayer. Income from one passive activity can be netted against a loss from another passive activity. Any excess losses can be carried forward to offset future passive income.

> **COMMENT**
>
> Passive activities in which loss deductions are restricted can arise in a number of situations. Generally, however, they can be grouped into two categories:
> - Passive investments in which the taxpayer is a "silent partner" or principally provides the capital for a particular profit-making undertaking;
> - Profit-generating activities that, by their nature, do not require much personal effort.

> **COMMENT**
>
> One of the most passive types of investments—shareholder interest in a corporation—carries its own separate set of rules that combine with the passive buying and selling of their other "capital assets." Net capital losses offset an individual taxpayer's ordinary income only up to $3,000 each year.

To defeat the IRS's assertion that a taxpayer may not deduct a net passive activity loss during a particular year, taxpayers may show that they *materially participated* in the trade or business during that year. If they fail do so, the taxpayers will be forced to carry over their loss into a subsequent tax year.

Tests of Material Participation

Taxpayers satisfy material participation tests by positive responses to any one of the following seven questions under the Code Sec. 469 regulations:

- Did the taxpayer participate in the activity for more than 500 hours during the year?
- Was the taxpayer's participation in the activity substantially all of the participation by all individuals involved?
- Did the taxpayer participate in the activity for 100 hours or more, and was this participation equal to or more than the participation of others?
- Did the taxpayer participate for more than 100 hours in several trade or business activities that add up to more than 500 hours?
- Did the taxpayer materially participate in the activity for at least 5 out of the 10 tax years that immediately preceded this tax year?
- Did the taxpayer perform personal services (e.g., law or medicine) as part of the trade or business and materially participate in the activity for any three tax years preceding this tax year?
- As a catchall, do the facts and circumstances suggest that the taxpayer participated through his or her personal efforts in the activity on a regular, continuous, and substantial basis?

If the taxpayer has met one of these tests, then the IRS will consider him or her to have materially participated in the activity. The taxpayer will then be able to deduct any resulting losses against nonpassive income.

> **EXAMPLE**
>
> During 2010, the Callahans, a married couple, purchase a small restaurant. They hire employees to manage the establishment, accountants to file its income tax return, and attorneys to handle its legal obligations. They do not work in the restaurant, but continue to work 40 hours a week at their normal occupations. For their role in the business, they only read reports from their employees and hire professional help. The restaurant incurs a net loss during 2010. It is likely that the Callahans did not materially participate in the operation of the business and may not claim a deduction for the restaurant's losses to offset the couple's wages. The loss stems from a passive activity.

Material participation is determined on an annual basis. Having passive activity losses in a past year does not relegate the activity to passive activity loss status in any current or future year.

> **EXAMPLE**
>
> During 2011, the Callahans quit their jobs and take a more personal approach to the business of the restaurant, working 45 hours a week as chef and maitre' d. Despite the owners' renewed efforts, the business experiences a loss during 2011 as well. Because the Callahans qualify as materially participating in the restaurant's business during 2011, they may claim a deduction for their 2011 losses.

Losses sustained in an activity in which the taxpayer does not materially participate may be carried over to a subsequent year in which the taxpayer does materially participate in that activity or they can offset passive activity income carried over into a subsequent tax year.

> **EXAMPLE**
>
> During 2010, Kim Lowell recognized $10,000, $20,000, and $20,000 in losses stemming from her laundry machine, plumbing, and tax preparation businesses. Kim spent 50, 300, and 140 hours, respectively, in each business during the year, managing employees, providing manual labor where needed, and performing payroll functions.

Kim will likely meet the material participation requirements for the plumbing and tax preparation businesses, but not the laundry machine business. Although she did not participate for 500 hours in any of the different activities, the facts indicate that she participated in the plumbing and tax preparation businesses for at least 100 hours. On these facts, she is entitled to claim deductions of $40,000 ($20,000 + $20,000). If Kim wanted to prove she materially participated in the laundry machine business, despite her failure to technically meet the requirements, she could attempt to fall under the catchall provision. She would try to show that the facts and circumstances of the business indicate that she participated on a regular, continuous, and substantial basis in the business. Yet, if she fails to prove this, she may still carry over the $10,000 loss from the laundry machine activity to a subsequent year.

The passive activity loss limitation applies to individuals, trusts, estates, personal service corporations, and closely held corporations. The limitation does not apply to S corporations and partnerships, but it does apply to taxpayers owning interests in these entities.

EXAMPLE

Haswell Corp., a Subchapter S corporation, owns resort property in Hawaii. It merely acts as a holding corporation and outsources all of the work associated with the property to local businesses. This includes reservations, marketing, cleaning, and landscaping services of the property. One of Haswell's shareholders, Thomas, materially participates in the business by meeting one of the seven tests. Shareholder, Terry, does not materially participate in the business. Haswell Corporation incurs a net loss for 2009 in its rental of the property.

The passive activity loss rules do not prevent Haswell Corp from recognizing the loss. However, although Thomas may claim a deduction for his portion of the Haswell's net loss, Terry may not claim a deduction because he did not materially participate in the S corp's business.

Passive Activity Presumptions

The law presumes certain business activities to be passive in nature. Taxpayers are automatically prevented from claiming net deductions against nonpassive income for losses stemming from these activities. Taxpayers may not overcome this presumption by showing that they materially participated in the business. One example is losses stemming from the rental of property (unless the taxpayer is a real estate professional). Another is losses stemming from a limited partnership interest.

EXAMPLE

Fairfax, LP, a Delaware limited partnership, delivers appliances. Ian Roberts and 10 other shareholders form a corporation to act as general partner. Ian also invests as a limited partner in Fairfax. Ian materially participates in Fairfax's business. Fairfax recognizes a net loss for 2009. Ian may not deduct his pro rata share of the losses as a limited partner, despite his material participation. The general partner's loss deduction is captured at the corporate level.

COMMENT

A recent opinion from the U.S. Tax Court (**Garnett,** 132 T.C. No. 19, June 30, 2009) determined that interests in limited liability partnerships (LLPs) and limited liability companies (LLCs) are not considered limited partnership interests for purposes of the passive activity loss rules. As a result, interests in LLCs and LLPS would not be presumed passive in nature and taxpayers may prove material participation in order to claim any resulting losses. A similar ruling was made by the U.S. Court of Federal Claims (**Thompson,** FedCl. July 20, 2009). That court decided that, to be a limited partnership under the passive activity loss rules, the entity must be treated as a partnership under state law, not merely taxed as one under the Internal Revenue Code. No official response to these rulings has been put forth by the IRS.

One limited dollar exception, however, allows taxpayers to overcome the presumption of passive activity loss by showing that they actively participated in rental of real property. A taxpayer that *actively participates* in rental real estate activities can deduct $25,000 per year of losses against nonpassive income. This allowance is phased out if the taxpayer's modified adjusted gross income exceeds $100,000. Active participation is a less stringent standard than material participation.

STUDY QUESTIONS

5. Taxpayers who have not participated in their business activity at all this year may yet satisfy material participation requirements if:
   a. They participated materially in the activity for 5 or more years out of the previous 10 years
   b. They performed personal services for 8 out of the previous 10 tax years
   c. The taxpayer participated actively in launching her first business during the last tax year

---

6. To which type of organization does the passive activity loss limitation **not** apply?

   a. S corporations

   b. Closely held corporations

   c. Estates

AT-RISK LOSSES

Another loss limitation is aimed at preventing taxpayers from claiming business losses to the extent they have no personal *investment* at stake. This differs from the passive activity loss limitation in which the taxpayer has an inadequate amount of personal *time and effort* invested in the business activity.

Individuals, trusts, estates, and certain closely held C corporations are subject to the at-risk loss limitations under Code Sec. 465. The rule also applies to losses from interests in partnerships and S corporations. The at-risk loss limitation is applied before applying the passive activity loss rules.

Amounts at Risk

The at-risk rules apply:

- Separately to each of five activities specified under Code Sec 465(c)(1), including
  - Holding, producing or distributing motion pictures or video tapes,
  - Farming,
  - Equipment leasing,
  - Exploring for, or exploiting, oil and gas resources, and
  - Exploring for, or exploiting, geothermal resources;
- Separately to all other activities other than the preceding, except collectively if either taxpayer actively participates in its management or the trade or business is carried on by a partnership or S corporation and 65 percent or more of the losses for the tax year is allocable to persons who actively participate in its management.

The at-risk rules limit taxpayers' deductions for losses to the amount they are financially "at risk" in the business. The taxpayer must first contribute money or property to the business in order to deduct any subsequent losses. Under the at-risk loss limitations, taxpayers are limited to claiming trade or business losses equal to money and the adjusted basis of other property contributed to the activity, plus certain borrowed amounts to the extent the taxpayer is liable for repayments. Any losses exceeding this total are carried over to the next tax year.

EXAMPLE

Lee and Cole Anderson each own 50 percent of Reinhart Corp., a Subchapter S corporation, to market a line of cosmetic products. During 2010, the corporation accumulates $20,000 in losses, with $10,000 allocated to each shareholder. Lee invests $1,000 cash and equipment with an adjusted basis of $5,000 in the company. Lee may only deduct $6,000 from Reinhart, the amount of money and the adjusted basis of the property he contributed. The remaining $4,000 of loss is carried over to the subsequent tax year.

COMMENT

To avoid the at-risk limitation, taxpayers are not specifically required to contribute money or property every tax year or even at the beginning of their involvement in the business. They must simply contribute capital to the venture before they attempt to claim any loss deductions related to their ownership interest.

COMMENT

The value of any personal services performed for the business, however, is not counted as a capital contribution. Instead, services would generate salary income that is first taxed as wages. The owners must draw reasonable compensation from the business.

Loans

A taxpayer borrowing funds that are contributed to a business must meet certain requirements to be at risk with respect to those funds or leveraged assets. The taxpayer must be personally liable for repayment of the funds or must put up property not used in the business as collateral to secure the loan. Taxpayers are not considered at risk for nonrecourse loans (for which they have no personal liability), guarantees, stop loss agreements, and similar arrangements made to secure financing or reduce losses from a business.

However, there is an exception for *qualified nonrecourse financing*, in which the taxpayer borrows funds to hold real property. The loan must be guaranteed or made by a federal, state, or local government. The taxpayer must also secure the loan with the real property and ensure the loan is not convertible.

> **EXAMPLE**
>
> During 2010, Jonathan Jones, a housing developer, borrows $110 million from several financial institutions to build single-family homes in a suburban area. Jonathan is not personally liable for the loans. The loans are secured by the land Jones purchased. Each loan was guaranteed by the local government to encourage the development. Jonathan reports a $5 million loss from his activity for the year. Jonathan may claim the loss despite the at-risk limitation because he satisfies the exception for qualified nonrecourse financing.

Generally, merely having borrowed funds will not place a taxpayer at risk within the business if the funds are loaned by someone with an interest in the business or from a related person. However, shareholders are at risk for loans they make to a corporation, despite their interests as owners.

> **EXAMPLE**
>
> In 2011, Justin Harris becomes an investor in Reinhart Corporation. Existing stockholder Lee borrows $50,000 from Justin and contributes the funds to Reinhart. Reinhart incurs a loss for the year. Lee's $50,000 contribution is not an amount at risk because the source of the funds was Justin, who also had an interest in the business.

Amount at Risk

The amount that a taxpayer is at risk is reduced by whatever loss the taxpayer claims for the tax year. As a result, in subsequent tax years, the taxpayer will be at risk for a smaller amount and can claim fewer losses (assuming that the taxpayer does not add more capital in the interim).

> **EXAMPLE**
>
> For 2012, Lee has an investment of $2,000 at risk in Reinhart Corporation. He is allocated $500 of the corporation's losses for the year and deducts that amount. For 2013, Lee will be at risk for $1,500 unless he makes further contributions to the S corporation.

However, if the taxpayer sells its interest in a business for a gain, the gain will be added to the amount at risk. This allows the taxpayer to claim a greater loss deduction.

EXAMPLE

For 2013, Lee is allocated $4,000 of Reinhart's losses. However, due to past loss deductions, he has no amount at risk within the organization. During 2014, he contributes $1,500 to the business. If Lee sells his interest in the corporation for a gain of $3,000 during 2014, he will then have $4,500 at risk and may deduct the entire $4,000 loss.

STUDY QUESTIONS

7. When a taxpayer claims a loss for the year, the amount at risk:
   a. Is reduced so the taxpayer may claim fewer losses in subsequent years
   b. Remains unchanged and does not affect future loss deductions
   c. Is increased so greater amounts may be considered at risk for future deductions

STOCK LOSSES

Another category of losses is the loss from the sale or exchange of a capital asset. One type of capital asset that has generated large losses in recent years is corporate stock. As a result, it is more important than ever to understand the timing restrictions and other limitations on claiming these losses.

Stock held for investment purposes is generally considered a capital asset under Code Sec. 1221(a). When selling stock, taxpayers must use their cost basis (purchase price plus any related fees) to determine gain or loss. Taxpayers realize a capital loss on the sale of stock when their cost basis exceeds the sales proceeds (selling price less expenses such as commissions).

COMMENT

Stocks form but one type of capital asset. Gain and loss from the sale of stocks must be combined with the capital gain and loss realized from all other capital assets required to be recognized under the tax code. What results is that individual's net capital gain or loss.

Deductible Amount

Similar to passive activity loss limitations, the amount of capital losses deductible by a taxpayer is generally limited to the capital gains the taxpayer realizes in the same year from the sale or exchange of capital assets.

The netting rules for capital assets first require gains and losses from long-term capital assets (those held for more than one year) to be netted against each other, and gains and losses from short-term assets similarly netted. Then those two groups are netted against each other. If a net capital loss results for the year, the net loss that is carried forward retains its character as long- or short- term, or a combination in case the net loss consists of some net long-term capital losses and some net short-term capital losses.

Net stock losses are generally nondeductible in the current year, with one *de minimis* exception. Individuals, trusts, and estates can deduct net capital losses up to $3,000 ($1,500 each for married individuals filing a separate return) against ordinary income. Any losses exceeding $3,000 in one tax year can be carried forward to the succeeding year to be included in the regular net capital gain and losses computation for that year.

COMMENT

Even though spouses may each have certain separate assets under a particular state law that include a stock portfolio, a single maximum $3,000 applies to a married couple collectively just as it does to a single individual; not $6,000 or something in-between in recognition of a couple being made up of two individuals.

Corporations cannot deduct net losses but can carry back any net losses on the sale of stock to the three previous years' returns and carry forward any net losses for up to five succeeding years. The loss must be applied to the earliest year for which the corporation had a net gain from the sale of stock. Corporations cannot increase their NOLs by carrying back losses from stock.

EXAMPLE

Elliot Sampson and his company, Telluride, Inc., both invest in corporate stock. Elliot sells his stock during 2010 at a $5,000 loss. Telluride sells its stock for a net $200,000 loss. Telluride may not claim a loss deduction for 2010 on the stock sale, whereas Elliot may claim a $3,000 deduction on the loss from his sale. However, Telluride may carry back or carry forward its $200,000 loss to a tax year in which the company had a net gain from its sale of corporate stock. Elliot may carry forward the remaining $2,000 of his losses on the sale.

Worthless Securities

Under Code Sec. 165(g), taxpayers do not always have to sell or otherwise transfer stock to deduct a capital loss. If the taxpayer invests in corporate stock and the stock later becomes worthless, the taxpayer may treat this loss of value as if he or she sold the stock on the last day of the tax year. This deemed sale results in a deductible capital loss. The stock must be *totally* worthless, and its worthlessness must be established by an *identifiable event*, such as bankruptcy or termination of operations.

> **EXAMPLE**
>
> During 2011, Benjamin Morris is a shareholder of a corporation that owns casinos, with a cost basis in his stock of $6,000. The corporation is forced into bankruptcy during 2011 and the stock becomes worthless. Benjamin must treat the stock as if he sold it for $0. Benjamin is allowed a worthless stock deduction of $6,000 on his 2011 return.

If a parent corporation owns stock in a subsidiary and the subsidiary becomes worthless, the parent can claim an ordinary loss instead of a capital loss. Instead of reducing the parent's tax liability at the lower capital gains rate (15 percent) and being netted strictly against capital gain, the worthless stock deduction reduces tax liability at the often higher ordinary income tax rate and across a wider base of taxable income.

> **COMMENT**
>
> Stock losses also may be entitled to ordinary loss treatment when realized within a trade or business if they form net Code Sec. 1231 losses. For further explanation, see the discussion of Code Sec. 1231 losses.

Denial of Losses

Wash sales. A *wash sale* occurs when a taxpayer sells stock at a loss and buys identical stock within 30 days before or after the sale. A taxpayer cannot deduct losses from wash sales, unless he or she is a dealer in securities. Instead, the amount of that loss increases the taxpayer's basis in the replacement shares.

Related parties. Losses are disallowed if stock is sold to a related party, such as a family member, a corporation more than 50 percent owned by the taxpayer, or two related corporations.

> **EXAMPLE**
>
> Andrew Hollister buys stock for $10,000. He then sells it to his brother Alexander for $7,600. Andrew cannot recognize as a deduction the $2,400 loss he realized on the stock.

Small Business Stock

Code Sec. 1244 special rules govern losses individuals claim on the sale of *small business stock*. A *small business* is a domestic corporation with aggregate paid-in capital of $1 million or less at the time the stock is issued. The losses are treated as ordinary loss. However, the ordinary loss deduction is limited to $50,000 ($100,000 in the case of a husband and wife filing a joint return).

> **EXAMPLE**
>
> Clark Nelson, a single taxpayer, pays $200,000 to buy all the stock of Phillips Corporation, a taxi company. In 2009, Clark decides to retire and sells the business for $130,000, incurring a $70,000 loss. Clark is entitled to claim a $50,000 ordinary loss deduction for 2009 related to the sale of his Code Sec. 1244 stock. He must recognize the remaining $20,000 as a capital loss.

> **COMMENT**
>
> The loss on Section 1244 stock that is characterized as ordinary is allowed as a deduction from gross income in arriving at adjusted gross income and thus is available to taxpayers regardless of whether they itemize deductions.

CODE SEC. 1231 LOSSES

Code Sec. 1231 is the best of both worlds: net gains from the disposal of Section 1231 property are taxed at capital gain rates, while net losses from the disposal of Section 1231 property are taxed as ordinary losses. If total Section 1231 gains exceed losses for the year, then all gains and losses are capital. If total losses exceed gains for the year, then all gains and losses are ordinary.

Code Sec. 1231 property is, generally, property used in the taxpayer's trade or business. Section 1231 applies to gains and losses from:

- The sale or exchange of ordinary property or a capital asset held for more than one year and used in a trade or business; and
- The compulsory or involuntary conversion (from destruction, theft, seizure, or government condemnation) of either type of property used in a trade or business.

Such property includes timber and coal, livestock, and unharvested crops. Code Sec. 1231 does not include inventory and property held for sale to customers, or copyrights, artistic compositions, and letters or memoranda.

Even though theft, casualty, or seizure by the government through condemnation or its exercise of eminent domain may destroy the property's usefulness, the taxpayer may still receive consideration for the property through a condemnation award. Code Sec. 1231 allows taxpayers to treat losses from these forced sales as ordinary losses if they exceed Section 1231 gains. Thus, the taxpayer will be able to net the loss against its other gross income.

> **EXAMPLE**
>
> Robinson Partnership, LP, owns property where the local government is planning to build a new intersection. The government asserts eminent domain over a large portion of Robinson's property. Although the government offers Robinson a condemnation award, the partnership reports a loss on the forced sale of the property. Code Sec. 1231 allows Robinson to treat the loss as an ordinary loss.

Recapture Rule

A taxpayer with Section 1231 gains for the current year has to treat them as ordinary income, rather than capital gains, if the taxpayer had Code Sec. 1231 losses in the previous five years. Any net Section 1231 losses that are not recaptured are carried forward for the remainder of the five-year period. Thus, Section 1231 gain is recharacterized as ordinary income until losses for the previous five years are completely recaptured. This is known as the *five-year lookback rule.*

> **EXAMPLE**
>
> Clifton Corporation runs an oil drilling operation in Tallahassee, Florida. In 2005, the business experienced a $10 million loss on the involuntary conversion of its Section 1231 assets, due a major natural disaster. The company treats the loss as ordinary. In 2009, the company decides to leave the area and sells its remaining Section 1231 assets for a net gain of $11 million. The taxpayer must recognize $10 million of this net gain as ordinary income. The remaining $1 million may be treated as capital gains. If, instead, the company realized $6 million of net gains in 2009, the $6 million would be characterized as ordinary gain. The remaining $4 million of net Section 1231 loss would be carried forward and applied to Section 1231 gains in 2010.

STUDY QUESTIONS

8. Which type of business property is *not* classified as Code Sec. 1231 property?
   a. Copyrights
   b. Capital assets involuntarily converted due to theft or condemnation
   c. Unharvested crops

9. Under the five-year lookback rule:
   a. Section 1231 gain is treated as ordinary income until losses from five years are recaptured
   b. Section 1231 losses are recharacterized as ordinary losses for five years
   c. Section 1231 net losses are nondeductible for five years after capital gains are reported

INVESTMENT THEFT LOSSES

Victims of investment schemes or fraud may find themselves under the casualty loss rules rather than using the net capital loss rules to salvage their position. Code Sec. 165(e) allows taxpayers to report a deduction for theft losses in the year in which a "reasonable taxpayer" discovers that the property is missing.

Rev. Rul. 2009-9 covers the tax treatment of fraudulent investment arrangements under which income amounts that are wholly or partially fictitious have been reported as income to the investors. In Rev. Rul. 2009-9, the IRS clarified that the investor is entitled to an ordinary theft loss rather than just a capital loss. Next, the IRS determined that the theft is not subject to the $100 floor ($500 in 2009) or 10 percent AGI limitation required for personal casualty losses (see discussion, below) because it arose in connection with a transaction entered into for profit and, therefore, is covered by Code Sec. 165(c)(2) rather than the personal casualty restrictions under 165(c)(3).

Discovered Thefts

Along with general theft loss relief comes a generous provision regarding the timing of the theft loss deduction. The tax code allows the taxpayer to report theft losses during the year in which they are discovered rather than when they occurred. This provision eliminates the need for the taxpayer to file an amended return to retroactively claim the loss in the tax year in which the theft actually occurred.

> **EXAMPLE**
>
> Over the span of several years, Adrian and Mary Ann Hastert, a married couple, are defrauded by an international broker claiming to sell priceless jewelry and gems. As a result of the scheme, they give the broker $400,000. In 2010, they consult an expert who determines that their purchased items are worthless fakes. The couple may claim a theft loss deduction in 2010, the year in which they discovered the loss. Adrian and Mary Ann are not required to carry back the loss to previous tax years, nor are they required to amend their income tax returns for those years to claim the losses and recompute their taxable income. In fact, they may not do so and are restricted in only claiming the loss in 2010. The 2010 deduction, however, may create an NOL that may be carried back.

Finally, although the investment theft loss is deductible in the year that the fraud is discovered (subject to reduction for amounts for which a reasonable prospect for recovery remains), the investment theft loss forms part of the taxpayer's net operating loss (NOL) that may be carried back or forward under normal NOL rules.

Ponzi Schemes

Under much pressure from Congress during 2009, the IRS issued several rounds of guidance (Rev. Procs. 2009-9 and 2009-20) allowing taxpayers to claim theft loss deductions for amounts lost from so-called Ponzi schemes, with the Bernard Madoff fraud victims its particular target for relief. These transactions are criminally fraudulent investment arrangements in which the organizer obtains cash and property from investors and reports fictitious earnings to them. Later, payments of "income" and "principal" are paid to the investors from cash or property paid into the scheme by other investors. The IRS specified that these losses qualify for the theft loss deduction because they arise from a criminal act and therefore do not qualify as capital loss.

> **EXAMPLE**
>
> Bucks, Ltd., an alleged stock brokerage firm, collects payments from customers for the purchase of securities and in payment of the company's transaction fees. Instead of using the funds for the purchase of the securities, Bucks uses them for the personal benefit of the owners. While engaging in this practice, the firm maintains records of customers' supposed investment transactions. When early-investing customers receive interest payments or return of their original principal invested according to the firm's fictional records, Bucks uses funds received from other, subsequent investors to cover their alleged investment payouts.

The amount of loss from a Ponzi scheme eligible for the theft loss deduction is equal to the initial amount "invested," plus additional "investments," less amounts withdrawn, reimbursements, recoveries, or claims that have the reasonable prospect of recovery. The deduction also includes "income" reported to the taxpayer by the Ponzi scheme organizer and subsequently reported on the taxpayer's tax return as gross income. This latter amount must have been reinvested into the fraudulent scheme.

EXAMPLE

The Thompsons, a married couple, invested $100,000 in what they subsequently discover is a Ponzi scheme. Before their discovery, they withdrew $5,000 from the scheme. They were also told by the scheme's organizers that they gained $10,000 of income on their investment. As a result, the Thompsons may report a theft loss deduction of $95,000 based on their invested principal ($100,000 – $5,000). They may also report a theft loss deduction for their increased income tax liability as a result of reporting the extra $10,000 of income.

Although this treatment is available to Madoff victims and similarly situated taxpayers, victims may elect not to adopt this treatment but rather file amended returns to recoup capital gains tax paid incorrectly on stock trades that actually never happened. Because the statute of limitations expired on all but the last three tax years, however, most victims of the Madoff scheme cannot recoup a greater portion of their tax losses through amended returns. Nevertheless, the amended return option remains open for those who can benefit.

COMMENT

The "Madoff-type" tax deductions are not allowed simply for individuals following bad investment advice. If the taxpayer's money is invested in stocks that plummet in value because of a broker's incompetence, only a capital loss is allowed. Likewise, any restitution paid by the broker would be considered capital gain.

STUDY QUESTION

10. Which of the following funds from a Ponzi scheme is **not** deductible as a discovered theft amount on the taxpayer's current return?

   a. Amounts from prior years discovered as thefts in the current tax year

   b. Amounts reported as gross income on prior returns but not reinvested in the fraudulent scheme

   c. "Principal" paid to investors in the fraudulent scheme

PERSONAL CASUALTY LOSSES

Types of Deductible Losses

Taxpayers may generally deduct losses that are sustained during the tax year and not compensated for by insurance or otherwise (Code Sec. 165). For individual taxpayers, categories of deductible losses include those incurred:

- In a trade or business;
- In transactions entered into for profit but not connected with a trade or business; and
- As the result of fire, storm, shipwreck or other casualty, or from theft (Code Sec. 165(c)), collectively caused personal casualty losses.

Personal casualty or theft losses are generally deductible only to the extent to which they exceed $100 per casualty or personal theft (except $500 for taxpayers in 2009), under Code Sec. 165(h)(1). Further, personal casualty losses for a tax year are deductible only to the extent the sum of the amount of personal casualty gains plus the amount by which the excess of personal casualty losses over gains is greater than 10 percent of the taxpayer's adjusted gross income (AGI).

Special Relief Provisions

Special relief is provided for taxpayers who sustain losses attributable to a disaster occurring in an area that is later determined by the president of the United States to warrant assistance by the federal government under the *Robert T. Stafford Disaster Relief and Emergency Assistance Act.* Under this provision, a taxpayer may elect to deduct a loss on his or her return for the immediately preceding tax year (Code Sec. 165(i)). This in effect allows taxpayers to get a fast refund for their loss.

In addition to the "normal" acceleration of tax benefits available to federally designated disaster areas, further disaster area relief has been provided on a temporary basis. Specifically, the 10 percent of AGI limitation applicable to personal casualty loss deductions has been waived under the *Emergency Economic Act of 2008* for personal casualty losses that are "net disaster losses." A *net disaster loss* means personal casualty losses attributable to a federally declared disaster occurring after 2007 and before 2010, and occurring in a disaster area, that exceed personal casualty gains. The 10 percent of AGI limitation continues to apply to casualty or theft losses that are not net disaster losses.

The $100 floor applicable to each casualty or theft is also temporarily increased to $500 for tax years beginning in 2009. The limitation amount for tax years beginning after 2009, however, will return to $100.

> **EXAMPLE**
>
> Sam Lincoln, an individual taxpayer having an AGI of $75,000, has the following personal casualty items during the 2009 tax year:
>
> - $5,000 personal casualty gain;
> - $15,000 allowable personal casualty loss attributable to a federally declared disaster ($15,500 less application of the $500 limitation per casualty under Code Sec. 165(h)(1), as amended by the Emergency Economic Act of 2008); and
> - An allowable personal casualty loss of $8,000 ($8,500 less application of the $500 limitation per casualty).
>
> Sam's deductible net disaster loss is $10,000 ($15,000 allowable disaster casualty loss – the $5,000 personal casualty gain). His deductible nondisaster casualty loss is $500 ($8,000 nondisaster casualty loss – $7,500 (his 10 percent of AGI limitation). Sam's deductible net personal casualty loss for the taxable year is $10,500 (the sum of the net disaster loss and the excess of the other casualty losses over the 10-percent limitation).

Although a casualty loss deduction is generally available only to those individuals who otherwise itemize their deductions, for tax years beginning after 2007, the amount of the standard deduction that may be claimed by a taxpayer who does not itemize deductions is increased by the amount of his or her disaster loss deduction resulting from a presidentially declared disaster under the *Robert T. Stafford Disaster Relief and Emergency Assistance Act.* Further, there is no limitation on how much of the disaster loss deduction may be added to the taxpayer's standard deduction. This relief was provided under the *Emergency Economic Act of 2008.*

BAD DEBT LOSSES

Ordinarily, owners of debt instruments, such as a loan, mortgage, lease, or bond agreement, possess an asset that may produce a steady stream of income over many tax years. During a down economy, however, these instruments may lose their value. The loss may be due to the debtor's failure to make good on its promise to pay under the associated agreement or simply because of the expectation that the debtor will not be able to pay.

Code Sec. 166, entitled "Bad Debts," generally controls who is entitled to a bad debt deduction and when a bad debt may be deducted. Code Sec. 166 conditions treatment generally on whether a bad debt is incurred in a trade or business. Further, Code Sec. 166 defers to Code Sec. 165 on the special treatment afforded to worthless securities (discussed earlier).

> **COMMENT**
>
> Uncollectibility differs according to whether the debt is wholly or partially worthless. This chapter discusses how taxpayers must prove uncollectibility.

Nonbusiness Losses

Noncorporate taxpayers cannot claim a bad debt deduction for nonbusiness debts (debts not created in connection with a trade or business or whose loss is not incurred within a trade or business). Instead, these taxpayers may claim a short-term capital loss deduction, as if they sold or exchanged the debt when it becomes totally worthless.

> **EXAMPLE**
>
> Abraham Yeager, a physician, loaned $20,000 to his neighbor, Bob Cooper. Bob declared bankruptcy during the year, and Abraham did not recover any of the funds loaned. The physician may not claim a bad debt deduction on the loan given to Bob, because it was not made within his trade or business. However, Abraham may report a $20,000 short-term capital loss deduction in the tax year in which his claim becomes uncollectible under bankruptcy law.

Business Losses

Under generally accepted accounting principles (GAAP), a business may elect to adjust its debt instruments periodically to reflect their fair value. As a result of this choice, debt holders may be subsequently forced to write down the value of these instruments where their market value has decreased.

It is important for business taxpayers to recognize that, not only may GAAP require the loss in value of a debt instrument to be reported as a financial loss, but doing so may create a tax benefit as well. Code Sec. 166 draws the dichotomy between completely worthless and partially worthless debt, with both types of loss deductible by a business but subject to different timing and substantiation requirements.

Code Sec. 166 allows taxpayers a deduction for completely worthless debt, debt which the taxpayer has no reasonable expectation of collecting. The deduction is equal to the taxpayer's basis in the debt instrument.

> **EXAMPLE**
>
> In 2010, Collins Bank issues a $50,000 loan to Drake Downy for use in his television repair business. Drake subsequently files for bankruptcy two months later. Collins reasonably estimates that, as a result, the bank will not be able to collect any amount of the loan. Collins will likely be able to claim a bad debt deduction for the completely worthless loan in the amount of $50,000.

Code Sec. 166 also provides a deduction for debt that becomes partially worthless. To claim the deduction, the taxpayer must prove to the satisfaction of the IRS that the debt is partially worthless. Additionally, the amount is limited to the total the taxpayer "charged off" during the year.

> **EXAMPLE**
>
> Assume the same facts as above for Drake's debt, except that Collins Bank reasonably expects it will collect $30,000 from Drake as a result of the bankruptcy proceeding. Collins reports on its books a bad debt loss for the remaining $20,000. Collins submits evidence of Drake's bankruptcy to the IRS to prove the loan instrument has lost its value. The bank will likely be able to claim a partially worthless bad debt deduction for the $20,000.

STUDY QUESTION

11. The *Emergency Economic Act of 2008* enables individuals who do not itemize deductions to add the amount of their disaster loss to their:

   a. Net operating loss carrybacks
   b. Standard deduction
   c. Tax credit totals

ABANDONMENT LOSSES

While a taxpayer conducts a trade or business, one or more items of business property may suddenly stop being useful. For a variety of reasons, the taxpayer may choose to stop conducting business with the property or permanently discard it. The IRS allows these taxpayers to claim an abandonment loss deduction under Reg. §1.165-2(a) for nondepreciable property or under Reg. §1.167(a)-8 for depreciable property. A sale or attempted sale is not necessary.

Whether abandonment has occurred depends on the facts and circumstances of each case. Generally, courts use a two-pronged test to determine abandonment.

- The taxpayer must show an *intent* to abandon the asset; and
- The taxpayer must overtly *act* to abandon the asset.

When courts use this two-part test, each part must be proved independently of the other. For the first prong, the taxpayer must show that it never intends to use the asset again. If the taxpayer merely sets the asset aside, with the possibility of its future use, that action will be insufficient to show abandonment. A taxpayer cannot merely declare that it has abandoned an asset; there must be an overt act. Additionally, abandonment occurs only if all of an asset's value is eliminated; mere *reduction* in value cannot result in an abandonment loss.

Buildings are a common example of an asset that a taxpayer may deem has been abandoned. Abandonment of a portion of a building may be treated as a retirement of the abandoned portion, but in addition to the abandonment, there must also be a sufficient segregation of the abandoned portion from the building as a whole. Abandonment can occur when a building is condemned as unfit for further occupancy or other use. However, difficulty or inability to rent out a building is not an abandonment of property.

> **EXAMPLE**
>
> Taxpayer Johnson Corporation, an agricultural company, hires an engineering firm to create a design for a new harvesting machine for $3 million. A natural disaster occurs in the area and destroys the majority of crops within Johnson's fields, forcing it to go out of business. Johnson is allowed to claim a $3 million loss deduction for the abandonment of the plans.

Similar to theft loss deductions, the taxpayer may claim the abandonment loss deduction outside of the actual tax year in which the property was abandoned. In one particular tax year the taxpayer may stop using the property for its business purpose or destroy it. The rules allow the taxpayer to claim a deduction for the related loss in a subsequent tax year.

Taxpayers abandoning property, however, must avoid an exception before claiming the abandonment loss deduction. Taxpayers cannot claim the loss deduction for abandoned property if they first claim a loss at the time of the sale of the property.

> **EXAMPLE**
>
> When the agricultural company, Johnson Corporation, went bankrupt because of a natural disaster, it sold the plans for a new harvester to another farming company in a different part of the country. Johnson reported a loss on the sale of the design. Johnson may not also claim an abandonment loss deduction for the cost it incurred for the plans.

A taxpayer may claim an abandonment loss for intangible property as well as tangible property. Abandonment of a partnership interest can give rise to a deductible loss.

STUDY QUESTION

12. An abandonment loss may **not** be deducted if:

  a. It occurred in a previous tax year
  b. Intangible property is abandoned
  c. A loss has been claimed on the sale of the property

GAMBLING LOSSES

Taxpayers must pay income taxes on all sources of income, even including income earned from gambling or wagers. Taxpayers may also be able to claim tax deductions for certain gambling or wagering losses, with certain limitations.

The principal tax code provision that restricts claims for losses from gambling or wagering is Code Sec. 165(d). That provision limits taking losses incurred in a wagering activity to the amount of any gains experienced. As a result, a taxpayer cannot claim a deduction for losses incurred while gambling or betting in excess of the amount they gained from that activity over the tax year.

> **EXAMPLE**
>
> Taxpayer Theodore Evans goes to Las Vegas and loses $5,000 gambling one evening. The next day, before his flight home, he wins $1,000. Theodore must report the $1,000 of income on his income tax return (the casino will also file a confirmation return with the IRS reporting those earnings). However, he may claim a deduction for $1,000 in gambling losses. He may not claim a deduction for the remaining $4,000 in losses, nor may he carry them over to offset any winnings in the following year.

Qualifying Gambling Income

One further twist to the wagering loss deduction is that the income the taxpayer receives must come from a wagering transaction. Although not specifically defined within the Internal Revenue Code or associated regulations, only certain transactions meet this qualification. The IRS has stated in Letter Ruling 200417004 that, according to the dictionary meaning of *gambling,* a wagering transaction must have three elements:

- A prize;
- A chance of winning the prize; and
- Required consideration in order to obtain the chance to win the prize.

Examples that meet these elements, the IRS stated, include income from entry into a sweepstakes, raffle, or lottery. In Rev. Proc. 77-29, the IRS listed keno, slot machines, table games, bingo, and betting on animal races as potential wagering transactions.

Substantiating Gambling Losses

More than for other types of losses, a deduction for wagering or gambling losses is rather difficult to substantiate. In Rev. Proc. 77-29, the IRS gave taxpayers guidance on how to substantiate losses from wagering transactions. The agency reported that, to adequately substantiate gambling losses, taxpayers should keep an accurate diary or similar record, supplemented with supporting evidence.

Generally, the record should contain at least the following information:

- Date and type of specific wagers or wagering activity;
- Name of gambling establishment;
- Address or location of gambling establishment;
- Names of other persons (if any) present with the taxpayer at the gambling establishment; and
- Amounts won or lost.

The IRS has identified supporting documents for certain gambling activities. These include:

- *Keno:* Copies of keno tickets purchased by the taxpayer and validated by the gambling establishment, copies of the taxpayer's casino credit records, and copies of the taxpayer's casino check-cashing records;
- *Slot machines:* A record of all winnings by date and time that the machine was played;
- *Table games of blackjack, craps, poker, baccarat, roulette, wheel of fortune:* The number of the table at which the taxpayer was playing, casino credit data indicating whether credit was issued in the pit or at the cashier's cage;
- *Bingo:* A record of the number of games played, cost of tickets purchased, and amounts collected on winning tickets. Supplemental records include any receipts from the casino or parlor;
- *Racing of horses, harness racing, and dog racing:* A record of the races, entries, amounts of wagers, amounts collected on winning tickets, and amounts lost on losing tickets. Supplemental records include unredeemed tickets and payment records from the racetrack; and
- *Lotteries:* A record of ticket purchases, dates, winnings, and losses. Supplemental records include unredeemed tickets, payment slips, and winnings statements.

Form W-2G

Form W-2G. Payers of winnings report winnings and any federal tax withheld on the winnings on Form W-2G, *Certain Gambling Winnings.* The requirements for reporting and withholding depend on the type of gambling, the amount of the gambling winnings, and generally the ratio of the winnings to the wager.

Gambling winnings are reported on Form W-2G if:

- The winnings (not reduced by the wager) are $1,200 or more from a bingo game or slot machine;
- The winnings (reduced by the wager) are $1,500 or more from a keno game;
- The winnings (reduced by the wager or buy-in) are more than $5,000 from a poker tournament;
- The winnings (except winnings from bingo, slot machines, keno, and poker tournaments) reduced, at the option of the payer, by the wager are
  - $600 or more, and
  - At least 300 times the amount of the wager; or
- The winnings are subject to federal income tax withholding (either regular gambling withholding or backup withholding).

Regular withholding. The payer may be required to withhold 25 percent of gambling winnings for federal income tax. This is known *as regular gambling withholding* (backup withholding at a higher rate is discussed below). The 25 percent rate applies if the winnings of more than $5,000 from:

- Sweepstakes;
- Wagering pools;
- Lotteries; or
- Other wagering transactions if the winnings are at least 300 times the amount wagered.

Backup withholding. However, *backup withholding* at 28 percent of winnings applies to winnings from bingo, keno, slot machines, and poker tournaments. Gambling establishments must withhold at the 28 percent rate if:

- The winner does not furnish a correct taxpayer identification number (TIN);
- 25 percent has not been withheld; and
- The winnings are at least $600 and at least 300 times the wager (or the winnings are at least $1,200 from bingo or slot machines or $1,500 from keno or more than $5,000 from a poker tournament).

> **COMMENT**
>
> Individuals who receive gambling winnings as a member of a group of two or more people sharing the winnings must complete Form 5754, *Statement by Person(s) Receiving Gambling Winnings.* Form 5754 is provided to the payer of the winnings to assist the payer in preparing Form W-2G for each winner.

Casual Versus Professional Gamblers

There is an important distinction between gambling losses claimed by casual gamblers versus those claimed by taxpayers who gamble as part of a trade or business; i.e., professional gamblers. Although gambling losses are only deductible to the extent taxpayers have gambling gains for casual gamblers, professional gamblers may claim gambling losses as loss from a trade or business. Thus, professional gamblers are not limited in the amount of wagering losses they may claim to the amount of their gambling-related income.

As a result, professional gamblers may offset other sources of business income with losses from their gambling trade or business. Additionally, excess gambling losses by professional gamblers are net operating losses that they may carry back to previous tax years or forward to subsequent tax years to apply against future gains. Casual gamblers do not have these options. The IRS will restrict taxpayers to casual gambler status and will demand strong proof to the contrary before deciding not to litigate the issue.

> **EXAMPLE**
>
> Reynolds plays professional blackjack for a living. He also receives a $500,000 salary from his company, Golden Chips Corporation, where he is a part-time consultant. During 2009, he reported an overall net tax gain (including his salary and blackjack winnings) of $2 million. During 2010, although he continued to receive a $500,000 salary, he also recognized a net loss from his blackjack activities of $3 million. Because Reynolds engages in wagering as a trade or business, he is not limited in claiming losses to the amount of gain for the tax year. Reynolds may offset his $500,000 salary with his blackjack losses for 2010 and carry back the remaining $2 million of his 2010 blackjack losses to 2009 for a refund. Reynolds may carry forward his remaining $500,000 of 2010 net operating losses to other tax years.

STUDY QUESTION

13. Professional gamblers:
  a. May not claim their losses as NOLs
  b. May offset other sources of business income with gambling losses
  c. May claim the same losses casual gamblers are permitted to deduct

HOBBY LOSSES

During an economic downturn, taxpayers may earn extra money through a favorite hobby or pastime. This may be profitable, but some taxpayers may lose money as a result. Taxpayers have to be careful that the IRS agrees that any net loss deductions they claim are related to an activity entered into with the intent to make money. After all, subject to exceptions, taxpayers cannot generally claim deductions related to personal expenses.

Code Sec. 183 generally denies loss deductions beyond income earned for activities in which the taxpayer fails to engage for a profit. These types of deductions are typically referred to as *hobby losses*. Generally, an activity is presumed to be carried on for-profit if it makes a profit in at least three of the last five tax years, including the current year. If an activity is not for-profit, losses from that activity may not be used to offset other income.

> **COMMENT**
>
> Hobby losses are the opposite of passive activity losses. Even though taxpayers may have a profit motive in conducting passive activities, they may lack the amount of active participation sufficient to claim any resulting loss deductions. Taxpayers engaging in hobbies may spend significant amounts of time pursuing their interest, yet hobbyists lack the profit motive sufficient to claim resulting loss deductions.

Taxpayers are generally considered to have engaged in an activity for profit based on nine different factors:
- The manner in which the taxpayer carries on the activity;
- The expertise or experience of the taxpayer's advisors;
- The time and effort the taxpayer spends on the activity;
- The expectation that the assets used in the activity may appreciate;
- The success of the taxpayer in carrying on similar or dissimilar activities;
- The taxpayer's history of losses from the activity;
- The amount of occasional profits earned;
- The taxpayer's financial status; and
- The elements of personal pleasure or recreation derived from the activity.

These factors are not exhaustive. The IRS looks at all the facts and circumstances of a taxpayer's activity. In some cases, several factors may predominate.

EXAMPLE

Neilson has a doctorate degree in paranormal psychology and spends the majority of his time as a professor on the subject at a local university. In his spare time, he hang-glides and travels around the country giving speeches about the topic. Occasionally, Neilson may receive a cash payment for speaking at an engagement if the organization chooses to compensate him. Because he gives the speeches for personal reasons, it is likely that his speaking engagements are not activities engaged in for a profit. Neilson most likely may not claim a tax deduction for any resulting losses stemming from this activity.

COMMENT

Taxpayers and the IRS have litigated many hobby loss cases in the courts. These cases are good guides for taxpayers. Taxpayers should prepare a business plan, keep detailed and accurate books and records, maintain separate checking accounts for each activity, advertise and promote the activity in a business-like manner, and make major decisions relating to the activity in a businesslike manner. Taxpayers should not commingle proceeds of the activity with personal funds, allow losses to grow without making efforts to change operations, or make major decisions about the activity based on personal enjoyment rather than business prospects.

Presumption of Profit

Although taxpayers would normally have to prove that an activity is for the conduct of a trade or business to avoid the hobby loss limitation, there is an alternative. Code Sec. 183(d) states that, if taxpayers can show that they actually received income from the activity for three or more consecutive years within the preceding five-year period, then they will be presumed to have engaged in the activity for a profit. In other words, if an individual makes enough money from a hobby, the IRS may eventually consider it a business. If so, then the taxpayer could begin claiming a tax deduction for any subsequent losses.

EXAMPLE

Between 2006 and 2010, Charlie Neilson reported income from his speaking engagements for all four years. During 2011, however, he incurred a net loss from his speaking tour due to many last-minute cancellations. Charlie may claim a loss deduction for 2011. Because his speaking activity was profitable for a period longer than that required under Code Sec. 183(d), his activity is presumed to be an activity engaged in for profit.

> **COMMENT**
>
> If an individual is launching a new activity to make additional money that may or may not be considered a hobby, the IRS allows taxpayers to file Form 5213, *Election to Postpone Determination as to Whether an Activity is Engaged in for a Profit.* The IRS will wait until after the fourth year the taxpayer conducts the activity to determine whether it is a trade or business what will produce acceptable loss deductions.

Deductions

If an activity is deemed to be a hobby, deductions are still available, but only if the taxpayer itemizes deductions on Schedule A, Form 1040, and then only in a certain sequence, and never in excess of the income that the activity generates. These deductions are taken in the following order and only to the extent stated in each of the three categories:

- **Category 1:** Deductions that a taxpayer may take for personal as well as business activities, such as home mortgage interest and taxes, may be taken in full irrespective of hobby income, but must reduce the amount of hobby income remaining available to offset deductions in Category 2 or 3;
- **Category 2:** Deductions that do not result in an adjustment to basis, such as advertising, insurance premiums, and wages, may be taken next, to the extent gross income for the activity is more than the deductions from the Category 1;
- **Category 3:** Business deductions that reduce the basis of property, such as depreciation and amortization, are taken last, but only to the extent gross income for the activity is more than the deductions taken in the Categories 1 and 2.

STUDY QUESTIONS

> **14.** Taxpayers seek to avoid classification of activities as hobbies because:
>
> **a.** No more than $500 per year may be deducted for hobby losses
> **b.** Deductions for hobby losses may not exceed the amount of gross income from the hobby activity
> **c.** Recordkeeping and record retention rules for hobby activities are stricter than for for-profit activities

> **15.** Category 1 deductions such as tax or mortgage payments:
>   **a.** Increase the gross income reportable as hobby income
>   **b.** Reduce the amount available to offset deductions in Category 2 or 3
>   **c.** May be claimed as itemized deductions only if hobby losses are claimed

CONCLUSION

It is important from a tax perspective for taxpayers to take advantage of losses they may experience from bad market conditions. Taxpayers should plan their business activities so that their losses remain deductible and capitalize on the timing rules so that they do not lose any tax benefits those losses may provide.

Special rules govern carrying forward and carrying back net operating losses. There are limitations on claiming deductions for other types of losses such as those for passive activities, losses from enterprises in which the taxpayer has little financial risk, and those in which taxpayers may engage for fun or leisure. Special rules also apply to loss deductions claimed after the sale of stock, theft, property abandonment, gambling, and the involuntary conversion of business property. Taxpayers who become aware of the relief provisions are positioned well to maximize the benefits of each of these tax losses.

MODULE 2: DEALING WITH ECONOMIC DOWNTURN — CHAPTER 5

Cancellation of Indebtedness Income: Rules and Exclusions

Individuals and businesses routinely go into debt. At any time, but particularly in the midst of a troubled economy such as the recent recession, some will have problems paying off their debts. Their creditors, such as mortgage lenders, credit card companies, merchants, or suppliers, may decide that the borrower is not going to pay the full amount of the debt. In that circumstance, a creditor may forgive or cancel part or all of the debt. This may occur whether the loan is personal or for business. Borrowing money does not give rise to income, because there is an offsetting liability, but a creditor's forgiveness of the borrower's debt can give rise to cancellation of indebtedness (COI) income for the borrower. COI occurs because the borrower gets to keep the funds (or, in most cases, does not have to pay back funds already spent). In many situations, however, the borrower does not have to recognize the income because of exceptions carved out under the tax law.

This chapter looks at the impact on the borrower of a cancellation of indebtedness: when cancellation is taxable, when it is excludible, and what offsetting adjustments have to be made. The chapter also looks at a provision enacted in 2009 that defers COI income realized from the forgiveness of certain business debt.

LEARNING OBJECTIVES

Upon completion of this chapter, you will be able to:

- Determine whether there has been a cancellation of indebtedness for tax purposes;
- Decide when the COI can be excluded from income;
- Describe how to reduce tax attributes when COI income is excluded;
- Explain the treatment of debt exchanged for stock or a partnership interest;
- Identify the effect of COI on partnerships and S corporations; and
- Apply the deferral of income to the reacquisition of business debt.

INTRODUCTION

COI income can be troublesome, because the income is not accompanied by a cash payment and it may be difficult for the debtor to pay the resulting tax liability. However, the tax code provides some relief by granting exceptions and exclusions from the recognition of income. Code Sec. 108

specifically provides these benefits: COI income may be excluded if the debtor is bankrupt (Code Sec. 108(a)(1)(A)), insolvent (Code Sec. 108(a)(1)(B)), a victim of terrorism (Code Sec. 101(i)), or victim of certain disasters (*Emergency Economic Stabilization Act*). Other exclusions apply if the debt is related to farming (Code Sec. 108(a)(1)(C)), real estate used in a business (108(a)(1)(D)), or a home used as a principal residence (108(a)(1)(E)). There also is an exception for student loans (108(f)).

If the COI income is not recognized, the debtor must reduce tax attributes (Code Sec. 108(b)). Many of these attributes are business-related, such as a net operating loss (NOL) or the general business credit. Another attribute, applicable to both individuals and businesses, is the basis (cost) of property. Reducing tax attributes has the effect of delaying the recognition of the excluded income, rather than avoiding recognition altogether. If all attributes have been reduced to zero, however, any amount of discharged debt that is left over is not taxable income and is disregarded as an item that otherwise would need to be "paid back" later through reduced tax benefits. There also is special treatment if a business debt, rather than being forgiven outright, is satisfied using stock or a partnership interest (Code Sec. 108(e)(8)).

A provision enacted in the *American Recovery and Reinvestment Act of 2009* (2009 Recovery Act) defers COI income if the income stems from the reacquisition of business debt (Code Sec. 108(i)). The income is then recognized over five years, beginning in 2014. The scope of this provision continues to be an issue. Sometimes one of the exclusions also applies, so a business may have to choose whether to exclude the income and reduce attributes or to delay recognizing the income and maintain attributes.

> **NOTE**
>
> COI income may also be referred to as *cancellation of debt (COD)* or *discharge of indebtedness (DOI) income*.

WHAT CONSTITUTES DEBT AND WHEN IT IS DISCHARGED

The provisions on COI apply to income from "the discharge (in whole or in part) of indebtedness." In many transactions it is clear when debt has been discharged. But there are circumstances in which it may not be obvious whether there has been a discharge. Such gray areas are explored here.

Debt

First, there must be a *debt:* an absolute obligation to pay a fixed amount on demand or within a given time, in cash or property. The characterization of the obligation as a debt is determined under federal tax law, but the rights of the parties initially are determined under state law. If there is a dispute as to the debt, a compromise in which the debtor pays less than the amount claimed by the creditor does not give rise to a discharge.

Discharge

A debt is clearly *discharged* when a creditor accepts less than the full amount of the debt in complete satisfaction. A debt is also discharged when it is clear that the debtor will never have to pay the debt. This situation may depend on the facts and circumstances concerning the likelihood of repayment or the worthlessness of the debt. An identifiable event may fix the debt loss with certainty, indicating a discharge. This includes a bankruptcy or debt discharge agreement. Failure to make payments for 36 months may be treated as an identifiable event.

However, a debt is not discharged if there is still a reasonable prospect that the debt will be paid even when it is "past due." Furthermore, an agreement to cancel a debt that is contingent on future events is not a discharge.

A debtor's acquisition of its own debt for less than its face value is a discharge. A debtor that issues a debt instrument in satisfaction of existing debt is treated as having paid an amount equal to the issue price of the new debt. This type of discharge is the subject of a 2009 Recovery Act tax provision that defers income from a discharge of business debt.

STUDY QUESTIONS

1. A debt is *not* considered discharged if:

  a. There is still a reasonable prospect a past-due debt will be paid

  b. The debtor reacquires its own debt for less than face value by issuing a debt instrument

  c. A related person of the debtor acquires the debt from an unrelated person

2. The 2009 Recovery Act addresses discharge of debt through:

  a. Offers in compromise

  b. Issuance of a debt instrument in satisfaction of existing debt

  c. Agreements to cancel debt contingent on future events

Related-Party Debt

The acquisition of debt by a person related to the debtor from an unrelated person is also a discharge (Code Sec. 108(e)(4)). The debt is treated as acquired by the debtor. A *related person* includes a family member, a member of a controlled group of corporations, a trade or business under common control, or a partner in a partnership controlled by the debtor.

> **EXAMPLE**
>
> P Corporation is the parent of S Corporation. S issues a bond to a third-party investor for $1,000. P acquires the bond for $900 on the open market. S has COI income of $100. Similarly, if P issued the bond and S acquired it, P would have $100 of COI income. In the latter situation, the IRS has also ruled that S's distribution of the note to P is a dividend, assuming S has earnings and profits, and that P has an interest deduction if the bond's value is greater than $1,000.

If a partnership acquires the debt of a partner and distributes the debt to the partner, this action extinguishes the partner's debt. The partner has COI income equal to the issue price of the debt reduced by its fair market value at the time the partnership distributed the debt.

Debt Reduction

A reduction in the debt amount can result in a discharge, provided the creditor is not the seller of the property. Seller financing of a purchase of property that is secured by the property gives rise to a *purchase money debt*. If the lender reduces a buyer's purchase money debt, the debt relief is treated as a reduction in the price of the property and does not give rise to COI income (Code Sec. 108(e)(5)). The buyer must reduce the basis of the property. This rule does not apply if the debt is reduced when the purchaser is insolvent or is in a Chapter 11 bankruptcy.

> **EXAMPLE**
>
> Alan buys a car for $10,000 and borrows the cost directly from the car dealer. The loan is secured by the car. Alan loses his job and cannot make the full payments on the loan for the time being. To help Alan pay the loan, the dealer agrees to forgive $2,000 of the debt. The transaction is treated as a reduction in the car's price to $8,000; Alan does not recognize any COI income. Alan's basis for the cost of the car is reduced from $10,000 to $8,000. (If, instead, the car loan had been made from a bank, the lender usually would not reduce the amount of the loan but simply would repossess and sell its security interest (the vehicle) and walk away from collecting any shortfall from the borrower. That shortfall becomes COI income to borrower.)

If a partnership that purchased property becomes insolvent, the seller's reduction of purchase money debt is treated as COI income that flows through to the partners. All of the partners must recognize the COI income and cannot treat the discharge as a reduction in the purchase price, because the partners are not the purchasers of the property.

Statute of Limitations

The running of the statute of limitations is a factor but is not itself conclusive. A writeoff by the debtor may merely reflect financial difficulties or may be evidence of a discharge. The writeoff of debt by the debtor before the statute of limitations has expired may trigger COI income if there is little chance of the creditor enforcing the claim. Under this rule, debts treated as discharged include:

- Unclaimed customer deposits to a utility company;
- Unclaimed, inactive and dormant bank accounts; and
- Unclaimed wages earned at least three years before the writeoff.

STUDY QUESTIONS

3. How is COI handled when a partnership purchases property, the partnership becomes insolvent, and the seller's purchase money debt is reduced?

   a. The partners recognize COI income and the discharge is not a reduction in purchase price

   b. The partnership recognizes the reduced purchase money debt and does not recognize COI income at the entity level

   c. The partners are considered the owners of the property and may reduce the purchase price by the discharge amount

4. A property seller's reduction of a buyer's purchase money debt:

   a. Gives rise to COI income for the buyer

   b. Is considered a reduction of the property's price

   c. Increases the buyer's basis in the property

RECOGNITION OF INCOME

Figuring COI

Generally, COI income is the difference between the face value of the debt and the amount paid by the debtor and accepted in full satisfaction of the obligation. This formula can apply whether the debt is recourse (secured by the borrower's personal note and, in many instances, a security interest in particular property owned by the borrower) or nonrecourse (secured only to the extent of the value of a particular property).

The amount taken into account in a discharge is adjusted for unamortized premium and unamortized discount on the debt discharged. Unamortized premium is added to the face value of the debt; unamortized discount is subtracted from the face value of the debt.

Transfer of Property

In many contexts, a sale of property (other than inventory) gives rise to a capital gain or loss, with the gain taxed at reduced rates and the loss generating a limited deduction from ordinary income. On the other hand, COI income, if taxable, is ordinary income. A transfer of property to the lender in satisfaction of debt may or may not give rise to COI income.

Nonrecourse debt. A transfer of property subject to nonrecourse debt (when the buyer is not personally liable on the debt) is a sale or exchange of the property and is not a discharge of indebtedness. The buyer treats the full amount of debt as an amount realized on the sale of the property, even if the property is worth less than the amount of debt. The buyer has a capital gain or loss.

Recourse debt. A transfer of property subject to recourse debt (the buyer is personally liable on the debt) is also a sale or exchange, provided the property's value equals or exceeds the debt discharged. The buyer has gain equal to the difference between the amount realized (which includes the face amount of the debt) and the adjusted basis in the property.

> **COMMENT**
>
> A forgiveness of debt and a transfer of property that occur several months apart may be treated as separate transactions that include a discharge of indebtedness.

However, if the recourse debt exceeds the value of the property, and the balance of the debt is forgiven, IRS regulations require that the transaction be bifurcated. Up to the fair market value of the property, the transfer is a sale or exchange on which gain or loss is recognized (generally capital). The amount of debt that exceeds the property's value gives rise to COI income, which is ordinary income.

> **EXAMPLE**
>
> Jeff buys a truck for $15,000 for his personal use. He borrows $14,000 from a credit union to pay for the truck and is personally liable for the loan. After one year, the loan principal is $10,000, and the truck is worth $8,000. Jeff stops making loan payments. The credit union repossesses the truck, which pays for $8,000 of the loan, and forgives the other $2,000 of loan principal. Jeff realizes a nondeductible personal loss of $7,000 ($15,000 basis – $8,000 amount realized). He has ordinary income of $2,000 from the cancellation of the debt.

EXCLUSIONS

Once it is established that a taxpayer has COI income, the next issue is to examine whether the taxpayer can exclude the amount from gross income. The tax code provides an exclusion in the following circumstances:

- Insolvency or bankruptcy;
- Qualified farm debt;
- Qualified real property business debt;
- Qualified principal residence debt;
- Certain student loans;
- Victims of terrorism and certain disasters;
- Gifts and bequests;
- Payment of the debt would have been deductible (Code Sec. 108(e)(2)); and
- General welfare payments.

The bankruptcy exclusion takes precedence over the insolvency and the other exclusions. Similarly, the insolvency exception takes precedence over the farm and business real property exclusions. However, the principal residence exclusion applies over the insolvency exclusion, unless the taxpayer elects otherwise. A solvent taxpayer cannot qualify for the bankruptcy or insolvency exclusions but may be able to use one of the other exclusions.

Reduction of Tax Attributes

To compensate for the benefit of many of the exclusions of COI income from tax, the debtor is required to reduce tax attributes such as NOLs or the basis of property. The reduction of attributes has the effect of postponing the recognition of COI income, rather than permanently excluding it, because the taxpayer will have fewer deductions to offset future taxable income. However, if the amount of the COI income exceeds the taxpayer's total tax attributes that can be reduced, the excess is permanently excluded from gross income. There are special attribute and basis reduction rules for some of the exclusions.

The amount excluded from income under the exclusions for bankruptcy, insolvency, farm indebtedness, and disasters must be subtracted from the taxpayer's attributes in the following order:

1. Any NOL for the year of the discharge and any NOL carryover to that year;
2. Any carryover of the general business credit to or from the year of discharge;
3. The minimum tax credit at the beginning of the year following the year of discharge;

4. Any net capital loss for the year of discharge and any capital loss carryover to that year;
5. The basis of the taxpayer's property (depreciable or nondepreciable), in the manner described in Code Sec. 1017;
6. Any passive activity loss (PAL) or credit carryover from the year of the discharge; and
7. Any foreign tax credit carryover to or from the year of the discharge.

These attribute reductions do not apply to the exclusions for real property business debt and principal residence debt. Instead, the basis of the real property securing the debt is reduced. Because the COI income may not exceed the available basis, the debtor may have to recognize some COI income for the balance of the debt. For example, the real property business debt exclusion cannot exceed the total adjusted basis of all depreciable property. If the debt forgiven exceeds the available basis, the excess is taxable and cannot be excluded.

A taxpayer must report the exclusion of COI income and the reduction of tax attributes on Form 982, *Reduction of Tax Attributes Due to Discharge of Indebtedness (and Section 1082 Basis Adjustment).* The taxpayer also must describe the debt cancellation transaction and identify the property whose basis is being reduced.

COMMENT

An IRS official noted that a taxpayer excluding COI income must reduce tax attributes and the IRS will be looking for Form 982. The lender that forgives the debt must file a Form 1099-C, *Cancellation of Debt,* with the debtor by February 1 and with the IRS by March 1 following the year of forgiveness.

For discharges after July 18, 2003, before reducing attributes, the taxpayer can determine his or her tax liability by using attributes (such as NOLs) that arose in the year of discharge or that carry over to the year of discharge or an earlier year.

EXAMPLE

In 2008, Acme Company has COI income of $2,000 that it excludes because it is insolvent. For 2008, Acme operates at a loss of $1,000, generating an NOL. Acme can use the NOL before it reduces attributes. Thus, Acme chooses to carry back the $1,000 NOL to 2007, when it had taxable income. Acme does not have to reduce the NOL to zero; instead, the company reduces other attributes, such as the basis of property, to reflect that Acme excluded $2,000 of COI income.

For an individual in Chapter 7 or Chapter 11 bankruptcy, the reduction of attributes applies to attributes of the bankruptcy estate, and not to any attributes of the individual that arise after the case began or that the taxpayer treats as exempt property. However, attribute reduction can apply to property transferred from the bankruptcy estate to the individual.

The reduction of basis applies to property held at the beginning of the year following the year of discharge. Thus, reduction does not apply to property sold in the year of discharge. Reduction under the general rule is limited to the aggregate bases of the taxpayer's property and the amount of money held after the discharge, reduced by the aggregate liabilities after the discharge.

> **EXAMPLE**
>
> In 2008, Carl has $1,500 of COI income that he excluded because he was insolvent. His only tax attributes are the bases of nonbusiness personal property. At the beginning of 2009, his assets consist of furniture with a cost basis of $4,500 and $600 in his savings account. He owes $5,000 on a student loan. He must reduce his basis in the furniture $100, the basis of property plus the amount of money he holds, reduced by the $5,000 student loan.

In the case of a foreclosure of a personal residence, the transaction is treated as a sale. If the fair market value of the property exceeds the balance of the loan, the debtor will realize a gain on the excess. However, up to $250,000 of gain ($500,000 if married) may be excluded under Code Sec. 121 as gain from the sale of a principal residence.

Under the general rule, the reduction applies in the following sequence:

1. Business or investment real property that secured the discharged debt,;
2. Business or investment personal property that secured the debt;
3. Other business or investment property;
4. Inventory; and
5. Personal use property. If both real and personal property secured the debt, the basis of the real property must be reduced first.

Generally, the attributes are reduced dollar-for-dollar for the amount of income excluded. However, for the general business credit, minimum tax credit, foreign tax credit, and PAL credit, the amount of the reduction is one dollar for every three dollars excluded. The reductions are made after determining the taxpayer's tax liability for the year of the discharge. The reduction in basis applies to property held at the beginning of the year following the year of discharge.

EXAMPLE

ABC Company has $2,000 of COI income. ABC excludes the income because it is insolvent; thus it must reduce its attributes by $2,000. It has the following tax attributes:

- An NOL of $200;
- A general business credit carryover of $500; and
- Property basis of $500.

ABC uses $200 of basis reduction to reduce its NOL to zero; it then uses $1,500 of basis reduction to reduce its business credit by $500, down to zero; and then the company uses the remaining $300 of basis reduction to reduce its property basis to $200.

Basis election. A taxpayer may elect to reduce the basis of depreciable property (including real property held as inventory) before reducing any other attributes. Code Sec. 1017 again applies. The election must be made on a Form 982 filed with the taxpayer's timely filed income tax return for the year of the discharge. IRS consent is needed for a late election. The reduction cannot exceed the aggregate bases of depreciable property held at the beginning of the following year and must reduce the depreciation or amortization that would otherwise be allowed.

Recapture. If the taxpayer reduces the basis of property and later sells the property for a gain, the taxpayer must recapture the amount of the reduction as ordinary income. This treatment applies to both depreciable and nondepreciable property, and applies even if recapture would not ordinarily apply to the sale of the property.

EXAMPLE

Donna buys and leases real estate. She buys Property B for $150,000. She borrows $135,000 from Bank B to buy that property. She pays $25,000 of principal on the Bank B loan, but then temporarily stops making payments after she loses several tenants. To help Donna, Bank B forgives $10,000 of its loan. Donna has $10,000 of COI income, but she qualifies for the exclusion for qualified real property business debt. She excludes the $10,000 of COI income, and she reduces the basis of Property B by $10,000 to $140,000. She subsequently sells Property B for $160,000. She has $10,000 of income that she must treat as ordinary income from the recapture of the basis reduction. The other $10,000 of income is capital gain.

Bankruptcy and Insolvency Exclusions

Bankruptcy. Debt canceled in bankruptcy (Chapters 7, 11, or 13) is excluded. The debtor must be under the jurisdiction of the U.S. bankruptcy court. The debt must be canceled by the court or the discharge must result from a plan approved by the court. A Chapter 11 proceeding can provide for either a liquidation or a reorganization. Individual debtors may also seek bankruptcy protection under Chapter 7 (liquidation) or Chapter 13 (wage earner's plan). In Chapter 7, an individual may be discharged from having to pay a debt. In Chapter 13, debts are not initially canceled and bankruptcy is not declared; future wages are collected by the court and used to pay the bankrupt's debts in part or in full. After all payments have been made, any remaining debts are canceled.

Insolvency. A debtor is insolvent if the total of the debtor's liabilities exceeds the fair market value of all the debtor's assets, as determined immediately before the debt is canceled. The insolvency exclusion is limited to the amount of the insolvency.

> ### EXAMPLE
> Betty's credit card company cancels $5,000 of her liability. Betty determines that her liabilities were $15,000 and the value of her assets was $7,000. Thus, Betty is insolvent by $8,000, which is in excess of the amount of the canceled debt. Betty can exclude the entire $5,000 from income. If, instead, Betty's total liabilities were $10,000, she would be insolvent by $3,000, and she could only exclude $3,000 of the $5,000 of canceled debt. Betty would then have to report the remaining $2,000 of canceled debt as income, unless another exclusion applied.

> ### COMMENT
> A taxpayer who is both bankrupt and insolvent can claim the bankruptcy exclusion and is not limited to the amount of the insolvency.

Assets include the value of everything owned, including assets that serve as collateral for debt and assets that cannot be reached by creditors, such as a pension plan benefit. Liabilities include the entire amount of recourse debts and the amount of nonrecourse debt that is secured by the value of property. The taxpayer can include excess nonrecourse debt that is discharged. Accrued liabilities, such as real estate taxes, are counted. Contingent liabilities are also counted if the taxpayer establishes that they are likely to be paid off.

> **COMMENT**
>
> The IRS provides a worksheet to calculate insolvency in Publication 4681, *Canceled Debts, Foreclosures, Repossessions, and Abandonments (for Individuals)*.

The value of appreciated assets is not reduced for any taxes that would be owed if the property were sold. The fair market value of property is not based on its liquidation or distressed sale value.

> **COMMENT**
>
> During an economic downturn in which determining the precise value of assets is difficult, more disagreements are evident between debtors and the IRS. As has always been the case, but is accentuated in the current economy, it is necessary to substantiate the value carefully and thoroughly using proofs such as comparables.

Qualified Farm Debt Exclusion

Farmers can exclude income from the cancellation of *qualified farm debt*. This includes debt on property and debt the farmer is personally liable for. The exclusion applies to debt incurred directly in the operation of a farming trade or business, provided that at least 50 percent of the taxpayer's total gross receipts for the three years before the debt is canceled were from the trade or business of farming.

> **COMMENT**
>
> Proceeds from the sale of inventory and from the sale of all the farmer's livestock and machinery are counted in gross receipts. Proceeds from renting farmland are not included.

A *qualified person* must have canceled the debt for the farm debt exclusion to apply. This includes an individual or organization who is actively and regularly engaged in the business of lending money. A federal, state, or local government (and governments' agencies and instrumentalities) is also a qualified person. The person cannot be related to the taxpayer, the seller of the property, or a person receiving a fee from the taxpayer.

> **COMMENT**
>
> The insolvency exclusion must be applied before the exclusion for farm debt. However, if the canceled debt exceeds the insolvency exclusion, the taxpayer can apply the farm exclusion to the remaining debt. The farm exclusion takes precedence over the real property business debt exclusion.

The farm exclusion is limited to the sum of the taxpayer's adjusted tax attributes and the total adjusted bases of qualified property held at the beginning of the year after the debt was canceled. The exclusion is computed after taking into account any reduction of tax attributes because of insolvency. Amounts exceeding the exclusion are taxable income.

Adjusted tax attributes include:

- NOLs;
- Capital loss carryovers;
- Passive activity loss carryovers; and
- Three times the sum of the general business credit carryover, the foreign tax credit carryover, the minimum tax credit available at the beginning of the following year, and the passive activity credit carryover.

Qualified property is property used or held for use in a trade or business or for the production of income.

STUDY QUESTIONS

> **5.** For an individual in a Chapter 7 or Chapter 11 bankruptcy, which tax attributes are **not** reduced?
>
> **a.** Attributes of the individual that arise after the bankruptcy filing
> **b.** Attributes of the bankruptcy estate
> **c.** Attributes for property transferred to the debtor from the bankruptcy estate
>
> **6.** A taxpayer who is insolvent:
>
> **a.** May not claim contingent liabilities
> **b.** May exclude assets that serve as collateral for purposes of the bankruptcy exclusion
> **c.** May include as a liability excess nonrecourse debt that is discharged when the insolvency exclusion is calculated
>
> **7.** Which of the following is **not** included in gross receipts when farmers claim the qualified farm debt exclusion?
>
> **a.** Proceeds from renting farmland
> **b.** Livestock sales
> **c.** Amounts exceeding the qualified farm debt exclusion

Real Property Business Debt Exclusion

Solvent taxpayers that are not C corporations can exclude a cancellation of real property business debt. The exclusion is elective. It does not apply to the extent that a taxpayer is insolvent.

The exclusion applies to *qualified acquisition debt*, defined as debt incurred or assumed to acquire, construct, reconstruct, or substantially improve real property used in a trade or business. The debt must be secured by the property. A taxpayer can also exclude debt used to refinance qualified debt incurred or assumed before 1993, up to the amount of the debt being refinanced. The refinancing exclusion does not apply to farm debt.

Limits on exclusion. The amount that can be excluded is limited to the debt's outstanding principal immediately before the discharge, reduced by the net fair market value of the real property. The net value is the property's fair market value reduced by any other qualified debt that secures the property and that was not discharged.

> **EXAMPLE**
>
> Curt uses a building worth $150,000 in his business. On the building he secures a first mortgage of $110,000 and a second mortgage of $90,000. The second mortgage holder reduces the debt to $30,000, creating $60,000 of COI income. Curt can exclude $50,000 of COI income: $90,000 (the debt's outstanding principal before the discharge), reduced by $40,000 ($150,000, the building's value, reduced by $110,000, the amount of other debt securing the property). Curt has to recognize $10,000 of COI income.

The amount excluded is also limited to the total adjusted basis of all depreciable real property held immediately before the discharge.

Reduction of basis. A taxpayer claiming this exclusion must reduce attributes by reducing the basis of any depreciable real property held by the taxpayer, in accordance with Code Sec. 1017. The taxpayer does not have to reduce the basis of the property securing the canceled debt. Generally, the reduction applies to property held at the beginning of the year following the discharge. Upon the sale or disposition of property with a reduced basis, the taxpayer may have to recapture the reduction as ordinary income under Code Sec. 1250.

Principal Residence Debt Exclusion

The discharge of qualified debt incurred to buy, construct, or substantially improve a principal residence can be excluded if the discharge occurs during the years 2007 through 2012. The residence must secure the debt. A taxpayer can also exclude the discharge of debt from the refinancing of qualified debt. All qualified debt protected by this exclusion cannot exceed $2 million ($1 million for married taxpayers filing separately). Any excess mortgage balance will be considered forgiven first and therefore taxable (unless the bankruptcy or insolvency exclusion applies). If only part of the debt was used for the principal residence, the exclusion applies to the amount of canceled debt that exceeds the loan amount not used for the principal residence.

> **EXAMPLE**
>
> Ken borrowed $100,000 from a bank and used $75,000 to renovate his home. Ken spent $25,000 on a new car. The lender canceled $30,000 of the loan. Ken can exclude $5,000, the excess of the canceled debt over the nonqualifying portion of the debt. Ken must recognize $25,000 of income.

If the taxpayer is bankrupt, the bankruptcy exclusion applies first. An insolvent taxpayer can elect to apply the insolvency exclusion before the principal residence exclusion. The residence exclusion is not available if the lender canceled the loan for services or because of a factor not related to the taxpayer's finances or a reduction in the residence's value (Code Sec. 108(h) (3)). Thus, if the taxpayer agrees to perform home repairs in exchange for loan forgiveness, the debt discharge will be taxable.

A taxpayer claiming the exclusion must reduce the basis of the principal residence by the excluded amount, but not below zero. Unlike other basis reduction rules that are applied in the next tax year, basis in the residence is reduced immediately. This helps homeowners in a foreclosure sale by sheltering any gain through the home sale exclusion (Code Sec. 121) and by not having to reduce other tax attributes that may eventually decrease other tax benefits.

STUDY QUESTION

8. When a taxpayer excludes COI income from the discharge of qualified debt on a principal residence, he or she must:
   a. Reduce the basis of the principal residence by the excluded amount
   b. Not use the residence to secure the debt
   c. Reduce other tax attributes before claiming the home sale exclusion

Student Loans

The discharge of a student loan is not taxable if all or part of the loan is canceled because the student works for a certain period of time in certain professions for any of a broad class of public service employers. Professions include doctors, nurses, teachers, and lawyers. The loan must have been made by:

- A federal, state, territorial, or local government, and their agencies and instrumentalities;
- A tax-exempt corporation that runs a state or local hospital whose employees are considered public employees;
- The school itself, but with funds provided by one of the above employers;
- The school itself, under a program to encourage students to serve in an occupation or geographic area with unmet needs, provided the employer is a charity or unit of government; or
- A school or charity that refinances the loan and imposes the same conditions as in the previously listed program.

An IRS ruling concerning attorneys identifies as a suitable employer for the exclusion to be a:

- Legal clinic;
- Government office;
- Prosecutor's office;
- Public defender's office; or
- Public interest or community service organization.

Payments made to a student by the National Health Service Corps Loan Repayment Program or a similar state program funded by the *Public Health Service Act* are not taxable if the student agrees to provide primary health services in an area with a shortage of health professionals.

If the COI income is excluded, the taxpayer does not have to reduce any tax attributes under this student loan exclusion.

The discharge of a student loan is taxable if the student must perform services for the school that made the loan. The student can exclude the income if another exclusion applies, however, such as the insolvency exclusion.

STUDY QUESTION

9. The discharge of a student loan is taxable COI income if:
   a. The former student gains employment in a government office
   b. The former student is required to perform services for the school that made the loan
   c. The former student works at a public service employer but eventually enters practice as a lawyer or physician

Victims of Disasters and Terrorism

In the past, Congress has provided temporary exclusions for victims of certain natural disasters and victims of certain terrorist acts. Individuals whose home was located in Midwestern disaster areas could exclude COI income from the discharge of debt. IRS Publication 4492-B identifies the states and disaster areas. This exclusion applied to discharges on or after the "applicable disaster date" and before 2010. This date was any of the dates when President Bush declared a disaster in various states (May 20, 2008, to July 31, 2008). Congress previously provided relief to victims of Hurricane Katrina whose debt was discharged on or after August 25, 2005, and before 2007.

In both cases, the relief was only available for personal debt (not business debt) that was discharged by a government agency or a financial institution, such as a bank, credit union, finance company, or credit card company. The exclusions did not apply to debt secured by property located outside the particular disaster area. Disaster victims claiming the exclusion were required to reduce tax attributes.

Congress also provided an exclusion for COI income from the discharge of debt of terrorist victims who died from the 1995 Oklahoma City bombing, the September 11 (2001) attacks, or because of illness stemming from an anthrax attack between September 11, 2001, and December 31, 2001. The exclusion was available to the spouse and the estate of the victim if they were also liable for the debt.

Other Exclusions

Gifts and bequests. A gift or bequest is not taxable income. Similarly, the discharge of debt as a gift or as a bequest is not taxable income. The gift exclusion usually does not apply to a business debt, because there must be donative intent, stemming from detached or disinterested generosity. A loan to a family member or friend to start or continue a business may be forgiven and considered a gift, but the debtor will have the burden of proof in those circumstances. There is no gift if a creditor cancels debt in the belief that the amount will never be paid.

Deductible debt. A cash-basis taxpayer does not recognize income from the discharge of a debt if payment of the debt would have been deductible. For example, the discharge of an accrued interest expense or a business expense is not income because the expense would have been deductible. This exclusion is not available for an accrual-method taxpayer, who would have already deducted the expense when it was incurred.

General welfare. A payment is not taxable if it is made by the government and promotes the general welfare. Thus, many government benefits are not taxable, such as housing assistance, job training, and veterans' benefits. In narrow cases, the IRS in the past has recognized a general welfare exclusion for forgiveness of debt by the government. The waiver of repayments of interim benefits paid under the *Public Safety Officers Benefits Act of 1976* did not generate COI income. The IRS has privately ruled that the Veterans Administration's discharge of a veteran's mortgage due to hardship was not taxable when the VA intended to reduce the veteran's future benefits for the amount of the debt forgiveness.

STUDY QUESTION

10. The exclusion for victims in 2008 disaster areas and victims of Hurricane Katrina applied to:

   a. Business as well as personal debt
   b. Debt discharged by a government agency or financial institution
   c. Discharges made only during the 2008 tax year

PASSTHROUGH ENTITIES

The COI income provisions contain special rules for partnerships and S corporations in determining treatment on the entity or partner/shareholder level.

Partnerships

COI income is recognized at the partnership level and each partner is allocated a share of the income as a separately stated item, increasing the partner's basis in the partnership interest. The amount of income does not have to correspond to the partner's share of the canceled debt. The basis of the partnership interest is also reduced by the partner's share of the debt that is canceled. This reduction is treated as a distribution of cash that occurs at the end of the partnership year.

The exclusions for bankruptcy, insolvency, real property business debt, and farm debt are then applied at the partner level. Attributes are also reduced at the partner level.

Depreciable property. With the partnership's consent, a partner electing to reduce basis before other attributes can treat the partnership interest as depreciable property, using the partner's share of the entity's depreciable property. This share is based on the depreciation deductions that the partnership expects to allocate to the partner over the life of the property. When the partner reduces basis, the partnership must also reduce the basis of the depreciable property allocated to that partner. The partnership does not reduce the overall basis of the property.

Business real property. The characterization of debt as real property business debt, and the amount of the exclusion, is determined at the entity (partnership or S corporation) level. However, an individual partner, not the partnership, elects whether to apply the exclusion and reduce basis.

S Corporations

The exclusions for bankruptcy, insolvency, real property business debt, and farm debt, and the corresponding attribute reductions are applied to the corporation, not to the shareholders. The S corporation must make the election to apply the exclusion for real property business debt and reduce the property's basis. COI income that is excluded by the S corporation does not flow through to the shareholders and does not increase the basis of the shareholders' S corporation stock.

For discharges on or before October 11, 2001, COI income excluded by the S corporation (for example, if the corporation were insolvent) will increase the basis of the shareholder's stock, based on the Supreme Court's decision in *Gitlitz* (2001-1 USTC ¶50,147). This decision also allowed shareholders to use the basis increase to deduct suspended losses (losses carried by the corporation and allocated to a shareholder who lacks sufficient basis to deduct the losses) before the corporation had to reduce attributes.

> **EXAMPLE**
>
> In the year 2000, an S corporation has an NOL of $2,000. It also has $6,000 of COI income from a discharge in bankruptcy in 2000. Its sole shareholder, Nathan, has a zero basis in his shares at the beginning of 2000 and has $3,000 in suspended losses. The corporation excludes the COI income, but the income passes through to Nathan, increasing his basis to $6,000. He now has sufficient basis to claim a $5,000 loss for the NOL and the suspended losses, leaving his basis at $1,000 at the end of 2000.

In 2002, Congress reversed *Gitlitz,* determining that the COI income does not flow through to the shareholders and that a shareholder should not be able to increase basis and deduct a loss which has no economic effect on the shareholder. The IRS has issued proposed regulations (NPRM REG-102822-08, August 6, 2008) that would reduce the corporation's deemed NOL when the S corporation excludes COI income. The *deemed NOL* equals the aggregate losses denied to the shareholders because the losses exceed their basis, reduced by the excluded COI income. Any remaining NOL is allocated to the shareholders but continues to be disallowed in the year of the discharge.

COMMENT

Some of the losses being reduced may be ordinary; others may be capital. The proposed regs require the reduction of all ordinary losses first. Practitioners have requested that the reduction be pro rata for ordinary and capital losses.

STUDY QUESTION

11. Since October 12, 2001, COI income excluded by an S corporation due to bankruptcy, insolvency, real property business debt, or farm debt:

   a. Is applied at the shareholder level and increases the basis of the shareholders' stock

   b. Does not flow through and thereby increase the basis of the shareholders' stock

   c. Increases the basis of the shareholders' stock , but suspended losses cannot be covered by the increase

DEBT FOR STOCK OR PARTNERSHIP INTEREST

As companies struggle to pay off their debts, an increasingly popular workout arrangement is to pay the debt with stock of a corporate debtor or an interest in a partnership debtor. The growth of passthrough entities such as partnerships and S corporations has also contributed to the increased use of this method.

Stock

A corporation that uses its stock to satisfy a debt is treated as having paid money equal to the stock's fair market value. Ordinarily, a corporation will not recognize gain or loss when its debt is converted into common stock. However, the IRS has ruled that a corporation had COI income on a conversion of debt when the adjusted issue price of the debt is greater than the fair market value of the common stock. The IRS has treated convertible preferred stock in the same manner, ruling that a debtor has COI income on the conversion if the stock's issue price is greater than the value of the stock. A bankrupt or insolvent corporation can exclude the income.

However, new Code Sec. 108(i), discussed below, would apply to a conversion of debt, and the corporation could defer the recognition of income until 2014.

Partnership Interest

A partnership's transfer of an interest in partnership profits or capital to a creditor to satisfy a recourse or nonrecourse debt is treated as a payment of money equal to the value of the partnership interest. If this value is less than the debt, the partnership must recognize COI income. The partners immediately before the discharge must recognize their distributive share of the income.

Proposed regulations (NPRM REG-164370-05, October 30, 2008) would treat the liquidation value of the partnership interest as its fair market value. The liquidation value is the amount a partner would receive if the partnership liquidated all its assets and paid all its liabilities. The use of liquidation value is considered an easier valuation method and is favored by practitioners. The IRS has already treated liquidation value as fair market value in guidance on the exchange of a partnership profits interest for services and probably would not question its use even before it issues final regulations.

The proposed regulations would treat the creditor's exchange of debt for a partnership interest as a nontaxable contribution to the partnership under Code Sec. 721, unless the debt is for unpaid rent, royalties, or interest or is an installment obligation. The basis of the interest equals the amount of the debt.

The regulations impose several conditions on the use of liquidation value:

- The partnership must determine and maintain capital accounts that comply with the accounting rules in the partnership regulations;
- All parties—the creditor, partnership, and partners—must use liquidation value as the fair market value of the interest;
- The transfer must be at arm's length; and
- The partnership interest is not cashed out—by a sale to a related party or a redemption by the partnership—to avoid COI income.

COMMENT

Practitioners have commented that the arm's-length requirement may be difficult to police, especially when an existing partner is also the creditor. The application of Code Sec. 721 is controversial because it denies a bad debt deduction to the creditor for the amount of debt that exceeds the value of the partnership interest. Moreover, if the creditor ultimately recognizes a loss on a sale of the partnership interest, the loss is capital, instead of the ordinary loss available for a business-related bad debt.

EXAMPLE

A creditor lends $100 to a partnership. The lender then contributes the debt to the partnership for a partnership interest with a liquidation value of $60, in effect forgiving $40 of the debt. Under the proposed regulations, the partnership has $40 of COI income, but the lender does not recognize its $40 loss. Instead, the lender has a partnership interest worth $60 with a basis of $100. If the lender sells or redeems the interest for $60, the lender will have a $40 capital loss.

> **COMMENT**
>
> The regulations are not scheduled to take effect until they are issued as final regulations. Nevertheless, taxpayers can probably rely on the proposed regulations. Taxpayers who choose not to follow the regulations should be prepared to litigate the issue; however, they have some chance of success because courts do not have to pay deference to proposed regulations (although the courts generally tend to respect the rationale behind the regs).

STUDY QUESTION

12. What are the tax consequences if a creditor exchanges a partnership interest for recourse or nonrecourse debt under the 2008 proposed regulations for Code Sec. 721?

  a. The exchange would be treated as a nontaxable contribution to the partnership if not for unpaid rent, royalties, or interest

  b. The creditor may claim a bad debt deduction for the amount that exceeds the value of the partnership interest

  c. Any loss the creditor incurs on the sale of the acquired interest is ordinary loss

DEFERRAL OF COI INCOME

A debtor that repurchases its own debt at a discount has COI income, generally equal to the difference between the adjusted issue price of the debt instrument and the amount paid. In the *American Recovery and Reinvestment Act of 2009,* Congress enacted Code Sec. 108(i), giving C corporations and businesses an election to defer COI income until 2014. This deferral option applies to COI income realized in 2009 or 2010 from the business's reacquisition of its own debt. The taxpayer then reports the income ratably over five years, beginning in 2014 and continuing through 2018.

> **COMMENT**
>
> Personal debt and debt incurred for investment do not qualify for the election.

> **CAUTION**
>
> Although there has been some discussion in Congress over extending this business deferral benefit for COI income beyond 2010, the law as it now stands only applies within a two-year window: 2009 and 2010.

Election

The deferral election is available as an alternative to any exclusion that applies under preexisting tax law. A taxpayer deferring the income therefore avoids having to reduce attributes if the taxpayer qualifies for one of the other Code Sec. 108 exclusions. The taxpayer makes the election on a timely filed return (including extensions) for the year of the reacquisition. The IRS granted an additional automatic extension of 12 months. A passthrough entity, such as a partnership or S corporation, must make the election itself. The election to defer COI income is irrevocable.

> **COMMENT**
>
> The election can be particularly beneficial if the taxpayer does not qualify for a COI income exclusion. A debtor that does qualify for an exclusion should compare the tax benefits between the election and the exclusion. If Code Sec. 382 will limit a C corporation's use of NOLs because of a change of ownership, it may be more beneficial for the corporation to recognize COI income (instead of deferring it) and use more of the prechange NOL to offset the income.

The taxpayer makes an election on an instrument-by-instrument basis. The IRS allowed taxpayers to elect to defer any portion of the COI income. Different elections can be made for different debt instruments. Taxpayers can elect to defer additional amounts if the IRS subsequently determines that the taxpayer understated the amount of COI income. Taxpayers can also make a protective election if the taxpayer concludes there is no COI income and the IRS later disagrees.

The debtor's election must identify the issuer of the debt, the debt instrument, the trade or business of an issuer that is not a C corporation, the debt reacquisition transaction, the total amount of COI income, the amount of COI income being deferred, and new debt instrument issued to acquire the existing debt.

> **COMMENT**
>
> There are additional reporting requirements for partnerships, S corporations, controlled foreign corporations, foreign partnerships and tiered passthrough entities. Rev. Proc. 2009-37 sets them out.

The IRS requires reporting of the election in the years after the election. The taxpayer must attach a statement to its return that, for each debt instrument, provides the deferred income included in income in the current year and the deferred income not yet included in income.

STUDY QUESTION

> **13.** Under Code Sec. 108(i), a business can elect to defer all or part of its COI income from the reacquisition of debt but cannot exclude any of the COI income from a debt reacquisition. **True or False?**

Eligible Taxpayers

Taxpayers that are eligible for deferral are a C corporation and any other person who issues a debt instrument "in connection with [that person's] conduct of a trade or business." The tax code defines *debt instrument* as a "bond, debenture, note, certificate, or any other instrument or contractual arrangement constituting indebtedness" (excluding annuities).

> **COMMENT**
>
> If a debt instrument issued to reacquire the debt has original issue discount (OID), none of the OID can be deducted while the COI income is deferred. Beginning in 2014, the OID can be deducted ratably over the five-year recognition period.

Acquisition. The debtor or a related person must acquire the debt. A related person is determined under Code Sec. 267, which limits losses between related persons, and Code Sec. 707, controlled partnerships. The acquisition generates COI income. An *acquisition* includes an acquisition for cash or other property, the exchange of the debt instrument for another instrument (including an exchange from a significant modification of the debt instrument), the exchange of the debt instrument for corporate stock or a partnership interest, the contribution of the debt instrument to capital, and the complete forgiveness of the debt. A significant modification includes a change in interest rate and/or a deferral of principal and interest payments.

> **COMMENT**
>
> If a debt instrument is issued for cash that is used to reacquire debt, the debt instrument is treated as if it were exchanged for the debt.

> **COMMENT**
>
> Practitioners have asked that the scope of an acquisition be expanded to other transactions. Government officials have indicated their willingness to do this, noting that the word *includes* suggests that the definition in the tax code is not exclusive.

Acceleration. Income or deductions that are deferred must be accelerated and recognized upon certain triggering events, such as the death of the taxpayer, the liquidation or sale of substantially all the assets of the taxpayer (including in a bankruptcy proceeding), the taxpayer's termination of business activity, and similar events. Items must also be accelerated if the owner of an interest in a passthrough entity sells, exchanges, or redeems the interest. Regulations can add acceleration events. The accelerated income is reported in the year of the triggering event. For a bankruptcy, this is the day before the petition is filed.

> **COMMENT**
>
> It is unclear whether a constructive termination of a partnership triggers acceleration. It is also unclear how much COI income is accelerated on a sale or redemption of stock of an S corporation shareholder.

Partnerships. A partnership, not the partners, must meet the trade or business test and make the election to defer COI income. COI income of the partnership must be allocated to the partners immediately before the discharge, in the same amounts that would have been allocated to the partners if the income had been recognized. Income that is deferred is not included in the partners' income and does not increase the partners' bases in their partnership interests until the partnership recognizes the income.

> **COMMENT**
>
> It is unclear whether debt of a partner or shareholder incurred to invest in a partnership or S corporation would qualify for the election.

To avoid prematurely triggering income, Code Sec. 108(i) defers the deemed distribution to a partner from the reduction of partnership liabilities until the deferred COI income is recognized, to the extent the deemed distribution would trigger income. Thus basis may still be reduced. The deferred distribution may also be reportable over the same five-year period as the deferred COI income.

> **COMMENT**
>
> COI income exclusions and attribute reductions are applied at the partner level, unlike the deferral election. The IRS provided significant relief in this area, however, for deferrals. The partnership can allocate any portion of the deferred income among each partner, regardless of its normal allocation of partnership income and deductions. Partners can communicate to the managing partners whether they are eligible for any COI exclusions and how much of the COI income they want to defer.

Corporations. One area where the IRS did not provide relief involves earnings and profits (E&P). Deferred income will increase E&P in the year realized, not in the later years it is included in income. Similarly, OID deductions will decrease E&P in the years normally reported. However, these rules do not apply to regulated investment companies and real estate investment trusts.

STUDY QUESTIONS

14. To become eligible for a deferral of COI income under Code Sec. 108(i), a business:
    a. Issues a debt instrument
    b. Reports the transaction as uncollectible bad debt
    c. Creates annuities totaling the amount being deferred

15. When a business reacquires debt using cash from a debt instrument, the instrument is treated as though it was exchanged for the debt. *True or False?*

CONCLUSION

The cancellation of indebtedness rules are complex. Although the creditor may report the COI income under IRS information-reporting requirements and thus usually take the guesswork out of determining whether there has been COI income, the debtor may have a difficult time trying to apply the numerous exclusions and meet the requirements to reduce attributes. The IRS National Taxpayer Advocate has pointed out some of the difficulties and has urged the IRS to improve its aid to taxpayers who may have COI income. The temporary provision deferring the reporting of certain business debt is also complex. However, the availability of both exclusions for COI income and the deferral of COI income can provide substantial tax benefits to those that qualify. Taxpayers will find it worthwhile to work their way through the rules and exclusions.

CPE NOTE: When you have completed your study and review of chapters 4-5, which comprise Module 2, you may wish to take the Quizzer for this Module.

For your convenience, you can also take this Quizzer online at **www.cchtestingcenter.com.**

Innocent Spouse Tax Issues

This chapter helps practitioners address recent developments that have helped significantly expand and revise the rules for innocent spouse relief.

LEARNING OBJECTIVES

Upon completion of this chapter, you will be able to:

- List the kinds of innocent spouse relief and their specific requirements;
- Recognize the differences among innocent spouse relief, separation of liability, equitable relief, and injured spouse relief;
- Describe how and when to present an innocent spouse claim for relief;
- Explain the procedures for, and the standard of review used in, an appeal the denial of an innocent spouse claim; and
- Explain how principles of innocent spouse relief are applied to parties within community property jurisdictions.

INTRODUCTION

The federal tax issues arising in connection with personal relationships have taken on increased significance over the past few years with the downturn in the overall economy. The IRS received a total of 33,389 innocent spouse claims during fiscal years 2003 through 2006. By requesting innocent spouse relief, a taxpayer may be relieved of responsibility for paying tax, interest, and penalties if his or her spouse, or former spouse, improperly reported or omitted items on a jointly filed tax return.

BACKGROUND AND OVERVIEW OF INNOCENT SPOUSE RELIEF

Whenever a married couple files a joint return, each spouse is jointly and severally liable for any federal income tax liability arising out of such return, even if all of the income giving rise to the tax liability is allocable to only one of them (Code Sec. 6013(d)(3)). This liability includes both the tax shown on the return as being due and also any additional liability the IRS assesses based on an underreporting of income, an incorrect deduction or credit, or an overstatement of tax basis.

A joint tax liability survives divorce, even if the divorce decree provides that only one spouse is responsible for the tax. Such clauses in divorce agreements may allow one spouse to pursue the other spouse for the unpaid taxes, but carry no legal weight in restricting the IRS from collecting the unpaid tax from one or both spouses. Innocent spouse relief may, however, be available under the tax code to a spouse or former spouse (a *requesting spouse* or *electing spouse*) to be relieved of joint liability with the other spouse or former spouse (the *nonrequesting spouse* or *nonelecting spouse*).

For liabilities existing on, or arising after, July 22, 1998, an expanded system of innocent spouse relief became available. There are now three forms of innocent spouse relief:

- General relief available to all joint filers (Code Sec. 6015(b));
- Separate liability relief available to joint filers who are treated as no longer married (Code Sec. 6015(c)); and
- Equitable relief for taxpayers who do not qualify for the other two types of relief (Code Sec. 6015(f)).

> **COMMENT**
>
> The operative Internal Revenue Code section for innocent spouse relief is Code Sec. 6015. However, nowhere in the Internal Revenue Code is the term *innocent spouse* used. The IRS does use the term generically at times to describe all three forms of relief and, in other instances, to mean only general innocent spouse relief, in contrast to *separation of liability relief* and *equitable relief*. Form 8857, *Request for Innocent Spouse Relief (and Separation of Liability, and Equitable Relief)*, includes requests for all three forms of relief; and IRS Pub. 971, *Innocent Spouse Relief*, also includes discussions of separation of liability relief and equitable relief.

TYPES OF INNOCENT SPOUSE RELIEF

General Relief

The general relief form of innocent spouse relief is available to all filers of joint returns if certain conditions are satisfied. This relief is not conditioned on the requesting spouse still being married to the nonrequesting spouse. Relief is available regardless of whether the couple is still married and living together, is separated, divorced, or one spouse is deceased at the time of the request. The qualifications for general relief are:

- The couple filed a joint return;
- An understatement of tax resulted from erroneous tax items attributable to the nonrequesting spouse;
- The requesting spouse did not know or have reason to know of the understatement when he or she signed the return;
- It is inequitable to hold the requesting spouse liable for the deficiency; and

- The requesting spouse elects innocent spouse relief no later than two years after the IRS commences collection activities and provides that spouse with notice of innocent spouse rights.

To be eligible to claim general relief the requesting spouse and the nonrequesting spouse must have filed a joint return that omitted an item of income or that contained an erroneous deduction item. A *joint return* is a return filed jointly with the nonrequesting spouse and signed under penalty of perjury. A return that, for example, deletes the penalty of perjury declaration is not a valid joint return (**M. James**, CA-9, 2009-1 USTC ¶50,345 [unpublished opinion]).

Reasons for the "erroneous tax item" attributable to the nonrequesting spouse can include:

- Failure of the nonrequesting to report income;
- Claiming a deduction to which the nonrequesting spouse was not entitled; and
- Overstating of a deduction or credit or basis used to compute gain or loss.

General innocent spouse relief only provides relief for *understatements* of tax, not *underpayments*. An *understatement of tax* is the difference between the tax as calculated on the return and the tax that should have been shown on the return. By contrast, an *underpayment* occurs when the requesting spouse and the nonrequesting spouse report an item correctly on an original or amended return but are unable to pay the tax resulting from such item. For underpayments, equitable innocent spouse relief (discussed below) may be available.

If the requesting spouse learns of the understatement (perhaps as a result of later disclosure by the nonrequesting spouse or as a result of audit) and files an amended return with the nonrequesting spouse reporting the item correctly, general innocent spouse relief is not available. Once the amended return is filed, there is only an underpayment and not an understatement. Again, in this instance equitable innocent spouse relief may be available.

However, if the requesting spouse first applies for innocent spouse relief following the resolution of an audit and consents to an assessment rather than filing an amended return to reflect the additional income, general relief may still be available. This is because consenting to an assessment by signing a Form 870, *Waiver of Restrictions on Assessment and Collection of Deficiency in Tax and Acceptance of Overassessment*, or similar form is not the same as filing an amended return. Signing a Form 870 or similar form causes the resulting liability to be considered an understatement and not an underpayment for purposes of general innocent spouse relief (**CCA Letter Ruling** 200922039).

Knowledge of understatement. The requesting spouse must have been unaware of the understatement, whether attributable to an omission of income or the overstatement of a deduction, credit, or basis. The burden of proof is on the requesting spouse to establish that when the joint return was signed, he or she did not know or have reason to know of the understatement. Lack of knowledge or reason to know cannot be established by a failure to read, review, or examine the return.

If the requesting spouse is aware that the nonrequesting spouse has received money or property that is not reported on the return but does not know of the source, the requesting spouse will not be considered to have knowledge of the item giving rise to the deficiency. The requesting spouse cannot, however, intentionally avoid learning about an item in order to gain protection from liability.

Ignorance of the tax consequences of an item generally does not qualify a spouse for relief unless the spouse did not know or have reason to know of the omitted income or erroneous deduction itself. Thus, if the requesting spouse knows the nonrequesting spouse has received a certain amount of cash, and the nonrequesting spouse only reports a portion of such amount on the return, claiming the remainder was not taxable income, the requesting spouse will likely not qualify for relief pertaining to the unreported portion. General relief is unavailable because the requesting spouse knew the full amount of the cash received, even if such spouse was unaware of the tax consequences attributable to the receipt of such cash.

A requesting spouse knows or has reason to know of an understatement if he or she actually knew of the understatement or if a reasonable person in similar circumstances would have known of the understatement. All the facts and circumstances are considered in determining whether the spouse had reason to know of the understatement, including:

- The amount of the item and its amount relative to other items;
- The couple's financial situation;
- The requesting spouse's educational background and business experience;
- The extent of the requesting spouse's participation in the activity that resulted in the erroneous item;
- Whether the requesting spouse failed to inquire, at or before the time the return was signed, about items on the return or omitted from the return that a reasonable person would question; and
- Whether the erroneous item represented a departure from a recurring pattern reflected in prior years' returns (e.g., omitted income from an investment regularly reported on prior years' returns).

EXAMPLE

Ken and Jemma Jones, a married couple, filed a joint Form 1040 return for 2008. Unbeknownst to Ken, Jemma sold stock she had purchased prior to their marriage. The stock was titled in Jemma's name and was sold at a gain of $100,000. Ken did not know or have reason to know that Jemma owned the stock; Jemma failed to disclose the sale to either Ken or their tax preparer. The IRS assessed a $20,000 deficiency, together with penalties and interest, against Ken and Jemma for tax year 2008. Six months after the return was filed, but before the IRS assessed the deficiency, Jemma revealed the sale to Ken. Ken is eligible for general innocent spouse relief because:

- There is an understatement relating solely to Jemma's failure to report the income; and
- Ken did not know or have reason to know about the underreporting of income at the time the 2008 return was filed.

The spouse need not prove that he or she was completely without fault and could not possibly have discovered the omission before executing the returns. Instead, the courts will look to the requesting spouse's specific situation to determine whether a reasonable person in the requesting spouse's situation would have known about the erroneous item. Using this standard, a spouse who is educated about, or familiar with, business matters, or is involved with the investment or other source of the income, will have a harder time showing that it was reasonable not to know about the understatement.

In one case, for example, a well-educated wife had some involvement in her husband's business affairs and knew that the couple was having issues with the IRS, and her husband did not hide information concerning the couple's investments. The wife could not avoid liability by claiming it was reasonable for her not to know about an understatement because she was raised in a culture that prohibited women from questioning their husbands about financial matters (*R.E. Alt*, CA-6 (unpublished opinion), 2004-1 USTC ¶50,279, 101 FedAppx 34).

Lack of knowledge at some time during the applicable year will not satisfy the burden of proof if the spouse learned of the income before the return was filed. Discovering the omission after the return is filed does not preclude innocent spouse relief. Similarly, ignorance of the tax consequences of an item generally does not qualify a requesting spouse for relief, unless the requesting spouse did not know or have reason to know of the omitted income or erroneous deduction itself.

Although the Tax Court applies the same standards in determining whether the requesting spouse had reason to know of an understatement regardless of whether such understatement arose from omitted income or erroneous deductions, other courts have applied a more lenient standard, the *Price standard,* to understatements arising from erroneous deductions. This standard entitles the requesting spouse to seek relief even if the spouse knew or had reason to know about the underlying transaction, as long as the requesting spouse reasonably did not know that the deduction would result in an understatement (***P.A. Price***, CA-9, 89-2 USTC ¶9598, 887 F2d 959).

In gauging the reasonableness of the requesting spouse's ignorance of the impropriety of the deduction courts look to factors such as the requesting spouse's:

- Education level;
- Involvement in the transaction giving rise to the deduction;
- Standard of living in comparison to historic income levels; and
- Degree of his or her evasive or deceitful behavior with respect to family finances.

The courts also look at the culpability of the nonrequesting spouse in taking a particular deduction; that is, whether it was fraudulent or taken out of ignorance of the proper requirement for taking the deduction.

Partial relief through apportionment. Regardless of whether relief is sought in connection with omitted income or erroneous deductions, innocent spouse relief is not an all or nothing proposition. If the requesting spouse demonstrates a lack of knowledge for only certain tax years but not others relief can be apportioned based on the tax years for which the requesting spouse did not have the requisite knowledge.

Apportionment is also available when the requesting spouse demonstrates knowledge of omitted income from one source, but did not know or have reason to have known of income from another source. Similarly, knowledge of one portion of an understatement, but a reasonable lack of awareness of other portions of the understatement, will allow the requesting spouse to seek relief from liability for those latter portions.

Facts and circumstances test. In addition to the above requirements for general relief, the requesting spouse must also show that under all the facts and circumstances, it would be inequitable to be held liable for the understatement. This aspect of general innocent spouse relief looks to similar factors considered in determining whether a spouse is eligible for equitable innocent spouse relief (discussed below).

The requesting spouse has the burden of proof on this "inequitable-to-be-held liable" issue. One factor many courts consider is whether the requesting spouse benefitted—directly or indirectly—from the understatement of tax. This determination may be made regardless of whether the requesting spouse knowingly shared in the nonrequesting spouse's income.

A *significant benefit* is any benefit in excess of normal support. Thus, it is common for courts to consider whether the requesting spouse's lifestyle or material possessions were enhanced by the financial gain arising from the erroneous item. However, if the nonrequesting spouse uses such gain to his or her own advantage, and not to the advantage of the requesting spouse, this circumstance will not cause the requesting spouse to be denied relief.

The regulations indicate that other facts relevant to the determination of equity include whether the requesting spouse was deserted by the nonrequesting spouse, and whether the spouses are divorced or separated (Treas. Reg. §1.6015-2(d)). Consideration may also be given to the same factors taken into account in determining whether a spouse is eligible for equitable innocent spouse relief.

Although general innocent spouse relief is designed to relieve the requesting spouse from personal liability for all or a portion of the tax liability incurred with the nonrequesting spouse, relief does not entitle the requesting spouse to a refund of his or her portion of community property taken to satisfy the nonrequesting spouse's remaining liability. This is because federal innocent spouse relief does not override state law concerning which property of a nondebtor spouse is liable for the debts of a debtor spouse (***Ordlock***, CA-9, 2008-2 USTC ¶50,457, 533 F3d 1136).

However, if innocent spouse relief is granted, the requesting spouse may be entitled to a refund of any amount of the tax liability previously paid by the requesting spouse. No refund is available for any portion paid by the nonrequesting spouse.

The right to receive a refund is limited by the normal refund statute of limitations. This means that if the requesting spouse files Form 8857, *Request for Innocent Spouse Relief (and Separation of Liability, and Equitable Relief)*, within three years after filing the return for which relief is sought, the refund cannot exceed that part of the tax paid within the three-year period (plus any extension for filing the return) before the Form 8857 was filed. If the Form 8857 is filed more than three years after the return was filed, but not more than two years after requesting spouse paid all or a portion of the tax, the requesting spouse is eligible to seek a refund of such amount.

STUDY QUESTIONS

1. General innocent spouse relief applies to:
  a. Underpayments of tax due to inability to pay a correctly listed liability on the return
  b. Understatements of tax liability on the return
  c. Both underpayments and understatements

2. Apportionment of general relief reduces the tax liability for a requesting spouse by:
  a. Splitting the liability equally between the requesting and nonrequesting spouse
  b. Applying relief to the tax years for which the requesting spouse did not have knowledge requisite to reporting the liability
  c. There may be no apportionment of the general relief form of innocent spouse relief

Separate Liability Relief

A separated or divorced requesting spouse may elect relief under Code Sec. 6015(c), a second kind of innocent spouse relief that allocates the tax liability between the *electing spouse* and the other spouse (who may also be an electing spouse if he or she files an election to allocate liability, or who would otherwise be a nonelecting spouse). If successful, the electing spouse is able to limit his or her liability to the portion of an assessed deficiency properly allocable to him or her. The electing spouse will be relieved of liability for the portion allocable to the other spouse.

> **COMMENT**
>
> Spouses who are divorced, legally separated, or living apart may file for separate liability relief regardless of whether they suspect any problems at the time. Some tax advisors recommend that these individuals file such an election as a matter of course. Although this election does not cover deficiency items of the other spouse to the extent the electing spouse had actual knowledge of them, it protects both against hidden assets as well as aggressive deductions taken by the other spouse that may withstand a future IRS audit. The portion of any deficiency attributable to actual knowledge (as opposed to simply a reason to know) then becomes the joint liability of both spouses, within the IRS's discretion about from whom it collects.

To be eligible for separate liability relief the electing spouse must satisfy one of these requirements:

- At the time the electing spouse files an election to allocate the liability, such spouse is no longer married to or is legally separated from the other spouse; or
- The electing spouse was not a member of the same household as the other spouse during the 12-month period ending on the date the election is filed.

> ### COMMENT
>
> The differences between general innocent spouse relief and separate liability relief are threefold. For a separate liability election:
>
> - The electing spouse must be separated or divorced;
> - The burden of proof is on the IRS and the standard of knowledge is actual knowledge versus the know-or-reason-to-know standard for general relief); and
> - The electing spouse is only relieved of the other spouses' portion of the liability using the formula for allocation specified under Code Sec. 6015(d).

Actual knowledge of item. The electing spouse in this situation does not have to show that it would be inequitable if such spouse had to pay the liability. However, the electing spouse will be denied relief if the IRS demonstrates that assets were transferred between the electing spouse and the other spouse as part of a fraudulent scheme, or to avoid collection of the tax.

Relief will also be denied to the extent that the IRS demonstrates that the electing spouse had actual knowledge of any item giving rise to any portion of the deficiency that the electing spouse is seeking to allocate to the other spouse. This actual knowledge standard is a stricter standard than the "knew or should have known" standard used for determining knowledge for general innocent spouse purposes (*S.M. McDaniel*, T.C. Memo 2009-137). Actual knowledge must be established by the evidence and is not inferred based on indications that the electing spouse had reason to know.

The IRS has both the burden of production and of persuasion on the question whether the requesting spouse had actual knowledge of an erroneous item. The IRS must establish, by a preponderance of the evidence, that the electing spouse had actual knowledge of the erroneous item in order to invalidate the election (Treas. Reg. §1.6015-3(c)(2)(i)).

If the item is omitted income, then in order to be denied relief the electing spouse must have knowledge of it, including knowledge of the receipt of the income Actual knowledge is not inferred from a mere reason to know of the omitted income (Treas. Reg. §1.6015-3(c)(2)(iii)).

> **EXAMPLE**
>
> Joanna and Jim, a married couple, filed a joint 2007 federal income tax return. On that return Jim failed to include in income $50,000 of taxable distributions he received from the ABC Partnership, and he did not attach the ABC K-1 form to the return. Joanna knew Jim had purchased the ABC interest, but she was unaware that ABC had made any distributions to Jim in 2007. Jim hid the K-1 from Joanna. In June 2008 the couple separated, and Joanna moved out of the marital home and into a separate apartment. In July 2009, upon learning of the omitted income, Joanna requested an allocation of liability based on the omitted income. Because Joanna did not have actual knowledge of the income, even though she knew about the source of the income, she is entitled to relief.

If the item is an erroneous deduction, relief will be denied if the electing spouse knew of facts that made the item not deductible (Treas. Reg. §1.6015-3(c)(2)(i)(B)(1)). If the item is a fictitious deduction, relief will be denied if the electing spouse knew that the expenditure was not incurred (Treas. Reg. §1.6015-3(c)(2)(i)(B)(2)).

> **EXAMPLE**
>
> Gill and Barbara, a married couple, filed a joint 2006 return on which Gill claimed a deduction for $10,000 of medical expenses that Barbara knew he never incurred, and a $5,000 deduction on Schedule C for the purchase of a new computer, purchased in July 2006, which Gill intended to use in his home business. Gill actually returned the computer to its place of purchase it in August 2006, claiming it was defective, and was refunded his entire purchase price. Barbara knew about the return of the computer. In 2008 Gill and Barbara divorced, and Barbara sought an allocation of liability for their 2006 return. Barbara is not eligible for an allocation of liability with respect to either the medical expense deduction or the computer expense because of her knowledge of the fictitious and erroneous deductions.

Many courts will deem the IRS to have satisfied its burden if it shows the electing spouse had knowledge of the erroneous item even if there is evidence that the spouse was unaware of how the item should have been reported on the return.

Duress. Relief will not be denied if the electing spouse can show that the joint return was signed under duress. Duress may involve a continued course of mental intimidation, as wells as threats of bodily harm. The electing spouse must prove that were it not for the threats, he or she would not have signed the return.

Formula for allocation. The portion of a deficiency allocable to the electing and to the other spouse, respectively, is the amount that bears the same ratio to the deficiency as the net amount of erroneous items allocable to such spouse bears to the net amount of all erroneous items. Code Sec. 6015(d) and the companion regulations provide that this formula is applied taking into account the following rules:

- The electing spouse must include any item giving rise to a deficiency (or portion thereof) that would otherwise not be allocable to such spouse but about which the electing spouse has actual knowledge;
- If the deficiency is attributable to the disallowance of a credit or to any tax required to be included on the return (other than regular tax and alternative minimum tax liability), then the deficiency is allocated to the spouse who is responsible for such credit or tax;
- If the deficiency arises from the tax liability of a child reported on the joint return, it will be allocated between the spouses as appropriate only after the allocation based on the items of the spouses is made;
- Any portion of the deficiency attributable to accuracy-related or fraud penalties is allocated to the spouse whose item generated the penalty; and
- The amount of the electing spouse's liability as computed using the above formula is increased by the value of any disqualified asset transferred to such spouse. A *disqualified asset* is any property transferred to the electing spouse by the other spouse if the principal purpose of the transfer was the avoidance of tax or payment of tax (including additions to tax, penalties, and interest).

CAUTION

Unlike the situation with general and equitable relief, no credit or refund will be allowed as a result of an election under Code Sec. 6015(c) (Treas. Reg. §1.6015-3(c)). Accordingly, the electing spouse should avoid payment or collection of the deficiency until after pursuing the election to allocate liability. If, instead the electing spouse pays the liability, and sues for a refund in a district court or the Court of Federal Claims, recovery will be barred by Code Sec. 6015(g)(3). This will be true even if the electing spouse also qualifies for equitable innocent spouse relief (T.D. 9003).

EXAMPLE

Hannah and William timely file their 2008 joint federal income tax return. They divorce in November 2009. On January 5, 2010, a $4,000 deficiency is assessed with respect to the couple's 2008 return. Of this deficiency, $1,500 results from unreported capital gain of $6,000 attributable to William, and $4,000 of unreported capital gain attributable to Hannah (both gains being subject to tax at the 15-percent marginal rate).

The remaining $2,500 of the deficiency is attributable to Hannah's $10,000 unreported gambling income subject to tax at a 25-percent marginal rate. William timely elects to allocate the deficiency and qualifies to do so. The three erroneous items are categorized according to their applicable tax rates, then allocated. Of the total amount of 15-percent tax rate items ($10,000), 60 percent is allocable to William and 40 percent is allocable to Hannah. Therefore, 60 percent of the $1,500 deficiency attributable to these items (or $900) is allocated to William. The remaining 40 percent ($600) is allocated to Hannah. The only 25-percent tax rate item is allocable to Hannah. Accordingly, Hannah is liable for $3,100 of the deficiency ($600 + $2,500), and William is liable for the remaining $900.

STUDY QUESTIONS

3. A request for allocation of liability relief may be invalidated if:

    a. The IRS establishes evidence that the electing spouse has actual knowledge of hidden assets or aggressive deductions

    b. The spouses are living apart but not divorced during the 12-month period ending on the date of election

    c. The IRS has indications or may infer that the electing spouse had reason to know of omitted income

4. Under the allocation formula applied to a spouse electing allocation of liability relief, receipt of a disqualified asset from his or her spouse:

    a. Increases only the nonrequesting spouse's allocated liability by the value of the asset

    b. Increases only the electing spouse's allocated liability by the value of the asset

    c. Increases each spouse's allocation of liability equally

Equitable Innocent Spouse Relief

Equitable innocent spouse relief may be available to a spouse who is otherwise ineligible for the other forms of relief. As a result, the typical situations unique to this third type of relief involve the underpayment of tax rather than a dispute as to the amount of tax liability for the year. Congress intended for the IRS to exercise discretion in granting equitable relief when a requesting spouse "does not know, and had no reason to know, that funds intended for the payment of tax were instead taken by the other spouse for such other spouse's benefit." Congress also intended for the IRS to exercise the equitable relief authority under Code Sec. 6015(f) in other situations where, "taking into account all the facts and circumstances, it is inequitable to hold an individual liable for all or part of any unpaid tax or deficiency arising from a joint return."

The situation that most frequently occurs in granting equitable relief under Code Sec. 6015(f), therefore, happens when money for payment of taxes as reported on the return never reaches the IRS but either gets misappropriated by the nonrequesting spouse for his or her personal use, or the nonrequesting spouse cannot pay for a unpaid liability that arises out of that spouse's income. This relief, therefore, may also be granted in addition to other innocent spouse relief, for example, when the requesting spouse seeks to be relieved from an *underpayment* of tax and not just an *understatement* of tax. A requesting spouse may also be eligible for equitable innocent spouse relief for interest even when the underlying taxes have been paid in full (***M.A. Kollar***, 131 TC ___, No. 12, Dec. 57,593).

As with the other forms of innocent spouse relief, the requesting spouse may still be married to the nonrequesting spouse, may be divorced or separated from such spouse, or may be widowed. As with general innocent spouse relief, to be eligible for equitable innocent spouse relief the requesting spouse and the nonrequesting spouse must have filed a joint return.

Threshold conditions. Rev. Proc. 2003-61, 2003-2 C.B. 296, sets forth the procedures used in determining whether the requesting spouse is entitled to relief. The revenue procedure lists six threshold conditions that must be satisfied before the IRS will consider a request for equitable innocent spouse relief:

- The requesting spouse filed a joint return for the tax year for which the relief is sought;
- The requesting spouse does not qualify for general innocent spouse relief or separate liability relief for the portion of the relief requested;
- No assets were transferred between the spouses as part of a fraudulent scheme by the spouses;
- The nonrequesting spouse did not transfer disqualified assets (property or property right transferred principally to avoid a tax or its payment) to the requesting spouse (if the requesting spouse did receive disqualified assets from the nonrequesting spouse, equitable relief is available only to the extent that the income tax liability exceeds the value of the disqualified assets);
- The requesting spouse did not file or fail to file the return with fraudulent intent; and
- The income tax liability from which the requesting spouse seeks relief is attributable to an item of the nonrequesting spouse, unless one of the following exceptions applies:
  - Attribution due solely to the operation of community property law,
  - Nominal ownership,
  - Misappropriation of funds, or
  - Abuse not amounting to duress.

Other considerations. After satisfying the threshold requirements, the requesting spouse must also prove that when all the facts and circumstances are taken into account, it is inequitable to hold such spouse liable and that the other forms of innocent spouse relief are not available. Although no single factor is determinative, some of the factors the IRS will consider include whether:

- The requesting spouse is separated (whether legally separated or simply living apart) or divorced from the nonrequesting spouse;
- The requesting spouse would suffer a significant economic hardship if relief is not granted;
- The requesting spouse received a significant benefit (beyond normal support) from the underpaid tax or item causing the understated tax;.
- The requesting spouse was abused by the nonrequesting spouse (but the absence of abuse is not a negative factor);
- The unpaid liability or item giving rise to the deficiency is attributable to the nonrequesting spouse;
- The requesting spouse was in poor mental or physical health on the date the return was signed or at the time relief was requested (but the absence of such issues does not weigh against relief); and
- The requesting spouse has made a good faith effort to comply with federal income tax laws in the tax years following the tax year or years to which the request for relief relates.

> **COMMENT**
>
> If an individual signs a joint return under duress, the election to file jointly is not valid and there is no valid joint return. The individual is not jointly and severally liable for any income tax liabilities arising from that return. Therefore, it that situation, innocent spouse relief is not necessary. However, less direct forms of intimidation would form part of the facts and circumstances relevant in determining equitable relief.

If the requesting spouse prevails in obtaining equitable innocent spouse relief, the requesting spouse's right to a refund of previously paid tax depends on whether the payment was made with respect to an underpaid tax or an understated tax. The requesting spouse may seek a refund of separate payments made but not for payments made with the joint return (including withholding tax and estimated tax payments), joint payments, or payments made by the nonrequesting spouse. The right to a refund is subject to the same limitations periods described above for general relief.

STUDY QUESTIONS

---

5. Which of the following is **not** a reason for which Congress intended equitable innocent spouse relief to be granted?

  a. The requesting spouse cannot pay the liability arising from the nonrequesting spouse's income

  b. The electing spouse is disputing the amount of the tax liability but the nonrequesting spouse is not

  c. The nonrequesting spouse misappropriated the money intended to pay the tax liability

6. If the electing spouse received disqualified assets from the nonrequesting spouse affecting the questionable tax return, equitable innocent spouse relief:

  a. Is not available for the requesting spouse that tax year

  b. Is applicable only for the difference between the tax liability and the disqualified assets' value

  c. The burden of proof lies with the requesting spouse to show no knowledge of the transfer

---

PROCEDURES FOR SEEKING INNOCENT SPOUSE RELIEF

Filing Form 8857

A spouse or former spouse seeking innocent spouse relief must first file Form 8857, *Request for Innocent Spouse Relief (and Separation of Liability, and Equitable Relief)*, or other similar statement, signed under penalty of perjury. If the requesting spouse is seeking general relief or allocation of liability, the form must be filed within two years after the first collection activity against the requesting spouse. However, in order for the two-year "clock" to start running, such collection activity must have been accompanied by notice of the right to pursue innocent spouse relief (*N. W. McGee*, 123 TC 314, Dec. 55,781).

CAUTION

The two-year period starts running when collection activity commences even if the requesting spouse was unaware of such collection activity at the time or does not actually receive collection notices, which might occur, for example, if the nonrequesting spouse hides collection notices from the requesting spouse (*D. Mannella,* 132 TC __, No. 10, Dec. 57,787).

If the requesting spouse is seeking equitable innocent spouse relief, the two-year deadline may not apply. In 2009, the Tax Court held that Treas. Reg. §1.6015-5(b)(1), which imposes a two-year limitation period on requests for equitable relief from joint income tax liability, was inconsistent with and was an invalid interpretation of Code Sec. 6015(f). Thus, the IRS abused its discretion by failing to consider all the facts and circumstances when it denied an individual's claim for innocent spouse relief solely on the basis that the claim was filed more than two years after the IRS's first collection action (*C.M. Lantz*, 132 TC __, No. 8, Dec. 57,784).

The IRS has, however, indicated that it will not follow the *Lantz* decision and will continue to maintain in litigation that the two-year deadline applies to equitable innocent spouse cases (*Chief Counsel Notice* CC-2009-012).

> **COMMENT**
>
> Rev. Proc. 2003-61, which identifies the threshold requirements for seeking equitable innocent spouse relief, refers to the two-year deadline as one of the requirements. However, this appears to be superseded by the *Lantz* decision.

The requesting spouse may request one, two, or all three types of innocent spouse relief in one request. If the IRS determines that a requesting spouse who requested only equitable relief might also qualify for other relief, the IRS cannot automatically grant such relief but may contact the requesting spouse and allow the request to be amended, with the amendment relating back to the original claim.

> **COMMENT**
>
> If the requesting spouse is a victim of domestic violence and fears that filing a claim for innocent spouse relief would result in retaliation, the requesting spouse should write the term "Potential Domestic Abuse Case" on the top of the Form 8857 and explain his or her concerns in a statement attached to the form, in addition to explaining the reasons for applying for innocent spouse relief.

While the innocent spouse request is pending, the IRS generally is required to suspend all enforced collection action, such as levying bank accounts or wages. However, interest and penalties continue to accrue on the underlying tax obligation.

PLANNING POINTER

Detailed information concerning eligibility to obtain innocent spouse relief and the preparation of Form 8857 is available in IRS Publication 971, *Innocent Spouse Relief.*

Nonrequesting Spouse's Right to Notice and to Participate

The IRS must send a notice to the nonrequesting spouse's last known address that informs the nonrequesting spouse of the claim for relief. The notice provides the nonrequesting spouse with an opportunity to submit any information that should be considered in determining whether the requesting spouse is entitled to innocent spouse relief. The nonrequesting spouse is not, however, required to submit information.

Upon the request of either spouse, the IRS will share with one spouse the information submitted by the other spouse unless doing so would impair tax administration. When abuse is alleged, however, IRS correspondence with the nonrequesting spouse is sent from the Cincinnati Centralized Innocent Spouse Operation, and identification information, such as the requesting spouse's new name, address, or employer, is omitted. The IRS examiner is also directed to contact the requesting spouse to determine whether additional precautions are needed to conceal his or her location.

COMMENT

Joint filer taxpayers who are no longer married or no longer reside in the same household have the right to request information regarding the IRS' efforts to collect delinquent taxes on their joint return liabilities (Internal Revenue Code Sec. 6103(e)(8)). Separated or divorced requesting spouses who are considering, or have filed, innocent spouse claims may also be interested in obtaining such information concerning the nonrequesting spouse.

Preliminary Determination Letter

The IRS issues a preliminary determination letter to the requesting spouse based on the merits of the claim and, at the same time, notifies the nonrequesting spouse of such determination. If the determination grants full or partial relief, the IRS suspends the processing of the claim for 45 calendar days and notifies the requesting spouse that the nonrequesting spouse has the right to separately protest the preliminary determination. The nonrequesting spouse may file a written protest and request an IRS Appeals Office conference to protest the preliminary determination that grants relief.

Although the nonrequesting spouse has notice and participation rights, the nonrequesting spouse does not have standing to appeal an IRS decision to grant innocent spouse relief to the requesting spouse. If the requesting spouse appeals the denial of relief, however, the nonrequesting spouse has the right to intervene to participate in the proceedings.

Judicial Appeal of Denial of Innocent Spouse Relief

If the IRS denies the requesting spouse's claim for relief, the requesting spouse may file a petition in Tax Court seeking review of the matter. Although ordinarily the Tax Court only considers defenses to a tax liability in connection with an underlying deficiency proceeding, it will consider "standalone" innocent spouse petitions in which the only issue is the requesting spouse's liability for the tax instead of also addressing the correctness of the underlying deficiency (*P.M. Friday*, 124 TC 220, Dec. 56,019).

The petition must be filed within 90 days following the date on which the IRS mails a final determination to the requesting spouse by certified or registered mail or, if the letter is not mailed within six months of the date that the election was filed, then any time after the six-month period from the date the election was filed and before the close of the 90th day after the notification is mailed (Code Sec. 6015(e)(1)(A) and Reg. §1.6015-7(b)).

> **CAUTION**
>
> The 90-day filing period begins the day the IRS mails the notice denying innocent spouse relief, not the day it is received by the taxpayer.

A requesting spouse who fails to file a petition within the 90-day period may not file a second innocent spouse request for the same liability, alleging essentially the same facts, and use a denial of such second request to restart the clock by seeking judicial review of the denial. In one case where a requesting spouse attempted to do this, the IRS claimed that such spouse had not met the jurisdictional requirements for judicial review, and the Tax Court similarly concluded that the IRS's second denial of the taxpayer's innocent spouse relief was not a "final determination letter" entitling the taxpayer to request judicial review (*J.A. Barnes*, 130 TC __, No. 14 (2008)).

During the 90-day period, in general the IRS may not levy against the property of the requesting spouse or take other enforced collection action to collect any portion of the underlying assessment; the requesting spouse may, however, waive this restriction on collection action. If the taxpayer files a petition with the Tax Court, these activities are generally barred until the Tax Court's decision becomes final, unless collection of the tax is in jeopardy.

Because of the general prohibition on collection action, the 10-year statute of limitations on collection under Code Sec. 6502 is extended for 90 days, plus an additional 60 days if no petition is filed. If a petition is filed, the collections statute is suspended from the date of mailing of the final determination until the Tax Court decision has become final, plus an additional 60 days. The collection statute is suspended for the entire deficiency, not just that portion from which the requesting spouse is seeking relief.

There had been some confusion about whether a spouse presenting a claim for equitable innocent spouse relief in which there was no underlying deficiency could seek review of a denial of the claim in Tax Court, because ordinarily the Tax Court's jurisdiction is limited to deficiency determinations. The *Tax Relief and Health Care Act of 2006* (P.L. 109-432) amended Code Sec. 6015(e)(1) to specifically provide that the Tax Court has jurisdiction to review such equitable innocent spouse cases.

Judicial review is also available in a refund suit filed in a district court or the Court of Federal Claims. It is necessary, however, to pay the full amount of tax assessed and to file a claim for refund. For those spouses who miss the 90-day deadline for Tax Court jurisdiction, this is their only judicial recourse.

A requesting spouse appealing the denial of equitable innocent spouse relief is entitled to have the matter considered *de novo* rather than reviewed under an abuse of discretion standard. In 2006, Congress amended Code Sec. 6015(f), which altered both the standard and scope of review from abuse of discretion to *de novo* review of the matter, with authority to consider matters outside of the administrative record (*S.L. Porter*, 132 TC No. 11, Dec. 57,792).

The IRS will continue, however, to litigate the issue of whether the requesting spouse in an equitable innocent spouse appeal is entitled to have the matter reviewed under a *de novo* standard. Following the *Porter* decision, the IRS issued guidance to its attorneys indicating that they should continue to argue that such cases should be reviewed under an abuse of discretion standard, with the scope of the Tax Court's review limited to issues and evidence presented before Appeals or Examination (*Chief Counsel Notice*, CC-2009-021).

STUDY QUESTIONS

> **7.** Interest and penalties continue to accrue on the underlying tax liability while an innocent spouse request is pending with the IRS, even though enforced collection actions are suspended. *True or False?*

---

8. Which avenue of appeal for denial of innocent spouse relief does **not** require the electing spouse to request a refund after paying the full amount of tax assessed?
   a. Court of Federal Claims
   b. District court
   c. Tax Court

INJURED SPOUSE

Although innocent spouse relief is designed to relieve a spouse from liability attributable to an understatement or underpayment on a jointly filed return, there is a separate avenue of relief for a spouse who files a joint return showing an overpayment, and the overpayment is applied, in whole or in part, in satisfaction of the noninjured spouse's unpaid support obligations or government debts (such as past-due federal tax, state tax, child support, or student loan obligations) (42 U.S.C. §664(a)(C)(3)).

To qualify for injured spouse relief, the requesting spouse must generally:

- File Form 8379, *Injured Spouse Claim and Allocation*, along with an amended income tax return Form 1040X;
- Not be obligated to pay the debt or obligation;
- Have received income, such as wages or interest;
- Have made tax payments, such as withholding or estimated tax payments, or claimed the earned income credit or other refundable credit; and
- Have filed a joint return that reported the income and tax payments and resulted in an overpayment, all or part of which was applied to the past-due debt of the taxpayer's spouse.

The injured spouse files Form 8379 by attaching it to the original return and writing "Injured Spouse" in the upper left corner of the return. Because the IRS processes the claim before making any offset, any refund may be delayed by six to eight weeks. If the injured spouse claim relates to a return that was already filed, the taxpayer mails the Form 8379 to the IRS Service Center for the location where the taxpayer lived when the return was filed.

RELIEF FROM COMMUNITY PROPERTY LAWS

Community property is generally defined as all property acquired by a spouse during marriage while domiciled in a community property state, other than property acquired as separate property. The community property states are Arizona, California, Idaho, Louisiana, Nevada, New Mexico, Texas, Washington, and Wisconsin.

For federal income tax purposes, spouses living in a community property state divide their community property income in equal shares. If a couple files separate tax returns, each spouse in a community property state must report his or her half of the combined community income and deductions in addition to his or her separate income and deductions. Each spouse is liable for the tax on his or her share of community income.

Under Code Sec. 66(c), community property laws may be disregarded for income tax purposes under specified circumstances. A spouse who files a separate return and meets statutory requirements may request either of two different kinds of relief under Code Sec. 66(c): traditional relief and equitable relief.

Traditional relief provides relief from deficiencies arising from understatements on the requesting spouse's separate return if such spouse meets the enumerated requirements. If traditional relief is not available, the requesting spouse may be entitled to *equitable relief,* which is similar to the equitable innocent spouse relief available under Code Sec. 6015(f) and includes relief from underpayments as well as understatements.

Traditional Relief

For traditional relief, the requesting spouse may be relieved of tax liability attributable to the income of the other spouse if the requesting spouse meets the following requirements:

- Did not file a joint return for the tax year;
- Establishes that the item would be treated as the income of the other spouse under the separate reporting rules of Code Sec. 879(a);
- Establishes that he or she did not know of, and had no reason to know of, the unreported community income; and
- Demonstrates that under the facts and circumstances, it is inequitable to include the item of community income in his or her gross income.

Similar to the standards used to determine "knowledge" for purposes of general innocent spouse relief under Code Sec. 6015(b), a spouse has knowledge of an item of community income if the spouse actually knew about it, or if a reasonable person in a similar situation would have known about it. If the requesting spouse is aware of the business activity that produced the income but is unaware of the particular amount involved, the IRS considers the spouse to have knowledge or reason to know of the item. Not knowing the specific dollar amount is not a basis for relief.

The IRS considers all relevant factors in making this determination, including:

- The amount of the item;
- The couple's financial situation;

- The taxpayer's educational background and business experience; and
- Whether the item was reflected on prior years' returns.

This is similar to the analysis applied to innocent spouse relief under Code Sec. 6015.

The requesting spouse files Form 8857, *Request for Innocent Spouse Relief*, once the IRS provides notice that a deficiency exists. The earliest time to request this kind of traditional innocent spouse relief is the date that the IRS notifies the requesting spouse that there may be an outstanding liability with respect to a particular year. A request submitted earlier than this notification date will not be considered.

The last date for requesting relief is six months before the statute of limitations on assessment expires for the nonrequesting spouse (generally three years from the due date of the return, plus extensions) or, if the IRS begins its examination of the return within that six-month period, within 30 days after the examination begins.

> **CAUTION**
>
> A spouse who has entered into a closing agreement or an offer in compromise with the IRS for a particular tax year is not eligible to request innocent spouse relief under Code Sec. 66 for that year with respect to the same liability. A spouse who has chosen to settle or seek to compromise a dispute cannot back out and seek relief as an innocent spouse.

Equitable Relief

Threshold conditions. A requesting spouse who is ineligible for traditional relief may be able to seek *equitable relief* from the operation of community property laws. To be eligible for equitable relief, the requesting spouse must have met these threshold requirements:

- Relief must be sought no later than two years after the date of the IRS's first collection activity against the requesting spouse;
- No assets were transferred between the spouses as part of a fraudulent scheme;
- No disqualified assets were transferred from the nonrequesting spouse to the requesting spouse for the purpose of avoiding tax. If the nonrequesting spouse did transfer disqualified assets to the requesting spouse by the nonrequesting spouse, relief is available only to the extent that the liability exceeds the value of the disqualified assets, as defined in Code Sec. 6015(c)(4)(B);
- The requesting spouse did not file (or fail to file) the return with fraudulent intent; and

■ The income tax liability from which the requesting spouse seeks relief is attributable to the nonrequesting spouse, unless one of the following exceptions applies:
— Attribution due solely to the operation of community property law,
— Nominal ownership,
— Misappropriation of funds, and
— Abuse not amounting to duress.

The IRS determines whether equitable relief should be granted after considering the same factors relevant to requests for equitable relief from joint liabilities arising from joint returns. These factors include:
■ The spouses' current marital status;
■ The requesting spouse's knowledge of the understatement or underpayment; and
■ The threat of economic hardship if relief is denied.

A requesting spouse will be considered to suffer an economic hardship if he or she is unable to pay his or her reasonable basic living expenses as described in the regulations that govern when the IRS should release a levy based on economic hardship (*Rev. Proc. 2003-61*, 2003-2 C.B. 296). Those regulations provide that in determining a reasonable amount for basic living expenses the director will consider any information provided by the taxpayer, including:
■ The taxpayer's age, employment status and history, ability to earn, number of dependents, and status as a dependent of someone else;
■ The amount reasonably necessary for food, clothing, housing (including utilities, homeowners' insurance, homeowners' association dues, and the like), medical expenses (including health insurance), transportation, current tax payments, alimony, child support, or other court-ordered payments, and expenses necessary to the taxpayer's production of income (such as dues for a trade union or professional organization);
■ The cost of living in the geographic area in which the taxpayer resides;
■ Any extraordinary circumstances such as special education expenses, a medical catastrophe, or natural disaster; and
■ Any other factor that the taxpayer claims bears on economic hardship (Treas. Reg. § 301.6343-1(b)(4)).

Additional considerations. Two additional factors weigh in favor of relief if they are present but do not weigh against relief if they are absent. The first is abuse. A history of abuse by the nonrequesting spouse may mitigate a requesting spouse's knowledge or reason to know.

The second is the requesting spouse's mental or physical health; that is, whether the requesting spouse was in poor mental or physical health on the date the return was signed or relief was requested. The IRS considers the nature, extent, and duration of the illness when weighing this factor.

As with traditional relief, a spouse seeking equitable relief files Form 8857, *Request for Innocent Spouse Relief*, or a statement containing similar information, signed under penalty of perjury. The Form 8857 or similar statement must be submitted within two years of the first collection activity against the requesting spouse.

> **PLANNING POINTER**
>
> A requesting spouse seeking equitable relief from an underpayment may attach Form 8857 to the federal income tax return when he or she files it; in that situation the spouse does not need to wait for collection activity to have commenced.

STUDY QUESTIONS

9. A requesting spouse has "knowledge" of a community income item under traditional relief rules:
   a. If the requesting spouse is aware of the business activity that produced the income
   b. Only if he or she knows the dollar amount of the community income item
   c. Only if the community property item was claimed on a previous federal income tax return

10. Equitable relief from community property laws under Code Sec. 66(c) is similar to equitable innocent spouse relief under Code Sec. 6015(f) and applies to understatements as well as underpayments. *True or False?*

CONCLUSION

The three kinds of innocent spouse relief and two types of community property innocent spouse relief provide important vehicles for relieving a spouse or former spouse of liability for a tax obligation. To obtain relief, taxpayers must meet certain eligibility requirements and satisfy their associated procedures.

Same-Sex Marriage/Domestic Partner Tax Issues

This chapter helps practitioners address tax issues of increasing concern to a growing segment of the taxpaying public arising out of the burgeoning recognition of domestic partners and same-sex couples under state laws.

LEARNING OBJECTIVES

Upon completion of this chapter, you will be able to:

- Describe current federal tax issues relevant to domestic partners and same-sex married couples (SSMCs), including claims to dependency exemptions, child credits, and head of household filing status;

- Explain the federal tax advantages and disadvantages same-sex married couples experience in comparison with husband–wife married couples with respect to the first-time homebuyer credit, passive losses, gain on the sale of a principal residence, and property transfers during marriage and incident to divorce;

- List the kinds of employee benefits received by same-sex married spouses or domestic partners that are treated differently for tax purposes from similar benefits received by a spouse in a husband–wife marriage;

- Explain select estate and gift tax issues relevant to same-sex married couples and domestic partners;

- Identify ways that transfers of property between same-sex married people or domestic partners may create additional tax liability or tax savings under Code Sec. 1239 rules; and

- Contract tax treatment of jointly owned property under a state's community property laws versus federal assessment and collection rules.

INTRODUCTION

The federal tax issues arising in connection with personal relationships have taken on increased significance over the past year with the recognition of domestic partnerships and same-sex marriages by a growing number of states. More than a one-quarter of U.S. states now recognize domestic partnerships, civil unions, or same-sex marriages. This recognition raises a number of important tax planning, employee benefit analysis, and compliance issues for such couples.

OVERVIEW OF INCOME TAX ISSUES RELEVANT TO DOMESTIC PARTNERS AND SAME-SEX COUPLES

Practitioners representing one or both members of a couple who have entered into a domestic partnership or same-sex marriage will have special planning and compliance issues to consider. This is a developing area of law, and there are several unanswered questions about how domestic partners (either a cohabiting male–female couple or unwed same-sex unmarried partners) and a same-sex married couple (SSMC) will be regarded for income, estate, and gift planning purposes. There are also a number of open issues concerning how such individuals will be treated for the purpose being assessed tax liabilities, and being subject to collection action for unpaid taxes.

As of the publication date of this course, Connecticut, Iowa, Maine, Massachusetts, New Hampshire (as of January 1, 2010), and Vermont recognize same-sex marriage. New Jersey offers civil unions—the legal equivalent of marriage. California, the District of Columbia, Maryland, Nevada (as of October 2009), Oregon, Wisconsin, and Washington offer domestic partnerships. California also recognizes the approximately 18,000 same-sex marriages entered into between June 16, 2008, and November 4, 2008, at which time California's constitution was amended prospectively to prohibit any further same-sex marriages.

> **COMMENT**
>
> The California Assembly is currently considering a bill that, if enacted, would amend California's Family Code to recognize marriages of same-sex couples performed out-of-state prior to November 5, 2008. It would further recognize marriages of same-sex couples performed out-of-state after that date as carrying all the same rights and responsibilities that spouses receive although without the designation of marriage (California SB 54, Marriage Recognition and Family Protection Act).

In California, Oregon, and Washington, domestic partnership is the legal equivalent of marriage, which includes community property rights, where applicable, and the right to receive support.

Hawaii recognizes reciprocal beneficiary registration, which provides certain state rights and benefits but is not the equivalent of either same-sex marriage or domestic partnership. Similar to Hawaii, Colorado allows same-sex couples to enter into a designated beneficiary agreement that grants limited rights, including making funeral arrangements, receiving death benefits, and intestacy rights.

> **COMMENT**
>
> California uses the term *registered domestic partners* to include both same-sex couples and husband–wife couples at least one of whom is older than age 62 and eligible to receive Social Security benefits. New Jersey previously offered domestic partnership to couples in both categories but, with its adoption of civil unions, now only allows new domestic partnerships to be entered into by husband–wife couples at least one of whose members is older than age 62. In California and New Jersey both categories of registered domestic partners are subject to the reporting and filing obligations described below.

In the following materials *spouse* refers to one of the two spouses in a same-sex marriage or civil union either contracted in, or recognized by, the state in which the spouses reside, and *domestic partner* refers to either of the partners in a domestic partnership regarded as the equivalent of a marital relationship under the laws of the state where the partners reside.

Impact of State Law

Prior to the adoption in 1996 of the *Defense of Marriage Act* (P.L. 104-199 (September 21, 1996), or DOMA for short, the IRS considered itself bound by state law rather than federal law when attempting to determine an individual's marital status (*Eccles,* CCH Dec. 19,508, 19 T. C. 1049, *aff'd,* CA-4, 54-1 USTC ¶9129, 208 F. 2d 796). Thus, for example, the IRS recognized common law marriage for federal income tax purposes if a state recognized common law marriage (Rev. Rul. 58-66, 1958-1 CB 60).

DOMA provides that in determining the meaning of any statute, ruling, regulation, or interpretation the word *marriage* means only a legal union between one man and one woman as husband and wife, and *spouse* refers only to a person of the opposite sex who is a husband or a wife (P.L. 104-199, Act §3). DOMA further provides that federal agencies cannot recognize any marriage other than one entered into between a man and a woman as husband and wife.

The IRS is, therefore, prohibited from recognizing SSMCs or domestic partners as married individuals. This is consistent with the Internal Revenue Code, which similarly prohibits two individuals who are not husband and wife from filing a joint return. Code Sec. 6013 provides "a husband and wife may make a single return jointly of income taxes." Thus, for all federal income tax purposes *husband* and *wife* are interpreted literally and are not considered to include SSMC spouses recognized as being married under applicable state law.

> **COMMENT**
>
> The Commonwealth of Massachusetts filed a federal lawsuit on July 8, 2009, seeking an order that the federal government be prohibited from enforcing Section 3 of DOMA against Massachusetts. Additionally, it seeks a declaration that Section 3 of DOMA, as applied to Massachusetts is unconstitutional. The outcome of this litigation will affect the 16,000 same-sex marriages that have thus far been performed in Massachusetts (*Commonwealth of Massachusetts v. United States Department of Health and Human Services et al.*).

Return Filing Requirements

SSMCs and domestic partners in jurisdictions regarding such partners as the equivalent of being married and that have a state income tax (California, Connecticut, District of Columbia, Iowa, Massachusetts, New Jersey, Oregon, and Vermont) must generally file their state income tax returns using either married filing jointly or married filing separately filing status. New Hampshire has no general state income tax, but its dividends and interest tax forms are filed by SSMCs using married status.

Maine generally requires taxpayers to use the same filing status for state purposes used for filing their federal returns. Thus, SSMCs living and working in Maine have to file as single taxpayers on both their federal and Maine returns.

Unlike requirements in most other jurisdictions that recognize domestic partnerships, in Maryland and Wisconsin domestic partners use single status on their state returns. Nevada and Washington have no state income tax, so state filing status is not an issue in either jurisdiction.

However, for federal tax return purposes, regardless of where SSMCs or domestic partners reside, they are not considered married and therefore each spouse/partner must file the federal return using single status instead of filing as married filing jointly or married filing separately.

Because most state taxing authorities base their joint return computations on the figures from a joint federal return, SSMCs and domestic partners will likely have to complete a total of four different tax returns in order to compute their federal and state tax liability in compliance with their filing obligations:

1. Each same-sex spouse/domestic partner must prepare and file an individual federal Form 1040 (or 1040-A or 1040-EZ);
2. Then the SSMC/domestic partners must prepare a hypothetical joint federal return combining income, adjustments, deductions, and credits; this return will not be filed but is used in the preparation of their state return(s);

3.   The SSMC/domestic partners then use the hypothetical joint federal
     return in order to prepare their state return.

> **COMMENT**
>
> Some states require that the hypothetical joint federal return be attached
> to the state return to show the computations. For example, for 2008
> returns Vermont instructed its civil union partners (Vermont began recog-
> nizing same sex marriage as of September 1, 2009, and recognized civil
> unions prior to that date) to mark their hypothetical 2008 federal return as
> "Recomputed for VT Purposes" and to use the recomputed information
> where federal information was requested on the Vermont return, attaching
> a copy of both the actual federal return filed with IRS, and the recomputed
> return, to their state return.

Some SSMC taxpayers are uncomfortable using a single filing status because
it does not reflect their marital status under state law. Moreover, tax return
information is often used as a basis for obtaining loans or other credit, the
applications for which will show the taxpayers as married, thus creating
what appears to be an inconsistency between their federal returns and their
credit applications. For these and other reasons, some SSMCs have elected
to indicate on their federal return that they are, in fact, married under state
law. This may be handled in a couple of ways:

- Including a cover letter or disclosure form (perhaps using Form 8275,
  Disclosure Statement, with the federal return stating that the taxpayer
  was married to a person of the same sex as of a certain date (possibly
  attaching a copy of the marriage certificate to the return), explaining
  that because of DOMA the taxpayer has filed as a single taxpayer; or
- Placing an asterisk in Box 1 (Filing Status) next to the "Single" box,
  indicating that the taxpayer is married to a person of the same sex, the
  date of the marriage, and that this designation as "single" is for federal
  income tax filing purposes only.

Tax Liability

The total tax liability that an SSMC or domestic partners will incur, in
contrast to what their federal tax liability would have been if they had been
entitled to file as married taxpayers, depends on what portion of their total
income each spouse/domestic partner earns. In general, for tax years after
2002 the standard deduction for a married couple filing a joint return is
roughly double the amount of the standard deduction for single taxpayers.
Thus, married taxpayers and two single taxpayers earning the same combined salaries would have the same total standard deduction.

The two lowest tax brackets (the 10-percent and 15-percent rates) for married taxpayers filing jointly are also roughly twice the amount of the brackets for those rates for single taxpayers. This parity between of the standard deduction and tax brackets for married couples and single taxpayers was designed to alleviate the "marriage penalty" that previously caused married couples to pay more in tax than two single taxpayers earning the same total amount.

> **EXAMPLE**
>
> In 2009, Lourdes and Miguel each have income of $50,000. They have no other credits, deductions, or adjustments. If they are unmarried and file as single taxpayers, they can each claim a standard deduction of $5,700, leaving them each with taxable income of $44,300, and a tax liability of roughly $7,263, for a total liability of $14,526. If Lourdes and Miguel are married, their joint standard deduction is $11,400, their joint taxable income is $88,600, and their joint tax liability is $14,525. Thus, their marriage has no impact on their tax liability.

In certain cases, however, relief from the marriage penalty can actually create a "marriage bonus" when income is earned disproportionately by the two spouses.

> **EXAMPLE**
>
> In 2009, Lourdes has income of $15,000, and Miguel has income of $85,000. If Lourdes and Miguel are married, their total joint tax liability is $14,525, just as it is if they each have $44,300 in taxable income. If Lourdes and Miguel are unmarried and file as single taxpayers (or if they were an SSMC or domestic partners treated as unmarried for federal income tax purposes) Lourdes' taxable income is $9,300 and her tax liability is $978, and Miguel's taxable income is $79,300 and his tax liability is $16,013, for a combined total of $16,991. Thus, being able to file a joint return gives Lourdes and Miguel a marriage bonus worth $2,466.

STUDY QUESTIONS

1. What federal law created nonconformity between federal tax treatment of same-sex couples and domestic partners and recognition of their status in many state laws?

   a. Pension Protection Act

   b. Defense of Marriage Act

   c. Worker, Retiree, and Employer Recovery Act of 2008 (WRERA)

---

2. One way an SSMC can indicate their spousal status when they file federal tax returns is:

   a. Attaching a description of their status on Form 8275, Disclosure Statement

   b. Filing with one partner claiming head of household status and the other, dependent status

   c. Filing the hypothetical joint federal return instead of two returns reporting single status

---

FAMILY TAX ISSUES

Dependency Exemption

SSMCs/domestic partners are not considered married for federal income tax purposes, and, therefore, the child of one spouse/domestic partner (Spouse A) would not, by virtue of the marriage, be considered for federal tax purposes the stepchild of the other spouse (Spouse B). Therefore, Spouse A's child who is not also the biological, adopted, or eligible foster child of Spouse B is not considered a child of Spouse B for federal tax purposes.

> **COMMENT**
>
> For this purpose an eligible foster child is a child who has been placed with the taxpayer by an authorized agency or by a judgment, decree, or other order of any court of competent jurisdiction (Code Sec. 152(f)(1)).

Because such child is not considered Spouse B's child, such child cannot be considered a qualifying child (as discussed below) of Spouse B for purposes of claiming head of household status, the child tax credit, or the earned income credit. However, such child may be considered a *qualifying relative* of Spouse B for purposes of claiming a dependency exemption.

To be considered a qualifying relative the child does not need to have any blood relationship to Spouse B. What is required is that the child:

- Live with Spouse B all year;
- Have less than $3,650 (for 2009) of gross income; and
- Receive more than one-half of his or her total support from Spouse B during the calendar year (Code Secs. 152(d)(1) and (d)(2)(H)).

This same standard would also apply if Spouse B were supporting Spouse A and wanted to claim Spouse A as a dependent on Spouse B's individual return.

> **EXAMPLE**
>
> Mary and Linda are a same-sex married couple who live together in Massachusetts. Prior to their marriage in 2008, Linda had a daughter, Neica, whom Mary has never adopted. After the marriage, Linda became a stay-at-home mother to Neica, who was five years old in 2008. In 2009 Mary provided all of the support for both Linda and Neica, neither of whom have any other source of income. Both Linda and Neica are qualifying relatives of Mary, who can claim them both as dependents on Mary's 2009 federal individual return.

> **COMMENT**
>
> If Mary and Linda had been considered spouses under federal tax law, Mary would not be eligible to claim Linda as a dependent because spouses are excluded from the definition of qualifying relatives (Code Sec. 152(d)(2)(H)).

Spouses/domestic partners are also eligible to claim a dependency exemption on their individual return for their biological, adopted, or foster child (a *qualifying child*). However, if a dependency exemption is claimed for a qualifying child, the other spouse/domestic partner cannot similarly claim the child as a dependent on his or her individual return.

If both spouses or both domestic partners are eligible to claim a biological, adopted, or foster child as a dependent, and the child lives with both parents the same amount of time during the year (which is likely when the SSMC/domestic partners and the child all live together), then only the spouse/domestic partner with the higher adjusted gross income is eligible to claim the child as a qualifying child (Code Sec. 152(c)(4)(A)).

> **EXAMPLE**
>
> In 2009, Micah and Ray, an SSMC, adopted Luis; all three live together. Both parents qualify for the dependency exemption with respect to Luis. Both Micah and Ray are employed. Micah's 2009 AGI is higher than Ray's. Because Micah and Ray both qualify for the exemption, both are parents, and they have equal custody of Luis, the exemption goes to Micah, the parent with the higher AGI.

> **COMMENT**
>
> Several states have adopted *presumption of parentage statutes*, which deem a child born during a same-sex marriage/domestic partnership to be the child of both spouses/partners. This is similar to the law in many jurisdictions which presumes that a child born during a husband-wife marriage to be the child of both spouses. It is unclear how presumption of parentage legislation in jurisdictions recognizing same-sex marriage or domestic partnership will affect the treatment of children born during such unions for purposes of the federal return dependency exemption, head of household filing status, and the child credit. The IRS has not indicated whether a child covered by a domestic partner presumption of parentage statute will be considered a qualifying child of both partners. Moreover, because of DOMA's prohibition on the IRS recognizing same-sex marriages, it would appear that a same-sex marriage presumption of parentage would not be respected by the IRS, and the child will only be a qualifying child if there is a biological, adoptive, or eligible foster relationship with such child.

Head of Household Status

By claiming head of household status instead of single status, a taxpayer is subject to lower marginal tax rates and a larger standard deduction. A spouse/domestic partner will be considered a head of household if:

- The spouse/domestic partner is considered unmarried on the last day of the tax year (which would be the case for federal income tax return filing purposes);
- The spouse/domestic partner paid more than half the cost of maintaining a home for the year; and
- A qualifying person lived with the spouse/domestic partner in the home for more than half the year.

For this purpose, a *qualifying person* includes a qualifying child or a qualifying relative under the dependency exemption rules, but not someone whom the spouse/domestic partner is eligible to claim as a dependent solely based on the person:

- Living with the spouse/domestic partner all year;
- Having less than $3,650 (for 2009) of gross income; and
- Receiving more than one-half of his or her total support from the spouse/domestic partner during the calendar year).

Expenses of maintaining a household include property taxes, mortgage interest, rent, utility charges, upkeep and repairs, property insurance, and food consumed on the premises. It does not include the cost of clothing, education, medical treatment, vacations, life insurance, or transportation (Treas. Reg. §1.2-2(d)).

If both spouses/domestic partners are the biological or adoptive parents of a child, or the child is an eligible foster child, and each parent files a federal return as a single taxpayer, then the child is a qualifying person and one of the two may be entitled to file as head of household. The parent claiming head of household status must provide more than 50 percent of the child's support.

> **EXAMPLE**
>
> Tara and Kisha are domestic partners living in Oregon, which recognizes domestic partners as the equivalent of being married for purposes of filing their state income tax returns. In 2009 Tara and Kisha adopted Josiah. Kisha does not work outside the home, whereas Tara, who does, provides all of the income for the family, including more than 50 percent of Josiah's support. On their Oregon tax return neither Tara nor Kisha may claim head of household filing status because Tara and Kish must file as married individuals, either jointly or separately. For federal purposes, however, they are not considered married and therefore Tara, whose income maintains the household, is entitled to claim head of household status.

Child Credit

The federal child tax credit may also be available to a same-sex spouse/domestic partner claiming a dependent child (Code Sec. 24). The credit is $1,000 annually per child through 2010 and, if not extended by Congress, will decrease to $500 per qualifying child in 2011. Eligibility as a qualifying child for purposes of the child tax credit is the same as for claiming a dependency exemption except that the child must *not* have attained the age of 17 by the end of the year. The federal child credit is, therefore, not available to a same-sex spouse/domestic partner who is not the biological, adoptive, or foster parent of the child.

The credit amount phases out when the same-sex spouse/domestic partner filing as single or head of household has a modified adjusted gross income (AGI) that exceeds $75,000. The credit is reduced by $50 for each $1,000, or fraction thereof, of modified AGI above the threshold amount. (*Modified AGI* is AGI without exclusions for foreign earned income, foreign housing expenses, and income of residents of U.S. possessions.)

> **EXAMPLE**
>
> Rafe and Sam are an SSMC. In 2009, Rafe's AGI was $50,000, whereas Sam's AGI for the year was $65,000. Rafe and Sam are parents to their adopted son, Paul. Paul meets the standard for being a qualifying child and is claimed as a dependent by Sam, who has the higher AGI. Sam is also eligible to claim the child tax credit for Paul.

Earned Income Credit

The earned income tax credit, which is a refundable federal income tax credit for low- to moderate-income working individuals and families, can be claimed by eligible individuals (Code Sec. 32). A larger credit is allowed if the taxpayer has one or more qualifying children. As is the case with head of household filing status and the federal child tax credit, a qualifying child includes a biological, adopted, or foster child of the taxpayer, but not a nonqualifying child even if the taxpayer can claim such child as a qualifying relative type of dependent.

> **EXAMPLE**
>
> Kara and Monica, who are an SSMC, live with Monica's biological daughter Lea, who is two years old. Kara has not adopted Lea. Kara supports the family by working as a waitress, earning $15,000 in 2009. Monica stays at home caring for Lea and does not have any source of earned income. Kara is ineligible to claim Lea as a child in computing Kara's earned income tax credit because Lea is not a qualifying child. Monica cannot claim the earned income tax credit because she is not earning income.

REAL PROPERTY TAX ISSUES

First-Time Homebuyer Credit

For 2009, taxpayers are eligible to claim a credit equal to 10 percent of the purchase price of a residence (Code Sec. 36(b)(1)(C)). For homes purchased after 2008 and before December 1, 2009, the maximum first-time homebuyer credit is $8,000. The credit is phased out for taxpayers with modified AGI in excess of $75,000 (or $150,000 for joint filers). The phaseout is complete when a taxpayer's modified AGI reaches $95,000 (or $170,000 for joint filers).

If a husband–wife married couple files separate returns, each spouse is only entitled to claim one-half of the credit. By contrast, if two or more taxpayers who are not married (or not recognized as being married, such as an SSMC or domestic partners) purchase a principal residence, the credit may be allocated between the taxpayers using any reasonable method (*Notice 2009-12*, IRB 2009-6, 446). A reasonable method includes allocating the credit between taxpayers who are eligible to claim the credit based on:

- The taxpayers' contributions toward the purchase price of the residence as tenants in common or joint tenants; or
- The taxpayers' ownership interests in the residence as tenants in common.

PLANNING POINTER

Allowing the credit to be shared may present an important planning opportunity to SSMCs and domestic partners. Such couples do not have to divide the credit evenly, as is the case with married couples filing separately. Moreover, if one spouse/domestic partner has an AGI in excess of $95,000, and the other's income falls below such cap, then depending on which basis they allocate the credit the spouse with the lower AGI may be able to claim more of the credit in order to help avoid the credit phaseout.

EXAMPLE

Alice and Betty are domestic partners. In 2009, Alice contributed $45,000 and Betty contributed $15,000 toward the $60,000 purchase price of a residence that they own equally as joint tenants. Alice and Betty may allocate the allowable $6,000 credit, with three-fourths to Alice and one-fourth to Betty based on their contributions, or one-half to each based on their ownership interests in the residence, or using any other reasonable method. If Alice's 2009 AGI is $60,000 and Betty's AGI is $105,000, allocating three-fourths of the credit to Alice would enable the couple to make greater use of the credit.

COMMENT

The amount of any liability on a mortgage note counts as part of any contribution, along with the down payments. Generally, cosigners of a mortgage are equally liable, jointly and severally, for payment.

STUDY QUESTIONS

3. A domestic partner cannot be considered a head of household for federal return filings. ***True or False?***

4. For an SSMC or domestic partnership, the federal child tax credit:
   a. May be available to the spouse or partner claiming the child as a dependent
   b. May be claimed in lieu of claiming the child as a dependent, but both breaks are unavailable to the same taxpayer
   c. May be claimed only by the spouse or partner who does not claim head of household filing status

Exclusion of Gain on Sale of Residence

A portion of the gain on the sale of a principal residence may be eligible to be excluded from recognition (Code Sec. 121). In order to be eligible for the maximum exclusion, a taxpayer must have owned and occupied the residence as a principal residence for an aggregate of at least two of the five years before the sale or exchange. The maximum exclusion is $250,000 of gain for a single taxpayer, but is $500,000 for a married couple filing a joint return. The exclusion amount is reduced in cases where the ownership and use requirement is not satisfied due to a change in place of employment, health, or certain unforeseen circumstances (Code Sec. 121(c)). A taxpayer may only use the exclusion once in any two-year period (subject to a partial-exclusion rule for certain situations within a two-year period).

For a husband and wife married couple filing a joint return, if one spouse owns the property, the other spouse is treated as owning it for purposes of meeting the two-year ownership requirement. Thus, to be entitled to the $500,000 exclusion:

- Both spouses must use the residence as their principal residence for two years during the five years prior to sale;
- One spouse must own the residence for at least two years during the five years prior to sale; and
- Neither spouse must have used the exclusion in the prior two years.

> **EXAMPLE**
>
> Orla purchased a home in 2004 for $200,000. Her boyfriend, Mal, moved into the home in June 2007. Orla and Mal married in October 2008. Orla sold the residence in August 2009 for $500,000. During the five years prior to the sale, Orla owned the home and used it as her principal residence. Mal used the home as his principal residence for two years prior to the sale. Mal is treated as owning the home for two years because his wife, Orla, owned the home for two years. Because they both qualify for the exclusion, they do not have to pay tax on any of the gain.

This presents certain planning pitfalls and limitations for SSMCs and domestic partners, who are not entitled to use the above rules concerning ownership and use of the residence.

> **EXAMPLE**
>
> Orla purchased a home in California 2004 for $200,000. Her girlfriend, Melonie, moved into the home in June 2007. Orla and Melonie were legally married in California in October 2008. Orla sold the residence in August 2009 for $500,000. During the five years prior to the sale, Orla owned the home and used it as her principal residence. Melonie used the home as her principal residence for two years prior to the sale.

However, because Orla and Melonie are not considered married for federal income tax purposes, Melonie is not treated as owning the home for two years even though Orla owned the home for two years. Because only Orla qualifies for the exclusion, she will have to pay tax on $50,000 of gain, the difference between the $300,000 of gain she has and the maximum $250,000 exclusion to which she is entitled as a single taxpayer for federal tax purposes.

Two special rules for divorcing taxpayers may present a significant benefit to husband–wife couples, but not to SSMCs or domestic partners. First, if a residence is transferred by a spouse incident to a divorce in a nonrecognition transaction under Code Sec. 1041 (see the discussion of property transfers below) the time during which the taxpayer's spouse or former spouse owned the residence is added to the taxpayer's period of ownership (Code Sec. 121(d)(3)(A)).

EXAMPLE

Delia and Dan became husband and wife when they married in July 2006. At the time of the marriage, Dan owned a home that he purchased in 2004, and which Delia and Dan use as a residence from the time of their marriage. In June 2007 Delia and Dan have a child, Ila, and in September 2008 they divorce. As part of the property division in the divorce decree Delia receives sole ownership of Dan's residence. Although Delia has lived in the house as her principal residence for more than two years, she has only actually owned the home since September 2008, the time when she received it as part of the divorce property settlement. Nonetheless, Delia is considered to have owned the residence for the entire time Dan owned it, and therefore she does not need to wait two years before selling the home in order to be entitled to exclude $250,000 of gain. If Delia and Dan had been an SSMC, however, they would not be considered to be married for federal purposes, and Delia would not satisfy the two-year ownership requirement, and therefore be eligible to exclude $250,000 of gain, until September 2010.

Moreover, a taxpayer who owns a residence is deemed to use it as a principal residence while the taxpayer's spouse or former spouse is given use of the residence under the terms of a divorce or separation instrument (Code Sec. 121(d)(3)(B)).

EXAMPLE

Lila and Ned are a husband and wife who were married in July 2008, at which time they purchased a principal residence. In July 2009 Lila and Ned separate, Ned moves out, and Lila is granted sole use of the residence under a separation instrument. Lila and Ned file for divorce in November 2010, which is also when they sell residence. Even though Ned has only actually lived in the house for one year at the time it is sold, he is deemed to have used it as his residence for the entire time Lila occupied it under the separation instrument, and therefore Ned and Lila will each be entitled to exclude $250,000 of any gain on the sale of the residence.

If Lila and Ned had been an SSMC, their situation might have caused significant challenges. An SSMC spouse would not, for federal income tax purposes, be considered to use the residence during the time the other spouse occupies it under a divorce decree or separation instrument. Moreover, if one spouse is granted exclusive use of the residence under such a decree/instrument, this could have the effect of causing the other spouse to no longer be able to satisfy the use requirement.

EXAMPLE

Lia and Nia are an SSMC were married in July 2008, at which time they purchased a principal residence. In July 2009 Lia and Nia separate, Nia moves out, and Lia is granted sole use of the residence under a separation instrument. Lia and Nia file for divorce in November 2010, which is also when they sell residence. Nia has only actually lived in the house for one year at the time it is sold and therefore has not used the residence for the required two year period that would entitle her to exclude $250,000 of gain.

EXAMPLE

Ria and Sia are an SSMC married in July 2008, at which time they purchased a principal residence. In July 2010 Ria and Sia separate, Sia moves out, and Ria is granted sole use of the residence under a separation instrument. Ria continues to live in the residence until July 2015, at which time Ria and Sia sell the residence. Sia is not considered to have occupied the residence during the time Ria lived in it between July 2010 and July 2015, and therefore will not have used the residence for the required two-year period that would entitle her to exclude $250,000 of gain on her share of the sales proceeds.

Passive Loss Limitations

Under the Code Sec. 469 passive loss rules, rental real estate losses up to $25,000 may be deducted in full against wages and portfolio income by a taxpayer whose modified adjusted gross income is less than $100,000. To qualify for this deduction, the taxpayer must actively participate, must own at least 10 percent of the investment, and must not be a limited partner in the real estate. The $25,000 exception is phased out at the rate of 50 cents for every dollar of modified adjusted gross income (AGI) exceeding $100,000. Thus, when the taxpayer's modified AGI exceeds $150,000, none of the $25,000 offset is allowed.

The computation of AGI is the same for single and married taxpayers. Thus, a married couple whose combined AGI exceeds $150,000 would not be entitled to deduct any otherwise qualifying rental real estate losses. By contrast, two single taxpayers, or two taxpayers who are treated as single such as same-sex spouses or domestic partners, each with an AGI of less than $150,000, may each claim up to $25,000 of rental real estate losses if they each satisfy the active participation standard, thereby giving them a potential advantage over a husband-wife married couple.

> **EXAMPLE**
>
> Jess and Jo are a husband and wife who file a joint return and have a combined 2009 AGI of $90,000, all of which is compensation income. In 2008 they purchased a 10-unit apartment building, which constitutes rental real estate. They each own 50 percent of the apartment building. Jess and Jo each actively participate, but they do not materially participate in the ownership of the building (they approve new tenants, decide on rental terms, and approve capital or repair expenditures). In 2009 the apartment building generated $60,000 of net losses (i.e., deductions in excess of rental income). Jess and Jo may deduct up to $25,000 of the losses on their 2009 joint return to offset their compensation income. They would each deduct $12,500 of the loss if they filed separate returns. But if Jess and Jo were, instead, domestic partners or an SSMC regarded for federal tax purposes as two single individuals, they would each be allowed to deduct $25,000 of rental real estate losses against other, ordinary income (including wages) on their individual federal returns—or a combined total of $50,000—twice as much as they would have been entitled to deduct if they were considered married for federal income tax purposes.

> **EXAMPLE**
>
> Les and Lu are a husband and wife who file a joint return and have a combined 2009 AGI of $180,000, half of which was earned by each, and all of which was compensation income.

In 2008 they purchased a six-unit apartment building which constitutes rental real estate. They each own 50 percent of the apartment building. Les and Lu each actively participate, but they do not materially participate, in the ownership of the building (they approve new tenants, decide on rental terms, and approve capital or repair expenditures). In 2009 the apartment building generated $50,000 of net losses (i.e., deductions in excess of rental income). Because Les and Lu have a combined AGI in excess of $150,000 they are not entitled to deduct any portion of the rental real estate losses. If Les and Lu were, instead, domestic partners or an SSMC regarded for federal tax purposes as two single individuals, they would each be allowed to deduct $25,000 of rental real estate losses on their individual federal returns—or a combined total of $50,000— because each has $90,000 of AGI, which falls below the AGI limit.

EMPLOYEE BENEFIT TAX ISSUES

Medical and Related Benefits

Employers may include employees' spouses or domestic partners in self-funded medical and dental plans. Because same-sex couples and domestic partners are not recognized as spouses such benefits are taxable to the employee. However, if such a spouse or domestic partner qualifies as the employee's dependent, the employee may be able to have the spouse/domestic partner receive medical insurance coverage under the employer's plan without triggering federal taxable income to the employee. The employee may also be able to pay the premium for medical benefits for such spouse/domestic partner dependents with pretax payroll deductions.

A *dependent* for these purposes is someone who resides in the employee's home as such dependent's principal residence for the entire taxable year and receives more than one-half of his or her support for the calendar year from the employee. The IRS does not require that the dependent's income fall below the $3,650 income test that is used to determine whether the individual is a qualifying relative for purposes of claiming the dependency exemption (*Notice 2004-79*, 2004-2 CB 898; Proposed Treas. Reg. §1.106).

Cafeteria plans may offer health insurance to employees, their same-sex spouses or domestic partners, and their dependents. The same-sex spouse/domestic partner may benefit from the employee's selection of family medical insurance coverage or of coverage under a dependent care assistance program.

COBRA Premium Subsidy

The *Consolidated Omnibus Budget Reconciliation Act of 1985* (COBRA) provides certain former employees, retirees, spouses, former spouses, and dependent children the right to temporary continuation of health coverage at group rates. The *American Recovery and Reinvestment Act of 2009* (2009 Recovery Act, P.L. 111-5) provides a 65 percent premium subsidy for nine months to employees involuntarily terminated between September 1, 2008, and December 31, 2009. If an eligible employee pays 35 percent of the premium, the group health plan must treat that individual as having paid the full premium required for COBRA continuation coverage.

Any COBRA-qualified beneficiary associated with the related covered employee who is covered immediately before the involuntary termination of the covered employee's employment is eligible for the COBRA subsidy. However, for this purpose an eligible *qualified beneficiary* only includes an opposite-sex spouse or dependent child of the terminated employee. Thus, a terminated employee's same-sex spouse or domestic partner would not satisfy the criteria for a qualified beneficiary.

STUDY QUESTIONS

---

5. An employee may include his or her same-sex spouse or domestic partner in an employer's self-funded medical or dental plan without the coverage being considered as federal taxable income:

   a. If the spouse or partner is the employee's dependent

   b. If the spouse or partner is considered married to the employee under state law

   c. A same-sex spouse or domestic partner may not be covered in such a medical or dental plan without federal taxation of the benefit

6. A same-sex spouse or domestic partner of an eligible former employee may also qualify for the COBRA premium subsidy if:

   a. The employer approves inclusion of the spouse or partner for the premium coverage

   b. The spouse or partner is considered married to the employee under state law

   c. A same-sex spouse or domestic partner may not be covered as a qualified beneficiary for the subsidy

---

GIFT AND ESTATE TAX ISSUES

Estate planning for SSMCs and domestic partners is beyond the scope of this course and requires consideration of both wealth transfer and decision-making authority (including medical decision-making authority if spouses/domestic partners were to become incapacitated or unable to manage their affairs). However, some general gift and estate tax considerations are pertinent here and should be considered.

For this purpose, assume same-sex Spouse A decides to give property to Spouse B. To give Spouse B an interest in real property, Spouse A creates a joint tenancy with right of survivorship with Spouse B—using either property previously owned by Spouse A or acquired using Spouse A's funds. Spouse A is deemed to have gifted 50 percent of the property to Spouse B if Spouse B has the right under local law to sever his or her interest in the joint tenancy. The amount of the gift is one-half the value of the property.

> **EXAMPLE**
>
> In 2007 Steven purchased a house in his own name; the house cost $300,000 and was acquired with Steven's own funds. In 2008 Steven and Tom were married in Massachusetts. In 2009 Steven transferred title to the house to himself and Tom as joint tenants with a right of survivorship. Under state law Tom has the right to petition a court to sever the joint tenancy, in which case he would receive one-half of the property free of the survivorship right. Steven has made a gift to Tom in the amount of $150,000.

Similarly, a mortgage payment by Spouse A may be deemed in part a gift to Spouse B. Placing a bank account or stock account in joint tenancy, however, probably does not constitute a gift because Spouse A retains the right to withdraw all of the money at any time. A gift will occur, however, at the time Spouse B withdraws any of the original owner's money. A gift of a jointly owned U.S. savings bond by Spouse A occurs when Spouse B redeems it for cash. A gift of stock is complete when a properly endorsed stock certificate is delivered by Spouse A to Spouse B or his or her agent.

Because Spouse A and Spouse B, as an SSMC, are not considered married for federal purposes, the Code Sec. 2523 unlimited marital deduction will not insulate Spouse A from the federal gift tax consequences arising from the transfer. Thus, any gratuitous transfer between same-sex spouses/domestic partners should be evaluated for potential gift tax consequences, particularly if the gift exceeds $13,000 in one year, the current annual threshold triggering consideration as a taxable gift.

Estate tax issues also lurk when a transfer at death is made between same-sex spouses/domestic partners, because no federal unlimited marital deduction applies to them. Thus, property titled in the name of one spouse/domestic partner will be fully includible in such individual's estate, unless the surviving spouse/domestic partner establishes one-half ownership in such property. The entire value of the property is again included in the surviving spouse/domestic partner's estate. The property, therefore, is potentially subject *twice* to estate tax!

Certain planning techniques might help to mitigate the gift and estate tax consequences of these transfers. For example, most states have adopted some form of the *Uniform Transfer-on-Death Securities Registration Act,* under which Spouse A can name Spouse B to inherit the former's stocks, bonds, or brokerage accounts upon death. Because no actual transfer takes place during Spouse A's life and Spouse A has the right to alter or amend the designation of who will inherit such brokerage assets at death, no immediate gift tax is triggered at the time Spouse A names Spouse B to inherit the accounts. However, because Spouse A will be deemed to own all the securities until death, the full value of those securities would be included in Spouse A's gross estate for estate tax purposes.

PROPERTY TRANSFERS BETWEEN SPOUSES/DOMESTIC PARTNERS

Transfers made during a husband–wife marriage or incident to divorce do not trigger gain or loss recognition pursuant to Code Sec. 1041. Thus, any sale of property between husband and wife has no federal income tax effect.

> **EXAMPLE**
>
> John and Jane are husband and wife. John owned an office building prior to marrying Jane. The property had a fair market value of $300,000 and an adjusted basis of $180,000 in June 2009, at which time John sold the office building to Jane for $300,000. Because Code Sec. 1041 terms apply to the transfer, John does not recognize $120,000 of gain on the sale, and Jane takes the office building with an $180,000 basis.

This treatment would not apply to SSMCs and domestic partners who are not recognized as being married for federal tax purposes The nonrecognition may present both challenges and planning opportunities.

Taxation and Basis

On the challenge side, any sale of property between spouses/domestic partners would be a taxable transaction.

> **EXAMPLE**
>
> Jane and Katrina are an SSMC. Katrina owned an office building prior to marrying Jane. The office building had a fair market value of $300,000 and an adjusted basis of $180,000 in June 2009, at which time Katrina sells the office building to Jane for $300,000. Because Code Sec. 1041 does not apply, Katrina must recognize $120,000 of gain on the sale, and Jane takes the office building with a $300,000 basis.

Related-Party Relationship Not Applied

On the other hand, SSMCs and domestic partners are not subject to certain tax code provisions that disallow losses on sales between related parties (Code Sec. 267), or that recharacterize what would otherwise be capital gain on the sale of depreciable property to a related party as ordinary income (Code Sec. 1239).

The disallowance of losses on sales to related parties is designed to prevent a taxpayer from claiming a tax loss on property that may have temporarily declined in value, without actually relinquishing the taxpayer's investment in the asset. For this purpose, if the taxpayer sells the property to a *related party*, which includes members of the taxpayer's family (brothers and sisters by whole or half blood, spouse, ancestors, and lineal descendants) and certain related entities, the taxpayer is not considered to have relinquished the investment in the property because of the close connection between the taxpayer and the purchaser. Same-sex spouses/domestic partners are not, however, considered married for this purpose, which creates the ability for one spouse/domestic partner to sell property at a loss to the other spouse/domestic partner.

> ### EXAMPLE
>
> Elias and Farrell are an SSMC. Elias owned an office building prior to marrying Farrell. The office building had a fair market value of $180,000 and an adjusted basis of $300,000 in June 2009, at which time Elias sold the office building to Farrell for $180,000. Because Elias and Farrell are not considered spouses for purposes of Code Sec. 267, Elias can recognize $120,000 of loss on the sale.

On the gain side, Code Sec. 1239 recharacterizes what would otherwise be capital gain, from the sale of depreciable property, to ordinary income when the seller and purchaser of the asset are considered related parties. For this purpose *related parties* include:

- A corporation that an individual is deemed to control by owning more than 50 percent of the stock; or
- A partnership in which the individual is deemed to own more than 50 percent of the profits interests.

In determining stock and partnership interest ownership, any stock or partnership profits interests owned by members of an individual's family (brothers and sisters by whole or half blood, spouse, ancestors, and lineal descendants) is considered owned by the individual. This is referred to as *attribution*. However, because same-sex spouses/domestic partners are not considered members of an individual's family for this purpose, SSMCs and domestic partners are not burdened by attribution, and therefore have greater potential avoidance for Code Sec. 1239 recharacterization.

EXAMPLE

Luke and Polly are a husband and wife married couple living in a noncommunity property state, who together own all of the outstanding stock of Remco, a C corporation. Polly owns 25 percent and Luke owns 75 percent of the Remco shares. Polly also owns a depreciable office building that she acquired in her own name prior to the marriage. In June 2009 the office building had a fair market value of $300,000, and an adjusted basis of $180,000, at which time Polly sold the office building to Remco for $300,000. Although Polly only owns 25 percent of the Remco shares directly, she is deemed to own 100 percent of Remco by attribution because she is considered to own the shares owned by Luke. A sale of the building to Remco therefore triggers Code Sec. 1239 recharacterization, and Polly recognizes $120,000 of ordinary income, instead of $120,000 of capital gain on the sale.

COMMENT

If in the above example Luke and Polly had been an SSMC, Polly would only be considered to own 25 percent of the Remco stock because there would be no attribution from Luke. Thus, a sale by Polly of the office building to Remco would trigger $120,000 of capital gain.

There are also potential planning opportunities with respect to corporate stock. Similar to the rules of Code Sec. 1239, an individual is generally treated as owning the stock owned by his or her spouse, children (including adopted children), grandchildren, and parents (Code Sec. 318(a)(1)). SSMCs and domestic partners are not, however, considered to be related parties for federal income tax purposes, which also means there should be no attribution of stock between such individuals.

EXAMPLE

Joel and Kyle are an SSMC. Each owns 50 percent of the stock of JK Corporation. Joel redeems all of his stock in JK. Joel is entitled to consider such transaction as the equivalent of a sale pursuant to Code Sec. 302(b)(3). By contrast, if Joel and Kyle were treated as spouses for federal income tax purposes, by virtue of attribution Joel would still be considered to own 100 percent of JK following the redemption, whereupon Joel would be considered to have received a dividend for any cash or property received in exchange for the redeemed shares.

STUDY QUESTIONS

---

7. Gift tax issues arise for an SSMC in which one spouse makes a deemed gift to his or her partner because:

    a. The unlimited marital deduction does not insulate the recipient from gift tax as it would a husband–wife spouse

    b. Unless the gift is held in joint tenancy, the recipient is considered to have received a taxable gift

    c. Spouses and partners recognized as married under state but not federal law must maintain their assets as separate property

8. A federal tax-planning opportunity occurs for SSMCs and domestic partners for property transfers:

    a. Because related party rules for losses and recharacterized gains do not apply to SSMCs and domestic partners

    b. Because sale of property between SSMCs or domestic partners are nontaxable transactions

    c. When their separate gross incomes are relatively equal and the ordinary gains and losses offset each other on federal returns

---

ALIMONY

Given that an SSMC is not considered to be married for federal income tax purposes, presumably a divorce of such couple is similarly not acknowledged. Thus, any court-ordered alimony payments made by one same-sex spouse to the other would not be eligible to be deducted as alimony under Code Sec. 215.

For the alimony-receiving former spouse in such situation, alimony would likely have to be included in income, because the transfer would not be considered a "gift." This is similar to the treatment of "palimony" paid by one unmarried long-term partner to another partner as a result of a termination of the marriage-like relationship.

SOCIAL SECURITY BENEFITS, PENSIONS, AND NONSPOUSAL ROLLOVERS

Same sex spouses and domestic partners are not eligible for Social Security benefits both because they do not meet the definitions of *husband* and *wife* under the Social Security Act, and because DOMA prevents the recognition of these benefits for such spouses. If a child of an SSMC or domestic partnership is not deemed the biological or legal child of a deceased spouse/partner, that child will similarly not be entitled to Social Security child benefits.

Because DOMA prohibits recognition of same-sex marriage, an employer is not required to comply with a qualified domestic relations order (QDRO) from a state court in which a spouse is named as an alternate payee of a pension benefit.

For spouses in husband–wife marriages, Code Secs.402 and 408 provide that upon the death of a spouse owning an interest in an individual retirement account (IRA), 401(a) plan, 403(a) or (b) plan, or eligible 457(b) government plans, certain distributions from the plan may be rolled over tax free within 60 days into an IRA by the surviving spouse. By rolling over the distributions the surviving spouse is able to avoid being taxed on a distribution from the plan. The rules concerning rollovers from qualified plans have been expanded to allow certain similar rollovers to nonspouses (therefore including SMCC spouses and domestic partners) but only if the distribution is from a 401(a) plan, 403(a) or (b) plan, or eligible 457(b) government plans, and not from an IRA.

COMMUNITY PROPERTY LAWS AND SAME-SEX MARRIAGE

There are nine community property states: Arizona, California, Idaho, Louisiana, Nevada, New Mexico, Texas, Washington, and Wisconsin. In community property jurisdictions SSMCs and registered domestic partners are normally required to split their income, deductions, and withholding credits if filing separately, and report such income, together with the income from separate property, on their state income tax returns. Such rules will not apply, however, for purposes of their federal returns. The IRS instructs SSMCs and registered domestic partners in such jurisdictions to report only their own income, deductions, and withholding on their individual returns.

Because the IRS does not recognize the marriage, presumably the jointly held property owned by an SSMC will not be considered community property for purposes of either assessment *or* collection. For a husband–wife couple, the interests in community property owned by the spouse who incurred the tax debt (the debtor spouse) as well as that of the other spouse (the nondebtor spouse) may be taken by the IRS to satisfy the debtor spouse's tax liability. However, for an SSMC, if the nondebtor spouse's interest in property is not considered to be community property for federal tax purposes, it should not be able to be taken by the IRS to satisfy the tax obligations of the debtor spouse.

CAUTION

For state purposes, an SSMC and certain domestic partners must generally file a married filing separately or married filing joint return. In California—a community property state recognizing domestic partnerships and certain same-sex marriages—all community property is liable for the tax obligations of either spouse, including any premarital/prepartnership tax obligations. If a California return results in a refund, and one spouse/partner has an outstanding federal tax liability, such refund will be paid by California to the IRS pursuant to an agreement between the state and the IRS. From California's perspective this is consistent with recognizing the relationship and the resulting class of community property it generates. However, although the IRS should not regard such property as community property, given that it does not recognize SSMCs or domestic partners as being married, there has been no formal indication that this will be how the IRS will regard the property owned jointly by same-sex spouses/partners. Until such clarification is forthcoming, the safest alternative may be to advise such couples to adjust their state withholding and thereby not wind up filing a state refund return.

STUDY QUESTIONS

9. Which of the following is **not** allowed a tax-free rollover for non-spouses?

a. IRAs

b. Code Sec. 403(a) plan

c. Code Sec. 457(b) government plan

10. Because same-sex couples are not considered married under DOMA, community property rules do not apply to their federal tax liabilities, with the result that:

a. State taxing agencies must treat the couple's community property in the same manner as the IRS treats such assets

b. A nondebtor same-sex spouse's property should not be able to be taken by the IRS to satisfy the tax obligations of a debtor spouse

c. Both spouses must report income, deductions, and withholding for community property on their federal returns

CONCLUSION

For individuals in same-sex marriages and domestic partnerships, the nonconforming filing status and tax treatment under state and federal laws requires careful consideration and planning. Resulting strategies may ameliorate some, but not all, federal tax restrictions, whereas being "unrelated parties" under federal law may sometimes bring some tax benefits unavailable to couples considered "married" under federal law.

MODULE 3: NEW CHALLENGES FOR INDIVIDUALS — CHAPTER 8

Rebuilding Retirement Savings: Tax Strategies

This chapter explores some of the tax planning techniques that can help individuals rebuild their retirement portfolios following the recent an economic downturn. Special attention is given to the features and key tax saving benefits of different retirement vehicles, as well as certain tax minimization and savings strategies to help rebuild and maximize the value of individual retirement accounts (IRAs). The role of Social Security and pension plans in planning for retirement is also highlighted.

LEARNING OBJECTIVES

Upon completing this chapter, the student will be able to:

- Compare/contrast the different retirement planning vehicles and their tax advantages;
- Understand the tax benefits associated with various retirement savings plans;
- Describe the ways to maximize the value of traditional IRAs and Roth IRAs;
- Identify circumstances that may reduce the value of retirement accounts; and
- Understand new rules affecting retirement savings and plans.

INTRODUCTION

In turbulent financial markets and market downturns, individuals and retirees need to learn how to rebuild savings they have lost. When the markets take a significant battering for an extended period of time, individuals who are close to, or in, retirement suffer serious—if not permanent—damage. The current economic downturn has presided over the losses of substantial value of most retirement accounts, contributing to the decline of individuals' retirement savings by more than 40 percent in many cases. Those individuals not nearing retirement age should also take heed of the recent economic meltdown, learning lessons of diversification both in terms of investments and investment/retirement savings vehicles.

This chapter will examine how income from different types of retirement vehicles are taxed, as well as the different tax strategies that may help individuals and retirees rebuild their retirement savings after their serious market downturn has reduced their retirement portfolios.

GETTING STARTED

An economic downturn can affect most, if not all, retirement savings vehicles. The portfolios of individuals who rely on their 401(k) plan accounts, stock and securities investments, and other retirement plans to finance their retirement are often hard-hit by a bear market. Rebuilding a retirement portfolio during and after an economic downturn should begin with a reassessment of what retirement vehicles an individual has used, and the tax strategies that can help him or her rebuild savings. Individual retirees often receive income from a number of retirement vehicles, including Social Security, distributions from pensions, annuities, 401(k) s, IRAs, and other retirement plans. They also have income from stocks, bonds, certificates of deposit (CDs), and mutual funds held outside of any tax-sanctioned plan.

STOCK AND STOCK LOSSES IN A DOWN MARKET

The ups and downs in the value of a retirement savings account come in two basic flavors:
- Regular, taxable accounts; and
- Tax-deferred or tax-free accounts.

Although a solid retirement savings plan should consist of tax-deferred retirement accounts (or tax-free in the case of Roth IRAs or Roth 401(k) s), regular investment savings also typically form a portion of the savings that will be used for retirement. This taxable portion of a retirement savings strategy may be the result of:
- Wanting to save more than what is permitted under the maximum annual contribution limits allowed for qualified retirement accounts;
- Maintaining an "emergency fund" that grows without emergencies; and/or
- Inheriting assets.

Also added to the list of significant assets used for retirement is a primary residence and/or vacation home that appreciates over the years as its mortgage is paid off.

No matter how much trading is done in any one year in the tax-deferred or tax-free account, nothing is currently taxable or deductible to the individual owner. Instead, the overall value increases or decreases each year tax-free, with a taxable event only caused at the time account funds are distributed to the owner. In the meantime, neither the trustee nor the owner of that account recognizes taxable capital gains or losses, or dividend and interest income, from it.

A downturn in the market will undoubtedly lead to losses in individuals' stock portfolios. Although most stock values will turn around as the market eventually recovers, investors harvesting stock losses within a taxable portfolio can realize some immediate tax benefits through two approaches:

- Offsetting gains from other stocks that may have increased in value over the course of several years or more and that are sold; and
- Offsetting at least a portion of an individual's ordinary wage income.

Both approaches can serve to lower current tax liability and enable an individual to channel those savings back into the portion of his or her retirement savings nest egg outside of the tax-deferred environment of a qualified retirement plan and account.

Capital Losses

Most retirement savings strategies call for a combination of regular taxable accounts as well as tax-deferred or tax-free accounts. First, recall that tax-protected accounts have an annual contribution limit; additional savings accounts funded by bonuses, gifts, and inheritances are not uncommon. In addition, early withdrawal penalties imposed on withdrawals from tax-favored accounts create a good reason to create—in addition to tax-favored accounts—a more liquid, nonretirement fund for certain emergencies.

Netting gains and losses. Long-term and short-term capital losses can be used to offset capital gains that are recognized during the tax year (Code Sec. 1211(b)). Additionally, up to $3,000 of any net capital losses ($1,500 for married individuals filing separately) that remain after reducing capital gains by capital losses can be used to offset ordinary income in any one year. If net capital losses exceed this $3,000 annual deduction limit, the Internal Revenue Code allows individuals to carry forward the excess losses to the next year (Code Sec. 1212(b)(1)). Excess losses that are carried over are then netted against capitals gains in that year. Any excess loss can then again be deducted against ordinary income, up to the $3,000 maximum.

EXAMPLE

During the tax year, Toby earned $40,000 from his job as a teacher.

He also sold shares of stock with the resulting long-term and short-term gains and losses: A total of $15,000 long-term gain and $8,000 in long-term losses; $14,000 total short-term losses; and $2,000 in short-term gain.

As a result, Toby has a net $5,000 short-term capital loss ($12,000 short-term capital loss – $7,000 long-term capital gain), of which $3,000 can offset his wage income (bringing his income down to $37,000) and $2,000 may be carried forward as a net short-term capital loss into the next year.

COMMENT

Unlike business losses, personal capital losses—such as from the sale of stock—can only be carried forward. However, losses that occur as a result of a *natural disaster* can be carried back to a limited extent as a net operating loss. Such disasters, however, do not include a stock market crash or similar *financial* catastrophe.

DOWNTURN STRATEGIES

The practitioner can evaluate the following methods for managing capital gains:

- Consider selling stock to realize a net loss at least to the extent of $3,000 for the year in order to offset wage income that is taxed at the higher income tax rates. The current maximum tax rate on wage income is 35 percent, whereas net long-term capital gains are taxed at a maximum 15 percent rate;
- In selling stocks, remember that a net long-term capital loss for the year can offset the same $3,000 of ordinary income as a net short-term capital loss. Short-term capital losses, because they offset short-term capital gains that would otherwise be taxed at the regular income tax rates, are potentially more valuable if timed correctly. On the other hand, although net long term capital gains are taxed at a maximum 15 percent rate, net long-term capital losses can offset $3,000 in ordinary income for the year, taxable at a maximum 35 percent rate; and
- In figuring the total tax on activity within a taxable portfolio, the impact of dividend income should not be overlooked. Whereas qualifying dividends are taxed at the long-term capital gain rate, neither net long-term or short-term capital losses can offset them for tax purposes except to the extent of the $3,000 limit.

> **EXAMPLE**
>
> Allison Johnson has qualified dividend income of $5,000 and a net long-term capital loss of $7,000. The net long-term capital loss absorbs only $3,000 of her dividend income. The remaining $2,000 in dividend income is taxed at a maximum 15 percent rate, and Allison must carry the $4,000 balance of net-long-term capital loss forward into the next year.

STUDY QUESTIONS

1. In non-Roth tax-deferred retirement accounts, tax is:

   a. Due at the time of contribution
   b. Due at the time funds are distributed
   c. Never charged because funds are earmarked for retirement

2. Qualified dividend income is taxed at a maximum of _____ for 2009.

   a. 15 percent
   b. 20 percent
   c. 25 percent

ANNUITIES

Many investors saving for retirement in the financial downturn are facing the possibility that they may outlive their retirement savings, especially if another market collapse takes place in the future. Many such investors are turning to annuities for safety. Under an annuity contract, an individual makes a lump-sum or other front-end investment, typically with an insurance company, and receives periodic payments starting at a certain date, such as when the individual retires. In contrast to a life insurance policy, which pays a beneficiary an amount of money on the death of the insured, an annuity pays a specified amount of money until the death of the annuitant or the expiration of a fixed term. Typically, an annuity provides for lifetime payments, so the total amount of annuity payments depends on the life expectancy of the individual who bought the annuity.

Taxation of Annuities

An investment in an annuity contract can be made as a lump-sum premium payment or as a series of payments before the annuity benefit start date. An advantage to an annuity held outside of a traditional tax-favored retirement vehicle such as an IRA is that an individual does not have to use the money until he or she actually wants or needs it. With a traditional IRA, on the other hand, the money grows tax-deferred, but individuals must start making withdrawals by the time they reach age 70½. Those required IRA withdrawals, whether through an annuity or periodic distributions computed according to life expectancy, can affect an individual's tax situation at distribution time.

An individual who receives an annuity payment can exclude part of the payment from gross income because part of each payment received is considered to be a return of capital and, thus, tax-free. This excluded amount is the annuity payment received multiplied by an *exclusion ratio*. The exclusion ratio is determined by dividing the investment in the annuity by the expected return under the annuity.

When distributions are deferred, a variable annuity (one with an account value and payout or rate of return that varies according to the securities market in which it is invested) will not affect an individual's ability to claim various deductions or credits on his or her federal income tax return. When annuity distributions occur, they may be subject to the alternative minimum tax (AMT). Variable annuities also generally have restrictive withdrawal options, especially if the owner is younger than age 59½. These annuities may require surrender charges. Further, earnings withdrawn will be taxed at ordinary income tax rates.

Two significant tax considerations should be taken into account when an investor decides between investing in a taxable account versus an annuity:

- The relative tax rates on income generated by the investments, and
- The ability to defer income.

A distribution from an annuity is subject to ordinary income tax, whereas qualified dividends and long-term capital gains in a taxable account enjoy lower capital gains rate. Generally, individuals approaching retirement age or working on "rebuilding" their retirement portfolio in light of an economic downturn that may have wiped out (or substantially depressed) their portfolio's worth may want to allocate a larger part of their investments to fixed-income securities and a smaller portion to stocks in their taxable accounts.

DOWNTURN STRATEGY

Investment in a fixed annuity can help diversify a retirement portfolio, especially for an individual who may have a 401(k) or other retirement plan. For instance, if an individual has a below-average return on his or her investments in a 401(k), he or she can also rely on the guaranteed stream of income from the annuity.

Annuities in IRAs

Individuals can also choose to place their annuity funds in an IRA. This maneuver has both tax benefits and disadvantages. Placing an annuity in an IRA allows an individual's contributions to the IRA-annuity to be tax deductible (to the extent allowed under the tax code). This benefits the owner because money contributed directly into an annuity is nondeductible. However, the individual must be eligible to make deductible IRA contributions in the first place.

On the other hand, because both IRAs and annuities are income tax-deferred investment vehicles, there is no additional tax-deferral advantage available when an annuity is created within in an IRA. Moreover, when an annuity is created inside an IRA, the annuitant will be required to take required minimum distributions (RMDs) beginning no later than age 70½, whereas an individual who has a non-IRA annuity is not required to take distributions at any time, until he or she so desires. Additionally, there are contribution limits to IRAs but no limit on the amount that can be invested in a non-IRA annuity.

STUDY QUESTIONS

---

3. An advantage of variable annuity contracts for retirement income generally is:

  a. They provide lifetime payments, as opposed to life insurance policies

  b. The annuity payments are tax-free, unlike traditional IRA distributions

  c. Withdrawals are not subject to alternative minimum tax

4. An advantage of creating an annuity within a traditional IRA is:

  a. The annuity offers additional tax-deferral features at the time of contribution

  b. The maximum traditional IRA contribution may be deducted from gross income, whereas direct contributions to annuities are not

  c. The annuitant is not subject to the RMD rule generally applied to commencing IRA distributions

---

401(K) RETIREMENT PLANS

A Code Sec. 401(k) plan provides participants with the opportunity to elect to receive pay in cash or contribute the compensation to the plan's trust on a pretax basis. Elective employee contributions (the amounts the participant elects to contribute to his or her 401(k) account) are excluded from the employee's current gross income and invested on a tax-deferred basis in the plan's trust. Although employees' elective deferrals are not included in their current gross income, are not subject to income tax withholding at the time of deferral, and are not reflected the individual's Form 1040, they are, however, included as wages subject to Social Security, Medicare, and federal unemployment taxes.

A 401(k) plan may also offer an employer matching contribution arrangement. The tradeoff for not being taxed on 401(k) distributions, however, is that upon the employee's retirement distributions are taxed as ordinary income.

Elective Contributions

Elective contributions to a 401(k) plan are subject to an annual limit. The limit applies to the aggregate amount of all the elective deferrals made by the employee for the year to all plans, not just to each plan to which the employee makes deferrals. Matching contributions made by the employer to a 401(k) plan are not subject to the annual limit on an employee's own contributions to the plan. Individuals who will be at least age 50 by the end of the tax year may make additional *catch-up contributions* to most types of retirement plans, including 401(k)s.

Employees can elect to defer a certain amount of their income annually, which is adjusted for inflation each year. In 2009, for example, employees can choose to defer up to the lesser of 100 percent of eligible compensation or $16,500 ($22,000 if 50 or older). Additional catch-up elective contributions of up to $5,500 in 2009 are available for those 50 or older as well.

Employer Matching Contributions

Use of matching contributions. In an economic downturn, individuals' retirement plans suffer not only losses from a significant downward spiral in the market, but also the loss or reduction of discretionary employer matching contributions to a 401(k) plan. Employer matching contributions that are discretionary are not required by law, but many employers match employee deferrals because they know they are a key to attracting and retaining employees (Code Sec. 401(m)(4)(A)). For example, a common employer matching formula has been 50 percent of 401(k) employee deferral contributions, based on a maximum employee deferral rate of 3 percent of compensation. But during economic times that call for companies to cut costs, one of the ways to do so is to reduce or altogether eliminate employer matching.

Freezing traditional versus safe-harbor matching contributions. Employers can freeze or terminate "discretionary" matching contributions to traditional 401(k) plans, as opposed to "safe-harbor 401(k) plans" at any time. Many companies do so in difficult economic times.

However, employers with safe-harbor 401(k) plans who want to reduce or suspend 401(k) safe-harbor matching contributions must amend the plan to provide for the reduction or suspension, and to satisfy certain applicable nondiscrimination tests for the entire plan year. A safe harbor 401(k) plan is similar to a traditional 401(k) plan, but, among other things, it must provide for employer contributions that are fully vested when made. These contributions may be employer matching contributions, limited to employees who defer, or employer contributions made on behalf of all eligible employees, regardless of whether they make elective deferrals. The effective date of the amendment must be at least 30 days after the plan notifies affected employees of the suspension or reduction, and the plan must continue to make all safe-harbor matching contributions up to the amendment's effective date.

Roth 401(k) Plans

Employees may also want to consider the relatively new *Roth 401(k)* option. This type of retirement plan option was first allowed beginning in 2006. Under a Roth 401(k) plan, a 401(k) (or 403(b) plan) may permit an employee to irrevocably designate some or all of his or her elective contributions under the plan as designated Roth contributions. The Roth 401(k) plan is essentially a type of hybrid 401(k) and Roth IRA retirement plan in which employees may make after-tax contributions to *designated Roth accounts.* The after-tax contributions are in lieu of all or a portion of elective deferrals that the employee is otherwise allowed to make under their applicable retirement plan. The earnings on the designated Roth 401(k) account grow tax-free, and qualified distributions are not included in gross income either, just as with a regular Roth IRA. However, Roth 401(k) plans are not subject to the restrictive adjusted gross income (AGI) limit to which regular Roth IRA contributions are subject.

However, employer matching is not permitted with a Roth 401(k), and pretax elective contributions under a traditional 401(k) plan may not be converted to a designated Roth account. Additionally, employees cannot take a deduction for contributions to the Roth account, as may be permitted with a traditional 401(k) plan. Thus, if an employee has both plans—a traditional 401(k) and a Roth 401(k) with equal amounts of money—the Roth 401(k) may be of greater value because earnings grow tax-free and distributions at retirement are tax-free as well.

STUDY QUESTIONS

---

5. An advantage of Roth 401(k) plans in 2009 is:

    a. For 2009 only, employees may deduct their contributions to a Roth 401(k) just as to a traditional 401(k) plans

    b. Roth 401(k) plans are not subject to the AGI limit applied to Roth IRA contributions

    c. Employer matching limits are higher with a Roth 401(k)

6. Employees may convert their elective contributions in traditional 401(k) accounts to Roth 401(k)s as long as funds are transferred to designated Roth accounts. *True or False?*

401(k) Hardship Distributions

During economic downturns, individuals may need to consider alternative sources of financing to reach their goals, make their mortgage or rent payments or pay other common monthly bills. An alternative source of financing may include the tapping of their retirement. There are three general ways that funds from a 401(k) can be withdrawn:

- Regular distributions;
- Hardship withdrawals; and
- Plan loans.

Many employers have adopted 401(k) plan provisions that permit employees to borrow money from their 401(k) account.

Eligibility for withdrawals. A hardship distribution from a 401(k) can be made only if made on account of an immediate and heavy financial need of the employee and a distribution is necessary to satisfy the financial need (Reg. §1.401(k)-1(d)(3)(i)). The amount distributed cannot exceed the amount of the employee's total elective contributions (plus earnings). Hardship distributions are further allowed only if, and to the extent, provided under the plan document. In the *Pension Protection Act of 2006* (P.L. 109-280), Congress directed the IRS to modify its regulations regarding hardship distributions from 401(k) plans for expenses relating to medical, tuition, and funeral expenses for a primary beneficiary under the plan, just as the distribution would be allowed for the accountholder.

    Hardship distributions are not tax-free. They are taxed to the recipient as ordinary income and are subject to income tax withholding. In addition, they may be subject to the 10 percent early withdrawal penalty if the reason for the withdrawal is not among those sanctioned for exemption.

Qualifying expenses. Types of expenses that qualify as a hardship distribution and are excepted from the additional 10 percent penalty include (Reg. §401(k)-1(d)(3)(iii)(B)):

- Medical expenses that exceed 7.5 percent of adjusted gross income (AGI) (Code Sec. 72(t)(2)(B));
- Qualifying first-time homebuyer purchases (capped at $10,000) (Code Sec. 72(t)(2)(F));
- Qualified higher education expenses (Code Secs. 72(t)(2)(E) and 72(t)(7));
- Disability (an individual is disabled if he or she is unable to engage in any substantial gainful activity by reason of a medically determinable physical or mental impairment that can be expected to result in death or to be of continuing and indefinite duration) (Code Sec. 72(t)(2)(A)(iii);
- Expenses to prevent or delay eviction or foreclosure with respect to a principal residence; and
- Expenses to pay for the repair of casualty damage to the employee's principal residence.

DOWNTURN STRATEGY

The tough rules for hardship withdrawals try to reserve such withdrawals as an option of last resort for participants...and they should be. The drawbacks of a hardship withdrawal are significant, all resulting in a permanently reduced retirement nest egg, as described here:

- An individual who takes a hardship withdrawal from his or her 401(k) is prohibited from making any contributions to the plan for at least six months;
- Income tax is due on the withdrawn amount, regardless of whether an early withdrawal penalty is also due;
- Makeup payments later on to build the account back up are not allowed; once that amount is withdrawn, it is not allowed back into the account and, therefore, foregoes the benefits of tax-deferred growth on that amount until retirement;
- The extent to which creditors can touch 401(k) assets and other retirement savings is generally a matter of individual states' laws, which vary. Declaring bankruptcy is of course an option to hardship withdrawals that has its own set of drawbacks; and
- Alternatively, declaring "insolvency" under the tax law when a creditor forgives a debt, wholly or partially, will help the individual avoid having to declare taxable income on that debt. However, under the insolvency exclusion of Code Sec. 108 the IRS generally insists on counting retirement assets in determining whether total liabilities of a particular taxpayer exceed total liabilities immediately before the debt in question is forgiven.

In addition to hardship distributions from 401(k) plans, individuals may also consider taking a loan from their 401(k) account when an economic downturn has limited their financing options. Like 401(k) hardship distributions, borrowing from a 401(k) plan also has financial and tax disadvantages. However, they do provide a viable option as long as the participant understands the parameters of the loan.

401(k) Plan Loans

Rules for taking a loan. A 401(k) plan document must provide for plan loans before they are allowed. A plan is not required to contain a loan provision. Generally, individuals can borrow up to 50 percent of the value of their vested benefit in a 401(k), or $50,000, whichever amount is less (Code Sec. 72(p)(2)(A)). Despite withdrawing the funds, the individual remains vested in the account, subject to the individual's obligation to repay the loan. Interest rates on loans are generally lower then many bank loans, and in this financial downturn, qualifying for a loan under a 401(k) plan is more likely, even for those with "bad" credit scores.

If certain requirements are not met, the loan from the 401(k) is treated as a premature distribution for tax purposes, subject to current income tax at ordinary rates, plus a 10 percent early withdrawal penalty on the amount distributed. Additionally, interest on a 401(k) plan loan is not deductible.

An individual must repay the loan within five years, subject to only one exception for plan loans used to make a first-time home purchase (for a principal residence, not a vacation or secondary home), which allows for a loan term as long as 30 years (Code Sections 72(p)(2)(B)(i) and (ii)). Loan repayments must be made at least quarterly, and are generally automatically deducted from the individual's paycheck.

Consequences of nonpayment. If an individual is unable to repay the loan and defaults, the IRS treats the outstanding loan balance as a premature distribution, subject to income tax and the 10-percent early withdrawal penalty.

Further, most plan terms require that the individual repay the entire remaining balance of the loan within 60 days if he or she leaves his or her job or is terminated. In a recession or economic downturn, when unemployment rates rise, this 60-day loan repayment provision can be significantly financially problematic if individuals lose their job. The remaining 401(k) balance, after income taxes and penalties are paid, may not be enough to cover the loan, creating a nightmare of cascading tax liability.

There are other significant tax and financial consequences to consider before a participant takes a loan from a 401(k). Often, many plans contain provisions that prohibit the employee or his or her employer from making contributions to the 401(k) until the loan is repaid, or for up to 12 months after the loan distribution. As such, the individual is not saving for retirement during the time the loan is being repaid and also may be forgoing matching contributions from an employer.

Additionally, the money borrowed will only earn the interest the individual pays on the loan. Typically, on a 401(k) loan, plan administrators use an interest rate of one to two percentage points above prime interest rates. Although the individual may believe paying a lower interest rate to himself or herself is better than paying a higher interest rate to a bank, that difference does not eliminate the disadvantages. The money the person uses to pay him or herself interest is taxed in his or her paycheck currently, then later when it is distributed from the plan in retirement as ordinary income. There is no relief currently from these provisions, so individuals should proceed cautiously when considering a loan from their 401(k), especially during an economic downturn.

DOWNTURN STRATEGY

Generally, commercial lenders will not accept a 401(k) plan account as collateral for a loan. Because the price for timely nonpayment of a 401(k) loan includes a 10-percent early withdrawal penalty, whereas a hardship withdrawal may not, an outright hardship withdrawal may be preferable when there is an immediate need and other resources are limited. More difficult to advise, however, are those participants who took out a 401(k) loan during the days of easy money and perhaps "invested" the proceeds in an asset that has itself now declined in value. Generally, those investment losses are capital losses that will not be able to offset the ordinary income realized from default on the loan.

Required Minimum Distributions from 401(k) Accounts

When an individual reaches age 70½ he or she must begin receiving required minimum distributions (RMDs) from his or her 401(k) account. Individuals must generally withdraw their first annual RMDs from their 401(k) by April 1 of the calendar year following the year in which the accountholder reaches ages 70 ½ or the calendar year in which the participant retires. However, the plan administrator can mandate that the participant begin taking RMDs from the 401(k) by April 1 of the year after the individual reaches age 70½.

Rollovers of distributions already made. The *Worker, Retiree and Employer Recovery Act of 2008* (WRERA) suspended RMDs for 2009 to give retirees a chance to keep more money in their retirement accounts in the hope of earning some of it back when the markets improved later in the year. Congress passed WRERA in late 2008, however, giving plan sponsors little time to adjust to the RMD suspension. The IRS reported it has received many questions from plan sponsors. Some sponsors wanted to give participants and beneficiaries the choice whether to continue or stop 2009 RMDs, but the sponsors could not act quickly. They have also questioned if they may offer direct rollovers when certain types of distributions include 2009 RMDs.

To provide relief from the tight deadlines, the IRS announced in September 2009 that it would allow taxpayers who took a required minimum distribution (RMD) from an IRA or certain retirement plans at any time in 2009 to retroactively take advantage of the 2009 RMD waiver opportunity by rolling over the distribution tax-free back into a tax-deferred account, if the individuals elect to do so through November 30, 2009 (or, under normal rules, within 60 days from the date of the distribution, if later). Alternatively, distributions that include 2009 RMDs from a plan could instead be rolled back into the same plan if the plan permits such rollovers. The IRS also issued sample plan amendments that plan sponsors may adopt to either stop or continue 2009 RMDs.

Other distribution rules. The required distribution from a 401(k) plan cannot be satisfied by taking a distribution from another plan. When a participant's 401(k) account balance is to be distributed, the plan administrator must determine the minimum amount required to be distributed to each calendar year. RMDs are discussed in greater detail later, as they relate to traditional IRAs.

As mentioned above, a recently permitted option under the tax law that is growing in popularity is the Roth 401(k). Contributions to a Roth 401(k), which is usually supplemental to a regular 401(k) up to the regular contribution limits, are made with after-tax dollars, but their withdrawal, as well as earnings attributable to those contributions, are not subject to tax at all…ever. In addition to being tax-free, one other powerful advantage of this plan type to those individuals older than age 70½ is that no required minimum distribution rules apply.

PLANNING POINTER

The full amount of the funds in a Roth 401(k) may therefore be left in the account and can continue to earn tax-free income until the retiree needs it, or until the retiree passes it to his or her heirs income tax-free at death.

STUDY QUESTIONS

---

7. Loans from a 401(k) plan account generally have a cap of 50 percent of the account's vested value or _____, whichever is less.

   a. $15,000

   b. $50,000

   c. $75,000

8. If an individual having a traditional 401(k) plan account acts before November 30, 3009, the IRS will allow him or her to:

   a. Roll over an RMD already taken for 2009 back into the traditional plan account

   b. Double the RMD for 2009 by taking a second distribution

   c. Roll over the RMD into a Roth 401(k) account

INDIVIDUAL RETIREMENT ACCOUNTS

Traditional IRAs

An *individual retirement account (IRA)* is a trust or custodial account set up for the exclusive benefit of an individual and/or his or her beneficiaries (Code Sec. 408). A *traditional IRA is* any IRA that is not a Roth IRA, a SEP, or a SIMPLE IRA. It may be an individual retirement account or annuity. An individual can establish and contribute to a traditional IRA if he or she has received taxable compensation for the year and has not reached age 70½ by the end of the year. IRA contributions by eligible participants in another retirement plan, however, are limited based upon participants' adjusted gross income.

Deductible contributions. Contributions to a traditional IRA are generally deductible. The deduction is taken from gross income to compute AGI. However, if the individual has attained age $70^1/_2$ before the end of the year for which the contribution is made, the contribution is not deductible. The amount of IRA deductible contributions is generally limited to the lesser of the individual's taxable compensation for the year or a specific dollar amount (e.g. $5,000 for 2009) (Code Sec. 408(o)). In general, a combined compensation limit applies for married couples filing jointly, so that the lower-earning spouse can take the other spouse's compensation into account in calculating the contribution limit.

The deduction for contributions made to a traditional IRA is phased out if an individual is an active participant (or eligible to be an active participant) in an employer's retirement plan for any part of the year, or the individual's modified AGI exceeds a specific amount (Code Sec. 219(g)). The applicable modified AGI limit depends on an individuals' filing status and generally increases annually. For example, in 2009 the phaseout began at a modified AGI of $55,000 for single individuals and $89,000 for married couples filing jointly. However, an individual, including an individual who is not able to fully deduct a contribution made to a traditional IRA, may be able to make nondeductible contributions to a Roth IRA.

DOWNTURN STRATEGY

Taxpayers who have lost their jobs during the year may be able to continue making contributions to an IRA. If a terminated employee has participated in a 401(k) plan, the 401(k) contribution limits also apply toward the maximum allowable contributions that would be permitted if he or she landed another job having a 401(k) plan in the same tax year. If the terminated employee has self-employment income during months otherwise unemployed, the maximum $5,000 IRA contribution limit would apply for deductible IRA contributions, but subject to the overall AGI limits for the year. That AGI amount includes all income for the year, including earned income as an employee, self-employment revenues, investment income, etc.

Nondeductible IRA contributions. An individual is permitted to make nondeductible contributions to an IRA. The amount of nondeductible contributions made for any tax year, however, cannot exceed the excess of the maximum contribution limit ($5,000 for 2009) over the amount of deductible contributions the individual is permitted to make for the same year. A taxpayer who makes both deductible and nondeductible contributions to an IRA must calculate the taxable and nontaxable portion of distributions when distributions begin.

Neither deductible nor nondeductible contributions can be made to a traditional IRA beginning in the year in which the individual turns 70½. However, Roth IRA contributions can be made as long as the individual has taxable compensation and AGI below a specified threshold.

Distributions. Distributions from a traditional IRA are taxed as ordinary income (Code Sec. 408(d)(1)). Once an individual reaches age 59½, distributions can be made from a traditional IRA without penalty. However, individuals who do not need to take distributions and can afford to leave their assets in the IRA account will benefit even more as the funds continue to grow. However, when an individual reaches age 70½, he or she is required to begin taking distributions from a traditional IRA (Code Sec. 401(a)(9)). These required minimum distributions (RMDs) are not required of Roth IRA owners, however. (RMDs are discussed in greater detail below.)

Premature distributions. If an individual takes a nonqualified distribution from his or her traditional IRA before reaching age 59½, he or she may be subject to a premature withdrawal penalty of 10 percent of the amount withdrawn, in addition to paying the income tax on the distribution. The tax on early distributions is reported on Form 5329, *Additional Taxes on Qualified Plans (Including IRAs and Other Tax Favored Accounts)*. However, there is no 10 percent additional penalty for *qualified distributions*.

IRA hardship distributions. The concept of hardship distributions based on financial need for purposes of distributions from 401(k) (as well as 403(b), 457, and 409A) plans does not carry over to IRA early withdrawals. Instead, certain events and expenses qualify for lifting the penalty, whether or not these circumstances precede a financial hardship. These events and expenses include hardship withdrawals for:

- Qualified higher education expenses;
- Qualified first-time homebuyer expenses (up to $10,000);
- Medical expenses in excess of 7.5 percent of AGI;
- Disability;
- Payment of health insurance premiums by certain unemployed individuals;
- Satisfaction of an IRS levy;
- A one-time rollover distribution to a health savings account (HSA);
- Reservists called to active duty for more than 179 days or an indefinite period; and
- Periodic payments made as part of a series of substantially equal periodic payments that are made at least annually and over the life or life expectancy of the individual or the joint lives or joint life expectancies of the individual and his designated beneficiary (Code Sec. 72(t)(2)(A)(iv).

PLANNING POINTER

A distribution after age 59½ is not considered premature.

However, once periodic payments begin, the individual cannot modify the payments in amount or duration within five years from the date the first distribution is made (for reasons other than death or disability). The 10-percent early withdrawal penalty tax applies if the method changes from the method requiring equal payments to a method that does not qualify for the exception to the tax.

Once an eligible hardship withdrawal is taken and 60 days have passed (two years for reservists), the withdrawn amount cannot be recontributed as an additional contribution after the individual accountholder gets back on his or her feet. In effect, the tax-deferred growth of those assets is foregone.

Withdrawal of prior contribution. The amount of any contribution that is distributed from an IRA before the due date, including extensions, of the return of the individual who made the contribution may be treated as an amount not contributed. The amount is not considered contributed if no deduction has been allowed for the contribution, and the net income attributable to the contribution is also distributed.

DOWNTURN STRATEGY

IRA account holders who suddenly find themselves unemployed, underemployed, underwater while they are subject to an adjustable rate mortgage, or otherwise in need of cash should consider taking back contributions made earlier in the year. They should clearly tell the bank or other trustee the nature of the withdrawal so an incorrect Form 1099-R is not sent to the IRS that would require additional explanations to avoid assessment of a 10 percent early withdrawal penalty. Unlike IRAs, however, contributions to a 401(k) or other employer-sponsored plan cannot be withdrawn after being made. Hardship withdrawals present the only avenue to relief for removing funds. Contributions made to a 401(k) plan that is rolled over into an IRA in the same year because the employee leaves employment also cannot be taken back without satisfying the hardship withdrawal tests.

Required Minimum Distributions

When an individual reaches age 70½ he or she cannot make contributions to a traditional IRA and must instead begin receiving required minimum distributions (RMDs) (Code Sec. 401(a)(9)). Individuals must start taking annual RMDs from their traditional IRAs by April 1 of the calendar year following the year in which the accountholder reaches age 70½. Failure to take the RMD exposes the individual to an excise tax of 50 percent of the excess of the amount that should have been withdrawn over the amount actually withdrawn. RMDs are calculated based on the account's balance as of the last business day (December 31) of the year prior to the year for which the RMD must be made.

PLANNING POINTER

Roth IRAs are not subject to the RMD rules. This RMD exception is so attractive to some retirees who don't need to immediately withdraw funds that they find it advantageous to convert traditional IRAs into Roth IRAs, even though income tax is due on the converted balance. For 2010 only, the tax law allows the income generated from any Roth conversion to be deferred and spread out between 2011 and 2012. This deferred tax, along with eliminating RMDs, will prompt many more conversions in 2010.

Lump-sum versus periodic distributions. Individuals generally may elect to take a lump-sum distribution, up to the full value of their account, from their retirement account in lieu of annual distributions, without penalty and at any time. However, the usual recognition of ordinary income on the taxable amount withdrawn remains. The entire value of the amount withdrawn will be included in taxable income as ordinary income in the year the money is withdrawn. As such, for many accountholders the recognition of ordinary income on the lump-sum distribution creates a financial disincentive for choosing this option.

RMDs have been suspended for 2009, under the *Worker, Retiree, and Employer Recovery Act of 2008*. The excise tax for not taking an RMD is also waived. Forgoing an RMD is elective, however, and individuals may choose to continue taking such distributions.

By late September 2009, the IRS acknowledged that the 2009 RMD waiver option may have taken many retirees and plan administrator by surprise, without adequate time to weigh the pros and cons of the option and act accordingly. In response, the IRS provided further relief from the deadline as well as easy ways to undo an RMD already paid out. Thus, taxpayers who took a required minimum distribution from an IRA or certain retirement plans at any time in 2009 were allowed to retroactively take advantage of the 2009 RMD waiver opportunity by rolling over the distribution tax-free back into a tax-deferred account, through November 30, 2009 (or, under normal rules, within 60-days from the date of the distribution, if later). Alternatively, distributions that include 2009 RMDs from a plan could instead be rolled back into the same plan if the plan makes arrangements to permit such rollovers. To facilitate relief, the IRS also issued sample plan amendments that plan sponsors may adopt to either stop or continue 2009 RMDs.

DOWNTURN STRATEGY

Not taking an RMD gives the account holder a chance to build up the account a bit more.

The lifting of RMDs for 2009 also has an indirect benefit in Roth rollover situations. Rollover of an RMD is prohibited. An individual who reached at least age 70½ by the end of the calendar year may not convert an amount distributed from a non-Roth IRA during that year to a Roth IRA before receiving his or her RMD with respect to the non-Roth account for the year of conversion. To be eligible for a conversion, the amount first must be eligible for rollover. This pitfall is therefore removed in 2009 by the temporary suspension of RMDs.

Effect of market decline on RMDs. The amount of a RMD is computed individually for each traditional IRA, when an individual owns more than one account. However, RMD amounts for each separate traditional IRA may be totaled and the aggregated RMD amount may be paid out from any one, or more, of the individual's traditional IRAs.

DOWNTURN STRATEGY

This RMD rule provides owners of multiple IRAs a certain flexibility in choosing the account(s) from which their RMD is taken. For instance, an individual with an IRA that comprises investments in stocks or mutual fund shares whose price has dropped due to market conditions can take the RMD instead from another IRA invested in a certificate of deposit CD that is set to mature in the near future. This move avoids selling the battered investments at market low and losing their future appreciation potential.

EXAMPLE

In 2008 Kelly O'Reilly had two separate traditional IRA accounts. The RMD from IRA X is $8,000. The RMD from IRA Y is $5,000. Kelly may take the total $13,000 RMD from either IRA X or IRA Y, or she may take distributions from both as long as the total IRA distribution payout is at least $13,000 for the year.

The rule allowing traditional IRA amounts to be aggregated for RMD purposes does not apply to IRAs held by beneficiaries; it applies only to the IRA owner.

IRA Losses

Losses on investments held in a traditional IRA, funded only by deductible contributions, are not recognized when the investments are sold within the account. If all amounts are distributed from his or her IRA, the accountholder cannot deduct a loss because there is presumed to be a zero basis in the account. On the other hand, if an individual makes nondeductible traditional IRA contributions and liquidates *all* of his or her traditional IRAs, a loss is recognized if the amounts distributed are less than the remaining unrecovered basis in the traditional IRAs. A loss in a traditional IRA is claimed on Schedule A, Form 1040, as a miscellaneous itemized deduction subject to the 2-percent AGI floor.

EXAMPLE

During 2008, Cheryl Swenson made $2,000 in nondeductible contributions to a traditional IRA. Her basis in the IRA at the end of 2008 is $2,000. During 2008, the IRA earned $400 in dividend income and Cheryl withdrew $600 from the account. As a result, at the end of 2008 the value of her IRA was $1,800 ($2,000 contributed + $400 dividends – $600 withdrawal). Cheryl computes and reports the taxable portion of her $600 withdrawal and her remaining basis on Form 8606, *Nondeductible IRA.*

In 2009, Cheryl's IRA lost $500 in value. At the end of 2009, her IRA balance was $1,300 ($1,800 balance at the end of 2009 – the $500 loss). Her remaining basis in the IRA was $1,500 ($2,000 nondeductible contributions – the $500 basis in the prior withdrawal). She withdrew the $1,300 balance remaining in the IRA. Cheryl can claim a loss of $200 (her $1,500 basis – the $1,300 withdrawn) on her Schedule A. The allowable loss is subject to the 2-percent floor on miscellaneous itemized deductions.

DOWNTURN STRATEGY

Individuals who made significant nondeductible contributions to an IRA during the last few years and who may be thinking of withdrawing the entire balance in all of their traditional IRAs before the end of the year in order to recognize a loss, should keep in mind that doing so will mean losing the opportunity to defer gain if the value of the investments in the accounts increases. Those withdrawn amounts cannot be recontributed at a later date. If they are placed in another IRA in a qualifying rollover transaction, on the other hand, no taxable event occurs and no loss deduction results.

STUDY QUESTIONS

9. An individual having one or more traditional IRA accounts:
  a. May make contributions as long as he or she has earned income
  b. Must begin taking required minimum distributions when he or she turns 70½ years old
  c. May contribute the $5,000 maximum to both a deductible and a nondeductible IRA accounts annually

10. A loss in a traditional IRA account:
  a. Is claimed on the individual's tax return in the year the loss occurs regardless of when distributions occur
  b. Is recognized if the entire nondeductible IRA account is liquidated
  c. Is recognized upon rollover to another traditional IRA

ROTH IRAs

A *Roth IRA* is a type of individual retirement account sometimes referred to as a "back-ended IRA" because its tax benefits occur when the individual takes distributions, not at the time he or she makes contributions to the account. Unlike a traditional IRA, contributions to a Roth IRA are never tax deductible (Code Sec. 408(A)(c)). However, interest, dividends, and appreciation accrue in a Roth IRA tax-free and qualified distributions are completely free from federal income tax as well.

Contributions

Contributions to Roth IRA may initially seem counterintuitive to those looking to rebuild their retirement savings most efficiently. After all, contributors to a regular IRA get a deduction in the amount of their contribution. Viewed from other angles, however, there are two possible advantages depending on the individual's situation. First, annual contributions to traditional and Roth IRAs are limited to the same combined $5,000. If someone has the available cash to contribute the full $5,000 without getting a tax deduction that effectively is "spent" elsewhere, a Roth IRA contribution in effect "spends" that potential tax deduction on the future: when distributions are made tax-free both from the initial contribution and the earnings from it; and when distributions can be delayed after retirement for as long as the individual wants to hold the balance in the Roth IRA.

Eligible individuals may make two types of contributions to a Roth IRA: an annual contribution and a conversion contribution.

Annual contributions. The annual contribution amount that an individual can make to a Roth IRA shares the same limit imposed on traditional IRAs. The maximum contribution that can be made in 2009 by an individual to both a traditional and Roth IRA is $5,000. Individuals age 50 or older by the end of the year can make catch-up contributions of up to $1,000 in 2009 as well.

Unlike traditional IRAs, individuals can continue to make contributions to a Roth account even after reaching age 70½, provided the taxpayer has earned income (Code Sec. 408(c)(4)). This allows an individual's account to continue to grow, tax-free.

DOWNTURN STRATEGY

Given the increased life expectancies to well over age 70½, retirees should preserve account balances as long as possible without withdrawals to take advantage of the tax-free growth and tax-free distribution of that growth available only through a Roth IRA. Not only should existing Roth IRAs be left untouched if possible, conversion of existing traditional IRAs to Roth IRAs should be considered to the extent those funds are not needed immediately after retirement by those now around retirement age.

Conversion contributions. Until 2010, eligibility to convert a traditional IRA to a Roth IRA depends on a taxpayer's adjusted gross income (AGI) and filing status. If a taxpayer's AGI exceeds $100,000, he or she has been ineligible to make Roth contributions. Joint return filers are held to the same $100,000 AGI limit based on their *combined* income. Additionally, individuals who filed their return as married filing separately also have not been able convert their accounts at all. However, these restrictions are permanently lifted for 2010 and beyond.

A conversion contribution is made by moving assets from a traditional IRA to a Roth IRA. Although income tax must be paid on the amount converted and is subject to ordinary income tax rates, the amounts in the Roth IRA attributable to the conversion receive the same favorable tax treatment as amounts that have been contributed directly to the Roth IRA. An individual can convert the entire amount in his or her traditional IRA, or only part of the amount, to a Roth IRA.

PLANNING POINTER

Both annual and conversion contributions must be accounted for on Form 8606, *Nondeductible IRAs,* with the IRS at the time of a distribution. Although annual and conversion contributions can be made to the same Roth IRA, the law treats conversion contributions differently from annual contributions, requiring separate accounting.

Distributions

Qualified distributions. Qualified distributions, as well as returns of capital contributions (subject to holding period requirements) from a Roth IRA are not includible in income or subject to the 10 percent early withdrawal penalty. A qualified distribution can be made after five taxable years beginning with the first taxable year for which the individuals contributed any amount to a Roth IRA. Each Roth IRA owner has only one five-year period for purposes of determining qualified distributions (Reg. §1.408A-6). The five-year period begins with the first tax year for which a contribution is made for any Roth IRA (Code Sec. 408A(d)(2)(B)). A conversion of a traditional IRA into a Roth IRA after the five-year period has begun will not start the running of a new five-year period for purposes of determining whether the distribution is a qualified distribution.

EXAMPLE

If an individual contributes to a Roth IRA on June 5, 2010, the five-year mandatory holding period would begin on January 1, 2010, and end on December 31, 2014.

Under Code Sec. 408(d)(2), a Roth IRA distribution will be treated as a *qualified distribution* after the five-year holding period has passed and may be made upon the occurrence of any one of the following:

On or after the date the individual turns age 59½ (Code Sec. 408(d)(2)(A)(i));

- To a beneficiary or to the estate of the IRA owner's estate on or after the death of the IRA owner (Code Sec. 408(d)(2)(ii);
- As a result of the individual becoming disabled (as defined under Code Sec. 72(m)(7)) (Code Sec. 408(d)(2)(iii)); or
- For a qualified first-time home purchase.

Nonqualified distributions. Withdrawals made from a Roth IRA that are not qualified distributions are subject to a 10-percent early withdrawal tax under Code Sec. 72(t), federal income tax on any appreciation of assets deemed withdrawn, and possible state and local income tax.

No required minimum distributions. Roth IRA accountholders are not required to take minimum distributions from a Roth IRA, unlike required distributions from traditional IRAs.

PLANNING POINTER

The full amount of the funds in a Roth IRA may therefore be left in the account and can continue to earn tax-free income until the retiree needs it, or until the retiree passes it to his or her heirs income tax-free at death.

STUDY QUESTIONS

11. Contributions to a Roth IRA are never tax deductible. *True or False?*

12. A conversion contribution from a traditional IRA to a Roth IRA:

    a. Is tax-free after remaining in the traditional IRA for five years
    b. Is subject to limits on the individual's AGI in 2009
    c. May be comingled with an existing Roth account

Roth IRA Losses

When an individual has losses on Roth IRA investments, he or she can only recognize the loss for income tax purposes if and when *all* the amounts in the Roth IRA accounts have been distributed and the total distributions are less than the individual's basis (e.g., regular and conversion contributions). This is the same rule followed when nondeductible contributions are made to a traditional IRA.

To report a loss in a Roth IRA, all the Roth IRAs (but not traditional IRAs) owned by an individual must be liquidated. The loss is an ordinary loss for income tax purposes, and can only be claimed as a miscellaneous itemized deduction subject to the 2-percent of AGI floor that applies to certain miscellaneous itemized deductions on Schedule A, Form 1040.

EXAMPLE

At the beginning of 2009, Jon Thompson's Roth IRA balances are $10,000, of which $6,000 is attributed to earnings and $4,000 is attributed to contributions. Because Roth IRA contributions are nondeductible, all contributions are considered after-tax amounts (basis amounts). During 2009, Jon's Roth IRA investments lost $2,000 in value, leaving him with a balance of $8,000. This amount is more than his basis ($4,000) in his Roth. If Jon withdraws his entire Roth IRA balance ($8,000), he will not be able to include the losses on his tax return because his remaining balance is more, not less, than his basis ($4,000).

DOWNTURN STRATEGY

The following may help to address issues from the recent hit Roth accounts experienced:

- Because all Roth IRAs must be completely terminated to generate a loss deduction, it generally provides small comfort for investments gone very bad. Generally, closing all Roth IRAs forgoes future appreciation on that amount. If the account balance is larger than a few years of maximum contributions, it is not worth the tax benefit of taking the loss unless the loss amount is very large in comparison. Ironically, possible future appreciation may no longer be a goal because of the account holder's age. (Elderly taxpayers as a group do not itemize deductions as frequently and, therefore, would not benefit from Roth IRA losses); and

- Unlike 401(k) plans under which loans may be made to the extent of a participant's account balance, no loans are allowed against IRAs. If an IRA account holder needs funds and his or her only source is the IRA, a distribution—as small in size as possible—is the individual's only alternative. Withdrawals first should be made from any Roth IRA because as it is net of taxes, less money needs to be taken from the IRA environment.

CONVERTING A TRADITIONAL IRA TO A ROTH IRA

Potential Benefits from Conversion

An IRA conversion enables individuals with a traditional IRA to switch to a Roth IRA. The conversion occurs by rolling over the funds from a traditional IRA account into a Roth IRA account. However, a conversion is not a nontaxable event. The amount switched to a Roth IRA is added to the owner's taxable income for the year. Thereafter, the individual possesses all the benefits of the Roth IRA, such as nontaxable growth and distributions. An individual can convert his or her traditional IRA to a Roth for any reason.

When the value of an individual's traditional IRA drops dramatically because of a market downturn, the potential tax benefits of converting to a Roth IRA are often highlighted as a way to soften the blow of tax-deferred retirement losses.

Special Traditional IRA-to-Roth IRA Conversions

Beginning in 2010, anyone can convert his or her traditional IRA to a Roth IRA, regardless of the accountholder's AGI or filing status. The *Tax Increase Prevention and Reconciliation Act of 2005* (TIPRA) eliminates the $100,000 AGI ceiling for converting a regular IRA to a Roth IRA for the 2010 tax year and tax years thereafter. The AGI limit, in addition to filing status preclusions, prevented taxpayers with AGIs of $100,000 or more, or married couples filing jointly, from contributing to, or converting to, a Roth IRA. Individuals can choose to convert only part of the funds in a traditional IRA into a Roth account. Conversion is not an "all or nothing" transaction, and there is no requirement that the *entire* IRA be converted to a Roth account.

Individuals who convert in 2010 (and 2010 only) can elect to recognize the conversion income in 2010 or recognize it ratably in 2011 and 2012. Amounts converted from a traditional IRA to a Roth IRA are subject to ordinary income tax. Therefore, if individuals convert plans in 2010, they can choose to recognize the conversion amount in ordinary income ratably in 2011 and 2012, or elect to recognize it all as ordinary income on their 2010 returns.

> **EXAMPLE**
>
> Beth Fieldcrest is in the 25-percent tax bracket. She has a traditional IRA with a value of $50,000, consisting of deductible contributions and earnings. She does not have a Roth IRA but, in 2010, she converts her traditional IRA into a Roth. As a result of the conversion, she has $50,000 in gross income, subject to her 25-percent tax rate. Unless Beth elects to recognize the entire $50,000 in income in 2010, $25,000 of the amount is included in her income in 2011, and $25, 000 is included in her income for 2012.

DOWNTURN STRATEGY

Individuals should also keep in mind that 2010 is the last year for the current, historically low income tax rates, which are scheduled to sunset in 2011 and likely will not be extended for high-income taxpayers—part of the group previously limited by the $100,000 AGI conversion ceiling. Therefore, the rush to do Roth conversions in 2010 may be historic, especially if Congress does not extend the lower tax rates.

To Convert or Not to Convert?

There are many reasons individuals may want to covert the assets in their traditional IRA to a Roth IRA. For example, individuals who want to remain in the market for the long haul may want to consider converting their assets from a traditional IRA that has been hammered by the stock market turmoil and lost significant value to a Roth IRA.

Factors. A key factor in determining whether to convert to a Roth IRA involves considering whether individuals anticipate being in a lower or higher tax bracket after retirement, when withdrawals will be made from their account. The tax deferral rules that apply to traditional IRAs work well for individuals who will be in the lower tax brackets during retirement, because the distributions from their traditional IRAs will be subject to the ordinary income tax rates in effect in the year the distributions are made. However, high-income taxpayers often end up in the same or higher bracket when they retire, and thus would benefit more from converting to Roth IRAs, from which distributions in retirement are tax-free.

Continuing contributions after age 70½. Second, converting to a Roth IRA gives individuals the ability to continue contributing to their account after reaching age 70½, or becoming an active participate in an employer-sponsored retirement plan. An individual who maintains a traditional IRA cannot make contributions to the account after reaching age 70½. Further, Roth IRA owners are not subject to the RMD rules that traditional IRA owners face.

Deciding whether to convert a traditional IRA into a Roth IRA involves assessing many important tax and financial factors. Some factors to consider include:

- The total income tax the individual will pay on the conversion (ordinary income tax rates apply);
- The miscellaneous costs that will be incurred due to the conversion (including transaction fees and sales charges);

- The individual's anticipated tax bracket at the time of receiving distributions from the traditional IRAs (at which time they will be subject to ordinary income tax rates);
- The anticipated return from the Roth versus the traditional IRA;
- The individual's age at the time of conversion; and
- The length of time it will take the individual (and the plan) to recoup the tax and other expenses caused by the conversion.

DOWNTURN STRATEGY

Many IRA accounts invested in the stock market have lost a significant percentage of their value during the past two years. Conversion of an IRA into a Roth IRA in those cases has the silver lining of generating a lower tax liability because the deemed ordinary income from the conversion is based on value at the time of conversion. Assuming that 2010 and 2011 will see better days in the stock markets, a conversion as soon as possible to catch the conversion at a low point would be advisable. For those taxpayers previously barred from conversions because of the $100,000 AGI limitation, doing the conversion immediately in January 2010 or soon thereafter (as opposed to later in 2010 or 2011 when values are higher) should prove a good bet in keeping the conversion tax as low as possible.

Recharacterizations of IRA Conversions

Many individuals who converted from a traditional IRA to a Roth in 2008 or early 2009 have seen their Roth IRA account balance drop substantially. However, these individuals must still recognize taxable income on the amounts converted to the Roth IRA based upon the value of the account on the date of conversion...unless the conversion is undone (recharacterized as a traditional type) in time.

Timing. The election to recharacterize a conversion *and* the transfer of the assets must both take place on or before the due date (including extensions) of an individual's federal income tax return for the year in which the initial conversion to the Roth IRA occurred, or the initial contribution was made to the IRA account. Generally, once a recharacterization election has been made, it cannot be revoked. For most taxpayers with initial 2008 conversions, the deadline to recharacterize the conversion is October 15, 2009.

Individuals who made a 2009 conversion may recharacterize the transaction on his or her federal income tax return filed on or before April 15, 2010 (or until October 15, 2010, if an automatic extension of six months is obtained to file the 2009 return). Form 8606, *Nondeductible IRAs,* is used to make the election to recharacterize.

DOWNTURN STRATEGY

If the value of assets in a traditional IRA that was converted to a Roth IRA has dropped significantly in value after the conversion, an individual may want to recoup the income taxes paid on the conversion by undoing, or recharacterizing, the conversion and reconverting the funds back to the traditional IRA. Generally in this situation, recharacterization may make sense if the amount of taxes paid on the conversion is more than the value of the Roth IRA after the conversion. Earnings (or losses) on the contribution also must be transferred. Unfortunately, the treatment of losses in this situation is the same as that when current contributions are taken back: the amount transferred is reduced by the losses on the contribution, but the losses are not deductible.

Amending a return. Individuals may need to file amended returns if they have already filed their return for the tax year in which the recharacterization is made. Filing an amended return will generate a tax refund if an individual is recharacterizing a Roth IRA contribution as a deductible contribution to a traditional IRA or recharacterizing a conversion from a traditional IRA to a Roth IRA. Alternatively, an individual will owe tax if he or she is recharacterizing a deductible traditional IRA contribution to a Roth IRA contribution.

Reconversions. A reconversion is a conversion from a traditional IRA to a Roth IRA of an amount that had previously been recharacterized as a contribution to the traditional IRA after having been earlier converted to a Roth IRA.

DOWNTURN STRATEGY

A reconversion may be beneficial for an individual's retirement portfolio if, for example, he or she converted a traditional IRA into a Roth in a year that market values were higher, thus paying higher taxes on the conversion. For example, individuals may want to consider reconverting their Roth IRA back to the traditional variety the following year, when market values may have declined, in order to take advantage of those lower market values.

STUDY QUESTIONS

13. Individuals converting a traditional IRA account to a Roth account in 2010:

  a. May convert the balance tax-free subject to AGI limitations

  b. May recognize ordinary income tax on the traditional account balance ratably on 2011 and 2012 tax returns

  c. Must include the balance of the traditional account as ordinary income on their 2010 return

14. The tax deferral rules for Roth IRA accounts work well for taxpayers:

  a. Who wish to begin taking distributions before age 70½

  b. Who expect to be subject to higher tax rates in retirement

  c. Who wish to withdraw more than the RMD when they retire

SAVER'S CREDIT

The *saver's credit* is a retirement savings tax credit that can save eligible individuals (typically lower- and middle-income taxpayers) up to $1,000 in taxes just for contributing up to $2,000 to their retirement account. The credit essentially rewards individuals for saving for retirement, including contributions made to traditional IRAs, Roth IRAs, 401(k) plans, and other account types, such as governmental plans.

The saver's credit is an additional tax benefit offered on top of any other benefits available for a retirement contribution. The retirement saving credit is a nonrefundable personal credit.

To qualify for the credit, an individual must be 18 years old (as of the close of the tax year of the contribution), not a full-time student, and not claimed as a dependent on another taxpayer's return.

The credit is determined as a percentage of the individual's *qualifying contribution*. A taxpayer's qualifying contribution is limited to $2,000 per year. The percentage varies depending on your adjusted gross income (AGI).

For married couples filing jointly, if joint AGI for 2009 is $33,000 or less, the credit percentage is 50 percent. For example, if each spouse makes the maximum $2,000 contribution for the credit, for a total of $4,000, the couple can claim a total saver's credit of $2,000 ($4,000 × 50 percent) on their joint return.) If AGI for 2009 is above $33,000 but not over $36,000, the credit is 20 percent of qualifying contributions ($800 in the above example: $4,000 × 20 percent). If AGI for 2009 is above $36,000 but not over $55,500, the credit is 10 percent of qualifying contributions. If AGI for 2009 is over $55,500, the credit is not available.

For single taxpayers, if AGI for 2009 is $16,500 or less, the percentage is 50 percent. If AGI for 2009 is above $16,500 but not over $18,000, the credit is 20 percent of qualifying contributions. If AGI for 2009 is above $18,000 but not over $27,750, the credit is 10 percent of qualifying contributions. And if AGI for 2009 exceeds $27,750, no credit is available.

WHITE HOUSE/IRS NEW RETIREMENT SAVINGS INITIATIVES

In early September 2009, the White House, Treasury Department, and the IRS unveiled new guidance to encourage retirement savings. The IRS issued seven rulings and notices to:

- Streamline automatic enrollment in 401(k) plans and SIMPLE IRAs;
- Facilitate contributions of unused leave and vacation time to a qualified retirement plan; and
- Allow the use of refunds to purchase U.S. savings bonds.

Likely, more guidance will be released over the coming year to follow through on these new retirement savings initiatives. Also likely, the focus will remain on reminding people of existing advantages and simplifying the procedures necessary to qualify for them.

Although automatic enrollment and use of vacation pay toward retirement contributions have been allowed previously, the new guidance released over Labor Day weekend makes it easier for small employers to implement them by providing automatic enrollment language and streamlined steps to convert unused leave into retirement savings. As before, however, each employer makes the final decision whether to make the necessary plan amendments to implement these savings enhancements.

> **COMMENT**
>
> These new measures are administrative actions and are separate from the president's fiscal year 2010 budget proposals to encourage retirement savings, which would require approval by Congress. President Obama has asked Congress to facilitate automatic enrollment in IRAs through payroll deductions for workers with no employer retirement plan; he also has proposed an expanded saver's credit.

STUDY QUESTIONS

> **15.** The maximum qualifying contribution for the saver's credit is _____ for a single taxpayer earning less than _____.
>
> **a.** $1,000; $16,500
> **b.** $1,500; $20,000
> **c.** $2,000; $27,750

CONCLUSION

Often, individuals feel helpless when a significant economic downturn tears away at their retirement portfolios and investments. However, economic downturns and market conditions inevitably turn around, although some storms last longer and the recovery much slower and harder than others. Even despite a lack of longevity, individuals' retirement portfolios—and therefore, retirement plans—inevitably suffer from a serious economic downturn. This chapter examined various tax-planning techniques, with a focus on application to popular retirement vehicles, that may help mitigate some of the damage and assist individuals with rebuilding their retirement portfolios.

CPE NOTE: When you have completed your study and review of chapters 6-8, which comprise Module 3, you may wish to take the Quizzer for this Module.

For your convenience, you can also take this Quizzer online at **www. cchtestingcenter.com.**

TOP FEDERAL TAX ISSUES FOR 2010 CPE COURSE

Answers to Study Questions

MODULE 1 — CHAPTER 1

1. a. *Incorrect.* If a nonresident alien's income is not connected with U.S. businesses, the revenue is not considered earned income.
b. *Correct.* A self-employed individual's net earnings from self-employment are considered earned income if they are taken into account in computing the individual's taxable income.
c. *Incorrect.* Pension or annuity payments are not considered earned income for MWPC eligibility.

2. a. *Incorrect.* A taxpayer who purchases his or her principal residence from a spouse, parent, grandparent, child, or grandchild cannot claim the first-time homebuyer credit.
b. *Correct.* A first-time homebuyer is an individual who has not held an ownership interest in any principal residence for three years before the date of purchase of the home.
c. *Incorrect.* Nonresident aliens are not considered qualified purchasers for the first-time homebuyer credit.

3. a. *Correct.* Students in graduate degree programs are ineligible to claim the AOTC.
b. *Incorrect.* The AOTC is available for each of the first four years of a post-secondary student's education, unlike the HOPE scholarship credit, which applied only to the first two years of post-secondary programs.
c. *Incorrect.* A student in a post-secondary program leading to an associate's degree is eligible for the AOTC.

4. a. *Correct.* The motor vehicle sales tax deduction's $49,500 purchase price limitation is imposed on a per-vehicle basis.
b. *Incorrect.* Taxpayers may purchase more than one vehicle and take advantage of the motor vehicle sales tax deduction on each of them.
c. *Incorrect.* The motor vehicle sales tax deduction is not limited to vehicles manufactured in the United States.

5. True. *Correct.* Under the 2009 Recovery Act, an individual must be involuntarily terminated from employment to qualify for COBRA premium assistance.

False. *Incorrect.* The triggering event for COBRA premium assistance is involuntarily termination from employment.

6. a. *Correct.* The 2009 Recovery Act authorizes the IRS to refund the employer's 65 percent share of COBRA premium assistance through a payroll tax credit.
b. *Incorrect.* Employers will recover their 65 percent share of COBRA premium assistance through a payroll tax credit and not through a one-time refund to be distributed in 2011
c. *Incorrect.* Under the 2009 Recovery Act, employers will be reimbursed for their 65 percent share of COBRA premium assistance through a payroll tax credit. Prior to passage of the 2009 Recovery Act, individuals paid 35 percent of their health insurance premiums and the HCTC program paid 65 percent. The 2009 Recovery Act raised the government-paid portion from 65 percent to 80 percent.

7. a. *Incorrect.* The 2009 Recovery Act raised the government-paid portion of the HCTC by a different percentage.
b. *Correct.* Before Congress enacted the 2009 Recovery Act, the government-paid portion of the HCTC was 65 percent. Congress increased the government-paid portion to 80 percent.
c. *Incorrect.* The 2009 Recovery Act does not provide for 100 percent government-paid HCTC.

8. a. *Correct.* A single unemployed individual may exclude up to $2,400, and unemployed spouses are each eligible for the $2,400 exclusion.
b. *Incorrect.* A different exclusion amount applies, which is available to each spouse if both receive unemployment benefits.
c. *Incorrect.* Congress rejected the proposal to exclude all unemployment benefits from taxable income, instead setting a maximum temporary exclusion amount.

9. a. *Incorrect.* The CARS Act applies a higher limit to the manufacture date of passenger cars eligible for the cash-for-clunkers program.
b. *Correct.* A passenger car that is traded in for a new fuel-efficient vehicle must have been manufactured less than 25 years before the trade-in date.
c. *Incorrect.* The CARS Act imposes a more recent cut-off date for the age of a trade-in passenger car.

10. a. *Incorrect.* The CARS Act provides a higher incentive for consumers to trade in clunkers for fuel-efficient vehicles.
b. *Correct.* **Taxpayers are eligible for a $3,500 voucher toward the purchase of a new fuel-efficient vehicle if the new vehicle has a fuel economy that is at least 4 mpg (but less than 10 mpg) higher than the trade-in vehicle.**
c. *Incorrect.* The CARS Act voucher is less than $4,500 if the new passenger automobile has a combined fuel economy that is at least 4 mpg (but less than 10 mpg) higher than the trade-in vehicle.

MODULE 1 — CHAPTER 2

1. a. *Incorrect.* The act extends the carryforward period to up to 20 years, not 10, applicable only to NOLs for tax year 2008.
b. *Correct.* **Businesses with average gross receipts of up to $15 million annually over a three-year period may elect an NOL carryback period of five years or fewer under the 2009 Recovery Act, applicable only to 2008 NOLs.**
c. *Incorrect.* The temporary extension applies only to 2008 NOLs.

2. a. *Correct.* **Businesses may claim bonus depreciation for regular tax and AMT for property placed in service before January 1, 2010 (2011 for qualifying property and certain noncommercial aircraft).**
b. *Incorrect.* The filing date for the business does not determine the applicability of the election.
c. *Incorrect.* The act uses a placed-in-service date for claiming bonus depreciation and does not extend through 2011.

3. a. *Incorrect.* The Code Sec. 179 deduction is reduced dollar-for-dollar when qualifying expenditures reach $800,000, but a higher cap applies to the total expenditure.
b. *Correct.* **The $250,000 ceiling for the deduction begins to phase out when qualifying expenses exceed $800,000 and is complete when purchases exceed $1,050,000.**
c. *Incorrect.* The 2009 Recovery Act uses $15 million as the maximum gross receipts for small businesses that claim the temporary NOL carryover, but the Code Sec. 179 expensing deduction is phased out completely at a lower expenditure level.

4. a. *Incorrect.* The 2009 Recovery Act offers employers of targeted groups a higher maximum percentage and dollar amount ceiling for the credit.
b. *Correct.* **Unemployed veterans and disconnected youth are two newly targeted groups for the WOTC added by the 2009 Recovery Act.**

c. Incorrect. The maximum percentage and maximum credit are lower, although employers of qualified veterans may claim a WOTC of up to $12,000.

5. a. Correct. An involuntary termination occurs when employment of the seasonal worker ends despite the fact that the worker is willing and able to continue employment.
b. Incorrect. A reduction of employee hours to zero is considered an involuntary termination, but if work hours are reduced less than that, no involuntary termination is considered to occur for purposes of COBRA premium assistance.
c. Incorrect. To qualify for the premium assistance, an individual's involuntary termination from employment must occur between September 1, 2008, and December 31, 2009.

6. a. Incorrect. Employers do not claim the credit as part of their annual federal return for tax year 2009.
b. Correct. The IRS revised Form 941-X for employers to use in claiming the credit.
c. Incorrect. Employers should not use Form 941c, *Supporting Statement to Correct Information,* or Form 843, *Claim for Refund or Request for Abatement,* to claim the COBRA premium assistance credit.

7. True. Correct. The 2009 Recovery Act allows business taxpayers to apply for federal grant monies instead of claiming the investment tax credit or the renewable energy production tax credit for property placed in service in 2009 or 2010. is available even if any other subsidized energy financing is used.
False. Incorrect. Business taxpayers have three options under the 2009 Recovery Act. They can claim the investment tax credit, the renewable energy production tax credit or apply for federal grant monies.

8. a. Incorrect. The effective date for repeal of IRS Notice 2008-83 for most prospective transactions is later in 2009.
b. Correct. In Notice 2008-83, the IRS provided incentives for the acquisition of struggling banks by exempting banks' built-in losses from the Code Sec. 382 limitation following an ownership change. Congress repealed IRS Notice 2008-83 effective January 16, 2009, for most prospective transactions.
c. Incorrect. Congress repealed IRS Notice 2009 as of an effective earlier in 2009 for most prospective transactions. The credits are available for 10 percent of the costs of new and converted vehicles but subject to lower maximums.

9. a. *Incorrect.* Build America Bonds (BABs), not QSCBs, offer higher interest rates than those of private issuers.

b. *Correct.* **QSCBs provide a tax credit to bond investors, whereas Build America Bonds offer a higher interest rate than taxable bonds from private issuers.**

c. *Incorrect.* Qualified Zone Academy Bonds, not QSCBs, are used for school renovations, equipment purchases, and curriculum development.

10. a. *Incorrect.* The credit is currently set to expire at the end of 2009.

b. *Correct.* The administration proposed to make the credit permanent.

c. *Incorrect.* The administration's proposal is not to extend the credit for one year.

MODULE 1 — CHAPTER 3

1. a. *Correct.* **Incurring the civil penalty under Code Sec. 6713 does not require knowing or reckless disclosure as do violations of Code Sec. 7216, but taxpayers may take civil actions against the preparer for the unauthorized disclosure.**

b. *Incorrect.* Knowing or reckless violations of Code Sec. 7216, not Code Sec. 6713, disclosure rules violate Circular 230 and may involve the Office of Professional Responsibility.

c. *Incorrect.* Code Sec. 6713 penalties do not apply to services provided without remuneration.

2. a. *Incorrect.* Disclosures to the IRS are specifically identified in the 2008 final regulations as permissible disclosures the preparer may make without prior consent of the taxpayer.

b. *Correct.* Statistical compilations of return information are considered tax information that requires the consent of the taxpayer for aggregation.

c. *Incorrect.* The 2008 final regulations permit disclosures to a taxpayer's fiduciary without the taxpayer's prior consent.

3. True. *Incorrect.* A preparer does not need prior consent to disclose return information to obtain legal advice or in connection with any court or grand jury hearing, even when the proceeding involves only the preparer.

False. *Correct.* An exception to the consent requirement applies for IRS or Treasury Department investigations or in connection with court or grand jury proceedings regardless of whether the investigation relates to the taxpayer or the preparer.

4. a. Correct. The disclosures are limited to the portions of return information needed by the whistleblower, and he or she must agree in writing not to otherwise use or disclose the information. Generally, the whistleblower agrees to permit an inspection of his or her premises by the IRS regarding the maintenance of the disclosed information.
b. Incorrect. The Whistleblower Office determines the need for assistance before disclosing the information to the whistleblower.
c. Incorrect. Disclosures may be made to assist in the investigation of a suspected criminal violation even if the suspicion proves incorrect.

5. a. Correct. Disclosures are prohibited for data related to the average refund, credit, or rebate amounts of client taxpayers.
b. Incorrect. The number of tax years used in the calculations does not determine whether or when disclosures of compilations are permitted.
c. Incorrect. The location of the preparers or clients does not determine whether or when compilations of such averages may be disclosed.

6. a. Incorrect. Simply obtaining consent from the taxpayer for the transmittal is insufficient under the data protection rules for SSNs.
b. Correct. Absent an adequate data protection safeguard, even when a taxpayer consents to disclose the SSN on a return, the number must be masked when the information is transmitted to another preparer located outside of the United States (unless the transmitting preparer initially received the SSN from that preparer).
c. Incorrect. If the preparer in the United States received the SSN from another preparer located outside of the United States, retransmitting the SSN to the preparer located outside of the United States is permitted.

7. a. Correct. A penalty against improper disclosure by an IRS employee applies under Code Sec. 6103(a)(3), as well as states employees and private persons to whom the IRS makes authorized disclosures under restrictions.
b. Incorrect. Unenrolled preparers are regulated by the compliance office of the IRS; IRS employees are not.
c. Incorrect. Circular 230 governs practice by attorneys, CPAs, and enrolled agents before the IRS and is not applicable to disclosures by IRS personnel or others who receive returns in the course of public business.

8. a. Incorrect. The OPR is authorized to issue a censure (public release of reprimand using the Internal Revenue Bulletin).
b. Correct. The OPR may issue a private reprimand, public censure, monetary sanctions, or suspension or disbarment of the practitioner violating Circular 230 rules.

c. Incorrect. The OPR may disbar practitioners, who may then seek reinstatement only after five years upon proof of good behavior.

9. a. Incorrect. Information communicated for inclusion on the tax return is intended for disclosure and is not privileged.
b. Correct. The privilege extends to communications with the accountant by the taxpayer or attorney when the attorney engages the accountant.
c. Incorrect. The privilege does not apply upon disclosure to such third parties.

10. a. Correct. The more likely than not standard (with a greater than 50-percent likelihood of sustainability) was higher than the substantial authority standard (having a 40-percent likelihood) for taxpayers; the more likely than not standard was replaced when Code Sec. 6694 was simplified.
b. Incorrect. The two standards are not equivalent.
c. Incorrect. The more likely than not standard is not lower (involve a lower percentage of sustainability) than the substantial authority standard for tax positions.

MODULE 2 — CHAPTER 4

1. a. Correct. Casualty losses arise when property is destroyed by fire, storm, or shipwreck and are deductible against gross income.
b. Incorrect. Types of losses deductible against gross income under Code Sec. 165(c)(1) are ordinary losses. A specific category of ordinary loss applies to property damaged by storm.
c. Incorrect. A different name applies to the category of loss occurring from storm damage.

2. a. Incorrect. NOLs may not be carried forward when an S corp converts to C corporation status.
b. Correct. Partners, S corporation shareholders, disregarded entity members, and sole proprietors may deduct NOLs from their entities.
c. Incorrect. C corporation NOLs do not apply when the entity becomes an S corp but remain available for deduction if the entity becomes a C corporation subsequently.

3. a. Incorrect. The Code Sec. 382 limitations do not prohibit application of the acquired corporation's NOLs to gains in the acquirer's future tax years.

b. *Correct.* **To prevent trafficking of NOLs, the tax code limits the carryforwards for the year of acquisition using this formula. NOLs exceeding the Code Sec. 382 limitation for the year** *after* **the ownership change may be carried over, however.**

c. *Incorrect.* The Code Sec. 382 rules impose a different limitation on use of these NOLs for the acquirer's current year.

4. a. *Correct.* **The** *2009 Recovery Act* **provided relief to banks having TARP-required restructuring agreements. The Code Sec. 382 limitation for NOLs does not apply because the government acquired the banks' stock using TARP funds.**

b. *Incorrect.* The *2009 Recovery Act* provisions for banks whose stock was purchased with TARP loans do not so apply the Code Sec. 382 limitation.

c. *Incorrect.* The *2009 Recovery Act* does not stipulate that bailout funds must be repaid before banks having these restructuring agreements may apply NOLs.

5. a. *Correct.* **If taxpayers fulfill requirements for material participation for at least 5 of the years between 1998 and 2008, they may deduct passive activity losses against nonpassive income in 2009.**

b. *Incorrect.* The requirement allowing netting passive activity losses and nonpassive income only requires providing personal services for any 3 years preceding this tax year.

c. *Incorrect.* Prior participation is considered material only when spread across certain multiple years.

6. a. *Correct.* **The limitation applies to the shareholders of S corporations, not the entities themselves.**

b. *Incorrect.* Closely held corporations are subject to the passive activity loss rules.

c. *Incorrect.* The passive activity loss limitation applies to both trusts and estates.

7. a. *Correct.* **Claiming a loss reduces the at-risk amount for subsequent tax years. Conversely, if the taxpayer sells its business interest for a gain, the gain is added to the at-risk amount, enabling a greater loss deduction.**

b. *Incorrect.* The at-risk amount is changed when the taxpayer claims a loss.

c. *Incorrect.* The at-risk amounts are not increased if the taxpayer claims a loss. Rather, a gain on the sale of the taxpayer's business interest is added to the amount at risk, so a larger loss may be deducted.

8. a. *Correct.* Copyrights and other property such as artistic compositions and memoranda are not considered Code Sec. 1231 property.
b. *Incorrect.* Trade or business property destroyed, stolen, seized, or condemned is a capital asset considered Code Sec. 1231 property.
c. *Incorrect.* Unharvested crops as well as livestock are considered Code Sec. 1231 property for preferable tax treatment.

9. a. *Correct.* Section 1231 losses for the previous five years must be completely recaptured.
b. *Incorrect.* The recapture rule does not recharacterize Section 1231 losses.
c. *Incorrect.* The Section 1231 rules apply to recapturing prior losses, not prohibiting deduction of future losses.

10. a. *Incorrect.* Taxpayers can claim the discovered theft on their current returns even when the theft(s) occurred in earlier years.
b. *Correct.* Amounts taxpayers reported as gross income on previous returns must have been reinvested in the fraudulent scheme to be deductible as theft amounts.
c. *Incorrect.* Payments of both "principal" and "income" from fraudulent investment arrangements may be reported as discovered theft losses in the current tax year.

11. a. *Incorrect.* The disaster loss deduction is not related to NOLs.
b. *Correct.* The standard deduction increases by the amount of the disaster loss deduction.
c. *Incorrect.* Tax credit amounts are not related to the deductible disaster loss nonitemizers may claim.

12. a. *Incorrect.* As is the case for theft loss deductions, a taxpayer may claim the abandonment loss in a later tax year.
b. *Incorrect.* The deduction for abandonment applies to both tangible and intangible property.
c. *Correct.* The taxpayer may claim an abandonment loss in a year subsequent to the loss but not if a deduction was taken for a loss on the property's sale.

13. a. *Incorrect.* Losses of professional gamblers are considered NOLs for carryback and carryforward purposes.
b. *Correct.* Professional gamblers may claim their losses as trade or business losses and may carry back or carry forward loss amounts as NOLs.

c. *Incorrect.* Treatment of losses differs for casual gamblers and professional gamblers who experience losses.

14. a. *Incorrect.* No such maximum deduction applies to hobby losses.
b. *Correct.* **Under the hobby loss limitation rules, deductions may not exceed income from the activity determined to be a hobby.**
c. *Incorrect.* All activities for which losses are claimed should substantiate expenses for five years. Activities are presumed to be for-profit if they are profit making for three of the last five years.

15. a. *Incorrect.* These deductions do not increase the taxpayer's gross income from hobby activities.
b. *Correct.* **Category 1 deductions reduce the amount by which hobby income may offset deductions in either Category 2 expenses or Category 3 for basis adjustments.**
c. *Incorrect.* Category 1 deductions may be itemized on Schedule A of Form 1040 regardless of whether the taxpayer has hobby activities.

MODULE 2 — CHAPTER 5

1. a. *Correct.* **A debt is discharged when it is clear the debtor will never have to repay the debt but not when a reasonable possibility of payment exists.**
b. *Incorrect.* This reacquisition is a discharge and is addressed in the 2009 Recovery Act.
c. *Incorrect.* Under Code Sec. 108(e)(4), such an acquisition of debt is a discharge.

2. a. *Incorrect.* The 2009 Recovery Act provisions are not focused on offers in compromise, which are used for negotiating tax liabilities.
b. *Correct.* **The debtor issuing a debt instrument to satisfy existing debt is considered to have paid an amount equal to the issue price, and under the 2009 Recovery Act, the income can be deferred.**
c. *Incorrect.* A debt cancellation agreement contingent on future events is not considered a discharge of the debt.

3. a. *Correct.* **Because the partners are not the purchasers, they may not treat the discharge as a reduction in purchase price and must recognize the COI income.**
b. *Incorrect.* The reduction of purchase money debt is not handled at the entity level, and the partnership recognizes COI income.
c. *Incorrect.* The partners are not the purchasers of the property and may not so reduce the purchase price.

4. a. *Incorrect.* When a lender reduces the buyer's purchase money debt, the debt relief does not give rise to COI income.

b. *Correct.* The reduction does not create COI income, and the buyer must reduce the basis of the property.

c. *Incorrect.* The buyer reduces, rather than increases, its basis of the property.

5. a. *Correct.* The reduction does not apply to attributes of the debtor once the case begins.

b. *Incorrect.* Attributes of the bankruptcy estate are reduced in Chapter 7 or Chapter 11 cases.

c. *Incorrect.* If property is transferred from the bankruptcy estate to the bankrupt individual, the property's attributes may be reduced.

6. a. *Incorrect.* The taxpayer may claim contingent liabilities that are likely to be paid off.

b. *Incorrect.* Assets for calculating the insolvency include all property owned, including assets used as collateral.

c. *Correct.* The taxpayer may include the excess discharged nonrecourse debt as a liability for the insolvency exclusion.

7. a. *Correct.* Such rental proceeds are not counted in gross receipts.

b. *Incorrect.* Proceeds from livestock sales are included in gross receipts.

c. *Incorrect.* Amounts in excess of the exclusion from tax attributes are considered taxable income and thus includible in gross receipts.

8. a. *Correct.* The basis must be reduced immediately, but not below zero.

b. *Incorrect.* The residence must secure the debt for the discharge to apply to a principal residence bought, constructed, or substantially improved during the years 2007–2012.

c. *Incorrect.* The principal residence debt exclusion helps to shelter any gain through the home sale exclusion under Code Sec. 121.

9. a. *Incorrect.* The discharge is not taxable if the former student becomes employed in a government office.

b. *Correct.* A taxable discharge is created if the student must perform services for the school that issued the loan unless another exclusion applies.

c. *Incorrect.* The discharge is not taxable if the lawyer or physician works for a certain period of time in one of these professions as long as the employer is suitable, such as a tax-exempt hospital, legal clinic, or public defender's office. As long as the required time of public service is fulfilled, the discharge is not taxed as income.

10. a. *Incorrect.* The exclusion applies only to personal debt.
b. *Correct.* **The exclusion is available to discharges by government agencies, banks, credit unions, finance companies, and credit card companies.**
c. *Incorrect.* The relief applies to discharges after the applicable disaster date and before 2010.

11. a. *Incorrect.* COI income is not applied at the shareholder level.
b. *Correct.* **Congress reversed the *Gitlitz* decision and determined that COI income does not flow through to shareholders or increase basis. The increase in basis applies to shareholders if discharges occurred on or before October 11, 2001.**
c. *Incorrect.* This exclusion situation applied to S corporations on or before October 11, 2001, when the *Gitlitz* decision by the U.S. Supreme Court also enabled suspended losses to be covered by the basis increase and deducted.

12. a. *Correct.* **The proposed regulations treat the exchange as a nontaxable contribution to the partnership under these circumstances.**
b. *Incorrect.* Code Sec. 721 denies a bad debt deduction to the creditor for the difference between the value of the partnership interest and amount of the debt.
c. *Incorrect.* A loss on the sale of the partnership interest by the creditor is capital, not ordinary, loss.

13. True. *Incorrect.* The taxpayer does not have to report the COI income if another exclusion applies.
False. *Correct.* **The taxpayer can claim any applicable exclusion for the income that is not deferred, such as bankruptcy or insolvency.**

14. a. *Correct.* **A business debt instrument may be a bond, debenture, note, certificate, or another arrangement constituting indebtedness. Annuities are excluded.**
b. *Incorrect.* The purpose of the election under Code Sec. 108(i) is to defer COI income recognition through the repurchase of the company's own debt.
c. *Incorrect.* Annuities are excluded from consideration in the debt repurchase.

15. True. *Correct.* **The reacquisition is considered an exchange of the debt instrument for the debt.**
False. *Incorrect.* The debt instrument is considered exchanged for the debt when the instrument is issued for cash.

MODULE 3 — CHAPTER 6

1. a. Incorrect. General relief does not apply to underpayments due to the taxpayers' inability to pay.
b. Correct. General relief is available only for the understatement of tax: the difference between the tax shown on the return and the actual amount of the liability.
c. Incorrect. General relief does not apply to both underpayments and understatements of the tax liability.

2. a. Incorrect. Apportionment does not pertain to splitting the percentages of liability between the requesting and nonrequesting spouse.
b. Correct. Apportionment may be available for certain tax years for which the requesting spouse reasonably lacked knowledge or for selective income sources of which the requesting spouse was unaware.
c. Incorrect. General relief may be apportioned regardless of whether the liability arises from omitted income or erroneous deductions, and the relief does not apply on an all or nothing basis.

3. a. Correct. The IRS bears the burden for both production of evidence and persuasion on the question of actual knowledge by the electing spouse.
b. Incorrect. The electing spouse may file for allocation of liability regardless of whether the spouses are divorced, legally separated, or living apart during the 12-month period prior to the election date.
c. Incorrect. Actual knowledge is not inferred if the electing spouse merely had a reason to know of omitted income.

4. a. Incorrect. The liability of the nonrequesting spouse making the transfer is not affected.
b. Correct. The liability of the electing spouse is increased by the value of any disqualified asset transferred to him or her by the other spouse.
c. Incorrect. The allocation for the value of the transferred disqualified asset is not equal.

5. a. Incorrect. Congress intended equitable innocent spouse relief to be available when the requesting spouse is unable to pay the tax liability arising from the nonrequesting spouse's income.
b. Correct. Equitable relief typically arises when the spouses underpaid the tax liability rather than understated its amount.
c. Incorrect. Congress intended for equitable relief to be available when the nonrequesting spouse misappropriates money intended to pay the liability reported on the joint return.

6. a. *Incorrect.* The electing spouse is not ineligible for equitable relief for the tax year if the nonrequesting spouse made the transfer.
b. *Correct.* **Relief is applied to the excess of the liability over the value of the disqualified assets.**
c. *Incorrect.* The threshold condition instead is that the transfer did not occur as part of a fraudulent scheme.

7. True. *Correct.* **Generally, the IRS must suspend actions such as levying bank accounts or the requesting spouse's wages during this period, but interest and penalties are not suspended.**
False. *Incorrect.* The underlying tax obligation continues to incur interest and penalties even though collection actions are suspended.

8. a. *Incorrect.* The electing spouse files a claim for refund after paying the full assessed tax when he or she pursues the case in Federal Claims Court.
b. *Incorrect.* The full amount of tax must be paid and a refund claim filed if the electing spouse appeals the case in district court.
c. *Correct.* **Judicial review in a district court or the Court of Federal Claims requires the electing spouse to pay the full tax liability and file a refund claim.**

9. a. *Correct.* **Even if the spouse does not know the dollar amount of the item, awareness of the business activity is considered "knowledge" for applying community property rules.**
b. *Incorrect.* "Knowledge" of the community income item is not based on knowing the specific dollar amount of the item.
c. *Incorrect.* Listing on a prior year's federal income tax return is not the sole determinant of "knowledge" for traditional relief rules.

10. True. *Correct.* **The IRS determination of equitable relief considers the same factors as those pertaining to requests for equitable relief from joint liabilities: threat of economic hardship, extent of knowledge of the understatement or underpayment, and current marital status.**
False. *Incorrect.* Equitable relief from applying community property rules involves the same considerations as for equitable relief from joint liabilities arising from joint returns.

MODULE 3 — CHAPTER 7

1. a. *Incorrect.* Although the PPA did not create the disparity of treatment on the federal and state levels, its rules are bound by the restrictions on marital status imposed by another federal law.

b. *Correct.* DOMA, enacted in 1996, prevents federal agencies (including the IRS) from recognizing any marriage except that between a man and woman. This definition for federal law purposes does not conform to state statutes that recognize the legal status of SSMCs and domestic partners.

c. *Incorrect.* Legislation enacted in a prior year defined marriage as between a man and a woman, creating nonconformity with state laws that recognize SSMC and the legal rights of domestic partners.. However, WRERA provisions for health benefits apply only to an employee, husband or wife spouse, and dependents.

2. a. *Correct.* The couple can attach Form 8275 to their federal returns to describe their marital status under state law. They may also attach a copy of their marriage certificate with their federal returns.

b. *Incorrect.* Although taxpayers in some SSMCs may in fact be eligible to claim the head of household status or dependent status, such filings are not the means by which SSMCs indicate their marital status under state law.

c. *Incorrect.* The hypothetical joint return should not be filed as the couple's federal return, but some states require the SSMC to attach the hypothetical return to the joint state return to disclose the computations.

3. True. *Incorrect.* The domestic partner may meet criteria to claim head of household filing status but may not also claim the child as a dependent.

False. *Correct.* The domestic partner may claim head of household status if he she is considered unmarried at the end of the tax year, paid more than half of home maintenance for the year, and a qualifying person lived with the domestic partner for more than half the year.

4. a. *Correct.* The credit may be claimed in addition to listing the child as a dependent as long as the child is younger than age 17.

b. *Incorrect.* Instead, the same spouse or partner cannot claim head of household status as well as claim the qualifying child as a dependent.

c. *Incorrect.* The dependency exemption, not the child tax credit, is unavailable to the spouse or partner claiming head of household status.

5. a. *Correct.* The dependent must reside in the employee's home for the entire tax year and receive at least half of his or her support that year from the employee.

b. *Incorrect.* Federal, not state, law regarding marriage determines the federal taxation of the health plan as an employee benefit.

c. *Incorrect.* Under certain circumstances, the spouse or partner may be covered under the employer's plan without creating taxable income from the benefit.

6. a. Incorrect. The 2009 Recovery Act rules, not the employer, set the requirements for qualified beneficiaries under the COBRA premium subsidy.
b. Incorrect. State law is not considered in determining those eligible as qualified beneficiaries for the subsidy.
c. Correct. Only an opposite-sex spouse or dependent child may satisfy requirements for a qualified beneficiary under the subsidy.

7. a. Correct. The Code Sec. 2523 federal unlimited marital deduction does not protect transfers in excess of $13,000 per year between unmarried partners.
b. Incorrect. Even when property is held in joint tenancy, the donor spouse is assumed to have gifted 50 percent to the recipient.
c. Incorrect. The federal treatment of asset transfers between same-sex couples and domestic partners does not require them to maintain all property under separate ownership but does apply federal gift and estate tax rules to transfers of money, property interests, savings bonds, and stock.

8. a. Correct. Related parties include family members and certain related entities but exclude domestic partners and same-sex spouses.
b. Incorrect. Such property sales are not eligible for the unlimited marital deduction available to husband–wife married couples, so sales have tax consequences.
c. Incorrect. SSMCs and domestic partners having roughly equivalent incomes do not benefit substantially overall by making such property transfers, because these taxpayers file federal separate tax returns.

9. a. Correct. Rollovers to nonspouses are tax-free from Code Sec. 401(a), 403(a), 403(b), or eligible 457(b) plans, but not from IRAs.
b. Incorrect. Rollovers from qualified 403(a) plans to nonspouses are tax-free.
c. Incorrect. Rules applied to eligible 457(b) government plans allow tax-free rollovers to nonspouses.

10. a. Incorrect. State returns and federal returns do not treat the community property of an SSMC the same as for husband–wife couples.
b. Correct. Jointly held property owned by an SSMC will not be considered community property for federal tax assessment or collection.
c. Incorrect. Federal tax law does not recognize community property as such for SSMCs.

MODULE 3 — CHAPTER 8

1. a. *Incorrect.* Only Roth IRA contributions are taxed when funds are contributed.
b. *Correct.* **Taxes for qualified tax-deferred retirement accounts other than Roth IRAs are paid when the taxpayer takes distributions from the account.**
c. *Incorrect.* Taxes must be paid on funds invested in qualified retirement accounts.

2. a. *Correct.* **Qualifying dividends, like net long-term capital gains, are taxed at a maximum of 15 percent.**
b. *Incorrect.* A different maximum tax rate applies to qualified dividends.
c. *Incorrect.* Qualifying dividends are subject to a lower maximum tax rate.

3. a. *Correct.* **Annuities provide an income stream during the annuitant's lifetime, unlike life insurance policies.**
b. *Incorrect.* Part of an annuity payment is not taxed because it is considered a return of capital, but the remainder is taxable.
c. *Incorrect.* Annuity distributions may be subject to the AMT.

4. a. *Incorrect.* There is no additional tax-deferral advantage of creating the annuity within an IRA, because both are income tax-deferred investments.
b. *Correct.* **Funds contributed to annuities directly are generally taxable, whereas contributions to annuities held in traditional IRAs are not.**
c. *Incorrect.* The IRA required minimum distribution rules apply to annuities held in IRA plans.

5. a. *Incorrect.* Pretax elective contributions apply to traditional 401(k) accounts; Roth 401(k) contributions are not tax deductible.
b. *Correct.* **Roth 401(k) plans are not subject to the same AGI limits applied to Roth IRAs in 2009.**
c. *Incorrect.* Employer matching is prohibited for Roth 401(k) plans.

6. True. *Incorrect.* Conversions to Roth 401(k) plans are not permitted. As with Roth IRAs, however, qualified distributions are tax-free.
False. *Correct.* **Pretax elective contributions from a traditional 401(k) plan may not be converted to a designated Roth 401(k) account.**

7. a. *Incorrect.* The loan may be greater than $15,000 as along as it does not exceed 50 percent of the account's value.
b. *Correct.* **The loan therefore may never exceed $50,000.**

c. Incorrect. A lower maximum loan amount is generally allowed for 401(k) account loans.

8. a. Correct. The rollover effectively enables individuals who already withdrew an RMD from their accounts to cancel the distribution for 2009 without penalty.
b. Incorrect. A double RMD is not permitted for 2009.
c. Incorrect. Rollovers from traditional to Roth 401(k) plans are not permitted by the IRS.

9. a. Incorrect. Individuals having earned income may continue to contribute to a Roth IRA account after reaching age 70 ½ as long as they have earned income, but not to traditional IRA accounts.
b. Correct. Individuals are required to begin taking RMDs when they become 70½, even if they continue to work. Employees may not continue to contribute to traditional IRA accounts once they reach age 70½.
c. Incorrect. The maximum annual total contribution is $5,000 if the individual is younger than age 55, and $6,000 if he or she is 55 years old or more.

10. a. Incorrect. If no distributions are made, losses are not recognized. Declines in value do not trigger deductions for tax purposes.
b. Correct. Recognition for nondeductible IRA losses occurs when all of the individual's traditional IRAs are liquidated and the amounts distributed are not more than the remaining unrecovered basis.
c. Incorrect. No taxable event occurs and no losses may be deducted when accounts are rolled over between traditional IRAs.

11. True. Correct. Roth IRA contributions are subject to income tax in the year of contribution, but the funds and all earnings are not taxed upon distribution.
False. Incorrect. Individuals are taxed on contributions to Roth IRA accounts, but qualified distributions of contributions and earnings are tax-free.

12. a. Incorrect. Income tax must be paid on the amount converted, with the converted amount being considered ordinary income. Funds must be held in a Roth IRA for five years to be considered qualified distributions not subject to an early withdrawal penalty.
b. Correct. Starting in 2010 the AGI limits will not apply, but for 2009 if a taxpayer's AGI exceeds $100,000, he or she is ineligible to make Roth contributions.
c. Incorrect. Separate accounting is required for conversion contributions.

13. a. *Incorrect.* The conversion amount is subject to income taxation.

b. *Correct.* For conversions in 2010, taxpayers may elect to spread the income recognition of the traditional IRA balance over two years for income tax purposes.

c. *Incorrect.* In 2010 taxpayers will not be required to immediately recognize the income from converting a traditional IRA to a Roth account.

14. a. *Incorrect.* The length of time for recouping the amount paid in tax on the Roth balance and allowing tax-free earnings to accumulate, not the age at which distributions commence, is a factor in the tax deferral features of Roth accounts.

b. *Correct.* If retirees will pay a higher percentage of income in taxes as they receive distributions, the tax-free withdrawals from Roth accounts apply to both investments and growth of the assets, thus affording a greater tax advantage than a current-year deduction from income taxed in at a lower rate.

c. *Incorrect.* Because Roth accounts do not require any distributions, the amount of withdrawals is not a key factor in using Roth IRAs for retirement savings.

15. a. *Correct.* A single taxpayer earning $16,500 or less may claim a saver's credit of $1,000.

b. *Incorrect.* Different qualifying contribution amounts and AGI limits apply.

c. *Incorrect.* Spouses each making retirement contributions of $2,000 may claim a total saver's credit of $2,000 on their joint return for 2009. Their AGI must be $33,000 or less. Different caps apply to single taxpayers.

TOP FEDERAL TAX ISSUES FOR 2010 CPE COURSE

Index

TOP FEDERAL TAX ISSUES FOR 2010 CPE COURSE

CPE Quizzer Instructions

The CPE Quizzer is divided into three Modules. There is a processing fee for each Quizzer Module submitted for grading. Successful completion of Module 1 is recommended for **6 CPE Credits.*** Successful completion of Module 2 is recommended for **6 CPE Credits.*** Successful completion of Module 3 is recommended for **7 CPE Credits.*** You can complete and submit one Module at a time or all Modules at once for a total of **19 CPE Credits.***

To obtain CPE credit, return your completed Answer Sheet for each Quizzer Module to **CCH Continuing Education Department, 4025 W. Peterson Ave., Chicago, IL 60646**, or fax it to (773) 866-3084. Each Quizzer Answer Sheet will be graded and a CPE Certificate of Completion awarded for achieving a grade of 70 percent or greater. The Quizzer Answer Sheets are located after the Quizzer questions for this Course.

Express Grading: Processing time for your Answer Sheet is generally 8-12 business days. If you are trying to meet a reporting deadline, our Express Grading Service is available for an additional $19 per Module. To use this service, please check the "Express Grading" box on your Answer Sheet and provide your CCH account or credit card number **and your fax number.** CCH will fax your results and a Certificate of Completion (upon achieving a passing grade) to you by 5:00 p.m. the business day following our receipt of your Answer Sheet. **If you mail your Answer Sheet for Express Grading, please write "ATTN: CPE OVERNIGHT" on the envelope.** NOTE: CCH will not Federal Express Quizzer results under any circumstances.

NEW ONLINE GRADING gives you immediate 24/7 grading with instant results and no Express Grading Fee.

The **CCH Testing Center** website gives you and others in your firm easy, free access to CCH print Courses and allows you to complete your CPE Quizzers online for immediate results. Plus, the **My Courses** feature provides convenient storage for your CPE Course Certificates and completed Quizzers.

Go to **www.cchtestingcenter.com** to complete your Quizzer online.

---

* Recommended CPE credit is based on a 50-minute hour. Participants earning credits for states that require self-study to be based on a 100-minute hour will receive ½ the CPE credits for successful completion of this course. Because CPE requirements vary from state to state and among different licensing agencies, please contact your CPE governing body for information on your CPE requirements and the applicability of a particular course for your requirements.

Date of Completion: The date of completion on your Certificate will be the date that you put on your Answer Sheet. However, you must submit your Answer Sheet to CCH for grading within two weeks of completing it.

Expiration Date: December 31, 2010

Evaluation: To help us provide you with the best possible products, please take a moment to fill out the Course Evaluation located at the back of this Course and return it with your Quizzer Answer Sheets.

CCH is registered with the National Association of State Boards of Accountancy (NASBA) as a sponsor of continuing professional education on the National Registry of CPE Sponsors. State boards of accountancy have final authority on the acceptance of individual courses for CPE credit. Complaints regarding registered sponsors may be addressed to the National Registry of CPE Sponsors, 150 Fourth Avenue North, Suite 700, Nashville, TN 37219-2417. Web site: www.nasba.org.

CCH is registered with the National Association of State Boards of Accountancy (NASBA) as a Quality Assurance Service (QAS) sponsor of continuing professional education. State boards of accountancy have final authority on the acceptance of individual courses for CPE credit. Complaints regarding registered sponsors may be addressed to NASBA, 150 Fourth Avenue North, Suite 700, Nashville, TN 37219-2417. Web site: www.nasba.org.

CCH has been approved by the California Tax Education Council to offer courses that provide federal and state credit towards the annual "continuing education" requirement imposed by the State of California. A listing of additional requirements to register as a tax preparer may be obtained by contacting CTEC at P.O. Box 2890, Sacramento, CA, 95812-2890, toll-free by phone at (877) 850-2832, or on the Internet at www.ctec.org.

Processing Fee:	**Recommended CPE:**	**Recommended CFP**
$72.00 for Module 1	6 hours for Module 1	3 hours for Module 1
$72.00 for Module 2	6 hours for Module 2	3 hours for Module 2
$84.00 for Module 3	7 hours for Module 3	3 hours for Module 3
$228.00 for all Modules	19 hours for all Modules	9 hours for all Modules
CTEC Course Number:	**CTEC Federal Hours:**	**CTEC California Hours:**
1075-CE-7963 for Module 1	3 hours for Module 1	N/A for Module 1
1075-CE-7953 for Module 2	3 hours for Module 2	N/A for Module 2
1075-CE-7943 for Module 3	3 hours for Module 3	N/A for Module 3
	9 hours for all Modules	N/A for all Modules

One **complimentary copy** of this Course is provided with certain copies of CCH Federal Taxation publications. Additional copies of this Course may be ordered for $33.00 each by calling 1-800-248-3248 (ask for product 0-0977-200).

Quizzer Questions: Module 1

> Answer the True/False questions by marking a "T" or "F" on the Quizzer Answer Sheet. Answer Multiple Choice questions by indicating the appropriate letter on the Answer Sheet.

1. For 2009 and 2010, the making work pay credit reaches _____ for married couples filing jointly.

    a. $100
    b. $400
    c. $800

2. The CARS Act allows taxpayers to trade-in "clunkers" for more fuel efficient:

    a. New domestic and foreign vehicles
    b. Domestic vehicles less than 25 years old
    c. New and used domestic and foreign vehicles

3. The 2009 Recovery Act enhanced all of the following features of the first-time homebuyer credit compared to the 2008 levels **except:**

    a. Raised the maximum amount of the credit
    b. Extended application of the credit to include homes purchased outside of the United States
    c. Removed the requirement to repay the credit for most 2009 purchases

4. The new motor vehicle state and local sales tax deduction applies to:

    a. Vehicles with a combined fuel economy of 18 mpg or more
    b. Up to $49,500 of the purchase price of the vehicle
    c. Principal and interest paid on vehicle loans between February 16, 2009, and January 1, 2010

5. Under COBRA premium assistance, eligible involuntarily terminated workers pay _____ of the COBRA premium, and employers or other entities pay _____.

    a. 25 percent; 75 percent
    b. 35 percent; 65 percent
    c. 50 percent; 50 percent

6. Which transportation fringe benefit was **not** raised by the 2009 Recovery Act?

    a. Van pooling
    b. Transit passes
    c. Qualified parking

7. The Code Sec. 25C energy credit for qualifying improvements is a:

    a. Fully refundable personal credit
    b. Nonrefundable personal credit
    c. 40 percent refundable credit

8. The *Worker, Retiree, and Employer Recovery Act of 2008* (WRERA) suspended required minimum distributions (RMDs) from IRA or other tax-deferred qualified retirement plans for:

    a. 2008 distributions only
    b. 2008 as well as 2009 distributions
    c. 2009 distributions only

9. The U.S. Department of Housing and Urban Development will allow taxpayers to monetize the first-time homebuyer credit when they finance homes through a state housing agency. **True or False?**

10. Under the CARS Act, the voucher for trading-in a "clunker" for a new fuel efficient vehicle is income to the consumer. **True or False?**

11. The temporary NOL five-year carryover treatment for small businesses applies:

    a. Only to 2008 NOLs
    b. To NOLs for the 2009 and 2010 tax years
    c. To tax years through 2014

12. Under the 2009 Recovery Act, the maximum amount of bonus depreciation businesses may claim is:

   a. $10,000
   b. $25,000
   c. There is no limit on the total amount of bonus depreciation businesses may claim in a given tax year

13. Which of the following is *not* a credit that may be claimed in lieu of bonus depreciation for businesses?

   a. Increased AMT credit
   b. Additional foreign tax credit
   c. Additional research credit

14. Under the 2009 Recovery Act, businesses can elect to defer recognition of cancellation of debt income from the taxpayer's reacquisition of an applicable debt instrument in 2009 and 2010. Taxpayers making this special election can report the deferred COD income over what period?

   a. 2010 through 2015
   b. 2011 through 2016
   c. 2014 through 2018

15. For sales in 2009 or 2010, the 2009 Recovery Act temporarily reduces the holding period for S corporation to avoid built-in gain tax on assets:

   a. From 10 to 7 years
   b. From 10 to 5 years
   c. From 8 to 3 years

16. The 2009 Recovery Act enhanced the work opportunity tax credit (WOTC) to include unemployed veterans and:

   a. Disconnected youth
   b. Recipients of federal aid to dependent children
   c. Individuals older than age 70

17. To jump-start the bond market and encourage construction projects, the 2009 Recovery Act created all of the following new bond types *except:*

    a. Qualified School Construction Bonds (QSCBs)
    b. Community Development Bonds (CDBs)
    c. Build America Bonds (BABs)

18. Under the Obama Administration's proposals for international business tax reform:

    a. Research and development deductions for foreign projects would be cut
    b. Deductions for items related to overseas profits would be deferred until earnings were repatriated
    c. Taxpayers will be able to deduct more of the expenses that support their overseas operations

19. Former employers report COBRA premium assistance on the recipient's 2009 Form W-2. *True or False?*

20. The 2009 Recovery Act allows certain producers of renewable energy property to claim the investment tax credit in lieu of the Code Sec. 45 production credit. *True or False?*

21. Under Code Sec. 7216 regulations, a preparer who knowingly or recklessly uses or discloses a client's tax return information can be fined up to _____ and up to _____ of imprisonment.

    a. $500; six months
    b. $1,000; one year
    c. $10,000; three years

22. The act of making tax return information known to any person in any manner is:

    a. Preparation
    b. Disclosure
    c. Use

23. When a tax return preparer uses a contractor to operate return preparation software:

   a. The contractor is a deemed preparer subject to the requirements and penalties of Code Secs. 6713 and 7215
   b. The preparer must obtain written prior consent from the taxpayer before obtaining the service
   c. The contractor must be an enrolled agent or certified practitioner

24. Any part of a client contact list:

   a. May never be transferred to another preparer or firm
   b. May be transferred only upon disposition of the return preparation business
   c. May be transferred only to collection agencies if the clients fail to remit their return preparation fees

25. Tax return preparers in the United States who disclose Social Security number information to preparers located outside of the United States must employ data security measures such as the European Commission's Directive on Data Protection, U.S. Department of Commerce safe harbor framework for data protection, or other program known as:

   a. The SSN protection protocol
   b. Administrative information redaction system
   c. An adequate data protection safeguard

26. Duties for preparers to exercise due diligence in preparing, approving, and filing tax returns are codified in the Code of Federal Regulations as:

   a. Circular 230
   b. 45 C.F.R. best practices
   c. Private cause damages subsection rules

27. A practitioner disbarred under Office of Professional Responsibility authority may seek reinstatement upon proof of good behavior only after:

   a. Five years
   b. Four years
   c. Two years

28. Under the final regulations, for disclosed positions the preparer must have _____ (a 15 percent probability of the tax position being sustained):

a. Reasonable basis
b. Substantial authority
c. More likely than not basis

29. An accountant or attorney may disclose taxpayer information to other officers, employees, or members of the same firm in the course of providing services such as estate planning or financial statement preparation. *True or False?*

30. A preparer must obtain written consent for disclosure of tax information to a client's fiduciary when the client becomes incompetent, insolvent, or bankrupt. *True or False?*

Quizzer Questions: Module 2

31. Which of these types of loss is not generally deductible under Code Sec. 165(c)(1) limitations?

- **a.** Casualty losses
- **b.** Property theft
- **c.** Passive activity losses

32. Net operating loss deductions differ from refundable tax credits because credits:

- **a.** Provide refunds to taxpayers even when they have no income tax liability
- **b.** Tax credits only offset tax liabilities
- **c.** Tax credits may be carried over to future tax liabilities

33. Net operating losses from product liabilities, workplace liabilities, and environmental remediation may be carried back to tax liabilities for _____ .

- **a.** 4 years
- **b.** 6 years
- **c.** 10 years

34. Which of the following is **not** entitled to deduct NOLs incurred by its entity?

- **a.** Disregarded entity member
- **b.** C corporation shareholder
- **c.** Sole proprietor

35. Passive activity losses of taxpayers who do not satisfy any material participation test:

- **a.** May not offset future passive income
- **b.** Must be netted against the taxpayers' income from passive activities
- **c.** Apply at the entity level for passthrough entities

36. The maximum deduction active participants may claim against non-passive income for losses from rental real estate activities is:

   a. $20,000
   b. $25,000
   c. $100,000

37. Under the at-risk rules of Code Sec., 465, taxpayers may deduct business losses up to:

   a. The amount for which the taxpayers are at risk financially in the business
   b. $50,000 per year
   c. $100,000 per year or 25 percent of secured debt of the business

38. To satisfy requirements for qualified nonrecourse financing of real property, the loan must:

   a. Not be guaranteed or made by a federal, state, or local government
   b. Secured with the real property to which the loan applies
   c. Be convertible

39. The maximum net capital loss deductible for the current tax year by individuals, trusts, and estates is:

   a. $3,000
   b. $2,000
   c. $1,000

40. The maximum small business stock loss that a married couple may claim as an ordinary loss is:

   a. $50,000
   b. $100,000
   c. $250,000

41. For 2009, the floor for deducting a theft loss is _____; in 2010, the minimum changes to _____.

   a. $500; $100
   b. $100; $500
   c. $250; $1,000

42. Under Code Sec. 166, when a business debt becomes partially worthless:

a. The taxpayer may deduct the debt amount charged off during the tax year

b. The bad debt totals of the business are unaffected because the debt is not completely worthless

c. The business reports the debt on its return as cancellation of debt income of the debtor

43. Regular gambling withholding of _____ applies to winnings exceeding $5,000 from gambling such as lotteries, but backup withholding by gambling establishments for winnings from games such as bingo or poker is _____.

a. 15 percent; 20 percent

b. 25 percent; 28 percent

c. 30 percent; 35 percent

44. An activity is considered as conducted for-profit and not as a hobby for deduction purposes if it makes a profit for _____, including the current year.

a. Two of the last three years

b. Three of the last five years

c. Five of the last seven years

45. Corporate taxpayers can increase their net operating losses for prior years by carrying back stock losses. *True or False?*

46. The 2009 Recovery Act allows COI income from reacquisition of business debt in 2009 to be deferred until the five-year period starting in the year:

a. 2013

b. 2014

c. 2015

47. A discharge of debt arises from:

a. An identifiable event

b. A compromise to a dispute resulting in reduced payment

c. An agreement to cancel a debt

48. When the seller of property finances the sale and secures the loan using the property, the debt is called:

   a. Seller-reduced purchase price
   b. Sales price discharged debt
   c. Purchase money debt

49. The first tax attribute reduced by subtracting the amount of COI income excluded from gross income due to farm indebtedness or disaster expenses is:

   a. Net operating losses or NOL carryovers for the year of discharge
   b. Passive activity loss or credit carryovers from the year of discharge
   c. Foreign tax credit carryovers to or from the year of discharge

50. If debt forgiven on real property business debt exceeds the debtor's total adjusted basis in depreciable property:

   a. The debtor may apply the exclusions to exclude the excess from gross income
   b. The debtor must recognize COI income for the excess
   c. The debtor must increase the basis of the real property securing the debt

51. Which of the following is *not* a requirement for taking the real property business debt exclusion?

   a. Securing the debt using the real property
   b. Operating as a C corporation
   c. Satisfying criteria of qualified acquisition debt on the property

52. The discharge of debt made as a gift or bequest:

   a. Occurs when a creditor cancels debt believing that it will not be repaid
   b. Is not taxable income
   c. Creates COI income for both business and nonbusiness recipients

53. A corporation using its own stock to satisfy a debt is:

   a. Treated as though the money paid equaled the stock's fair market value
   b. Taxed on the conversion if the preferred stock's issue price is less than the value at payment
   c. Allowed a deferral on recognizing COI income for three tax years

54. The five-year deferral of COI income recognition allowed by Code Sec. 108(i) applies to:

   a. Debt incurred for investment
   b. Businesses repurchasing their own debt
   c. Personal debt, including student loans

55. The Code Sec. 108(i) election for deferral of COI income:

   a. Is made for COI income for 2009 and 2010 as a whole
   b. May be applied to selected instruments and any portion of COI income
   c. May not be taken if the IRS subsequently concludes the taxpayer has COI income

56. If a business reacquires its debt by issuing a debt instrument that has original issue discount:

   a. The OID may not be deducted during the deferral period for COI income
   b. The OID is deducted ratably through the deferral period for COI income
   c. The OID may not be deducted, even following the deferral period

57. Upon the taxpayer's termination of business activity, COI income or deductions that were previously deferred:

   a. Are accelerated and recognized
   b. The former business files subsequent returns in order to continue recognize the items during the original deferral period
   c. Receive revised bases using fair market value for tax purposes

58. A taxpayer that defers COI income on the reacquisition of debt, using an instrument with OID:

  a. Can also defer increases to earnings and profits (E&P) until the income is reported
  b. Must increase earnings and profits in the year that the COI income is realized, but can reduce E&P as the OID deductions are realized each year
  c. Must increase earnings and profits in the year realized and but cannot reduce E&P until the income is reported

59. When a taxpayer is both bankrupt and insolvent, it can claim the bankruptcy exclusion up to the amount of insolvency. *True or False?*

60. Each partner's basis in the partnership interest must be increased for COI income of the partnership, with the partner's share of income corresponding to that partner's share of the canceled debt. *True or False?*

Quizzer Questions: Module 3

61. The form of innocent spouse relief under Code Sec. 6015 for taxpayers who do not qualify for the other two types is:

   a. Equitable relief
   b. General relief
   c. Separate liability relief

62. The requesting spouse must elect general relief within _____ year(s) after the IRS provides notice of innocent spouse rights.

   a. One
   b. Two
   c. Three

63. When a requesting spouse applies for general innocent spouse relief for understatements arising from erroneous deductions on the tax return, some courts have applied:

   a. The liberal *Price* standard
   b. The single liability standard
   c. The nonfraudulent intent rule

64. Which form of innocent spouse relief does **not** allow a credit or refund to be recovered if the electing spouse pays the tax deficiency before he or she pursues the election?

   a. Equitable relief
   b. General relief
   c. Separate liability relief

65. Typically, an electing spouse requests equitable innocent spouse relief when:

   a. Funds for paying the spouses' tax liability has been misappropriated by the nonrequesting spouse
   b. The spouses understated, rather than underpaid, the tax liability
   c. The spouses filed separate returns for the tax year of the liability

66. Which of the following types of tax payments may be refunded if a requesting spouse obtains equitable innocent spouse relief?

    a. Joint payments
    b. Separate payments by the electing spouse
    c. Withholding tax paid with the joint return

67. A requesting spouse may petition a Tax Court review for denial of innocent spouse relief:

    a. If the petition is filed within a year following mailing of the final determination by the IRS
    b. That suspends the collections statute of limitations until the Tax Court decision becomes final
    c. Except in requests for equitable relief

68. Which of the following is *not* a type of relief from community property laws?

    a. Traditional relief
    b. Equitable relief
    c. Injured spouse relief

69. The formula applied in allocation of liability relief for innocent spouses equally divides the tax liability arising from disallowance of a credit between the electing and nonrequesting spouses. *True or False?*

70. A requesting spouse may be eligible for equitable innocent spouse relief for the interest imposed on his or her tax liability even when the underlying taxes have been paid. *True or False?*

71. The general conformity between federal and state tax law treatment of marital status was changed by what act?

    a. *Defense of Marriage Act*
    b. *Uniform Transfer-on-Death Securities Registration Act*
    c. *Consolidated Omnibus Budget Reconciliation Act*

72. A husband–wife married couple may be entitled to a "marriage bonus" on federal returns that is unavailable to same-sex married couples whose total income is the same if:

a. The husband–wife spouses earn income disproportionately so one spouse is taxed in a lower bracket

b. The same-sex filers have roughly equivalent incomes reported using the single status for federal returns, which taxes each partner at the same higher bracket

c. Husband–wife married couples have a higher federal standard deduction unavailable to that for two single filers

73. To be considered a qualifying relative of a supporting same-sex married couple (SSMC) spouse or domestic partner in 2009, a child may have a maximum of _____ in gross income.

a. $2,750

b. $3,650

c. $5,550

74. Which same-sex spouse or domestic partner is eligible to claim the dependency exemption on a federal return when a qualifying child lives with both partners the same amount of time during the year?

a. Only the partner having the higher adjusted gross income is eligible

b. Either partner is eligible

c. Only the partner having the lower adjusted gross income is eligible

75. For claiming head of household status, expenses of maintaining a household include:

a. Medical expenses

b. Cost of clothing

c. Property taxes and insurance

76. First-time homebuyers who are an SSMC or domestic partners claim the first-time homebuyer credit for 2009 by:

a. Each claiming half of the credit amount if their combined income does not exceed the modified AGI cap, just as husband–wife couples filing separately do

b. Allocating the credit using any reasonable method, regardless of relative contributions or ownership percentages in the home

c. Allocating three-quarters of the credit to the higher-income spouse or partner

77. An advantage under the passive loss limitation rules applies to single filers such as an SSMC or domestic partners because, unlike husband–wife joint filers, each actively participating partner may deduct up to _____ in rental real estate losses.

    a. $10,000
    b. $25,000
    c. $35,000

78. All of the following benefits are restricted for SSMCs and domestic partners under the Defense of Marriage Act (DOMA) and subsequent laws **except:**

    a. Deduction of palimony payments made by the donor
    b. Tax-free rollovers from qualified plans to a same-sex spouse or partner
    c. Social Security benefits to the child of a deceased parent if the child is not legally or biologically related to the deceased

79. Because states recognizing same-sex married couples usually base joint return computations on figures from a joint federal return, SSMCs often prepare a hypothetical joint federal Form 1040 as a basis for their state return, but file separate Form 1040s for their actual federal return. **True or False?**

80. The federal child tax credit may only be claimed by the SSMC spouse or domestic partner who does **not** file as head of household on federal Form 1040. **True or False?**

81. Joint-filing couples or individuals can use up to _____ of net capital losses each year to offset their ordinary income.

    a. $1,000
    b. $3,000
    c. $5,000

82. For 2009, the maximum tax rate on wages is _____; capital gains are taxed at a maximum rate of _____.

    a. 35 percent; 15 percent
    b. 30 percent; 15 percent
    c. 25 percent; 20 percent

83. The portion of annuity payments not included in gross income is:

   a. The payment times the exclusion ratio
   b. The percentage of adjusted basis of the annuity balance at commencement of payments
   c. The percentage of payments constituting appreciation of the assets

84. A disadvantage of annuity contracts compared with other retirement investment types is:

   a. A distribution from an annuity is taxed as ordinary income, not at a lower dividend or capital gains tax rate
   b. The income stream of annuities fluctuates more than distributions from 401(k) plans or securities' dividends
   c. Annuity contracts have fixed age requirements for commencing distributions, whereas other retirement plans such as traditional IRAs or 401(k) plans do not

85. Employees younger than age 50 may for the 2009 tax year elect to defer income in their 401(k) plan up to 100 percent of eligible compensation or up to _____.

   a. $12,000
   b. $16,500
   c. $22,000

86. After-tax contributions are made by employees to their Roth 401(k) plan's:

   a. Defined benefit account
   b. Designated Roth account
   c. Deferred vesting Roth account

87. Hardship distributions from 401(k) plans:

   a. May be replaced without penalty within six months
   b. Are taxed as ordinary income and subject to income tax withholding
   c. May not be applied to costs of casualty damage to an individual's primary residence

88. Unless the loan is used to make a first-time home purchase, loan funds from a 401(k) plan:

    a. May not exceed $10,000
    b. Are treated identically with hardship distributions
    c. Must be repaid within five years to avoid income taxation and the early withdrawal penalty

89. The maximum deductible contribution to a traditional IRA for individuals younger than age 55 is _____ for 2009.

    a. $5,000
    b. $6,000
    c. $10,000

90. The *Worker, Retiree, and Employer Recovery Act of 2008*:

    a. Prohibits terminated employees from contributing to a traditional IRA in 2009
    b. Allows traditional IRA distribution recipients not to take a required minimum distribution in 2009
    c. Prohibits traditional IRA distributions for 2009

91. To report a loss in a Roth IRA account, the individual:

    a. Simply lists the loss as an itemized deduction on his or her tax return for the year the loss occurs
    b. Must liquidate all of his or her Roth IRAs (but not traditional IRAs)
    c. Takes the loss as a long-term capital loss at the time distributions commence

92. All of the following are new rulings and guidance in White House initiatives for retirement planning issued in September 2009 *except:*

    a. Converting unused vacation time into qualified retirement plan contributions
    b. Streamlining automatic enrollment for both SIMPLE IRAs and 401(k) plans
    c. Permitting rollovers of traditional 401(k) account funds into Roth 401(k) accounts

93. Elective 401(k) employee contributions are not subject to income tax at the time of deferral but are taxable wages for other (e.g., employment) tax purposes. *True or False?*

94. Employers may make matching contributions to Roth IRAs provided they stay within the same maximum as for safe-harbor 401(k) plans. *True or False?*

95. When an individual reaches age 70½ he or she cannot continue to make contributions to a traditional IRA, even if he or she continues to work. *True or False?*

TOP FEDERAL TAX ISSUES FOR 2010 CPE COURSE   (0796-3)

Module 1: Answer Sheet

NAME _____

COMPANY NAME _____

STREET _____

CITY, STATE, & ZIP CODE _____

BUSINESS PHONE NUMBER _____

E-MAIL ADDRESS _____

DATE OF COMPLETION _____

CFP REGISTRANT ID (for Certified Financial Planners) _____

CRTP ID (for CTEC Credit only) _____(CTEC Course # 1075-CE-7963)

On the next page, please answer the Multiple Choice questions by indicating the appropriate letter next to the corresponding number. Please answer the True/False questions by marking "T" or "F" next to the corresponding number.

A $72.00 processing fee wil be charged for each user submitting Module 1 for grading.

Please remove both pages of the Answer Sheet from this book and return them with your completed Evaluation Form to CCH at the address below. You may also fax your Answer Sheet to CCH at 773-866-3084.

You may also go to **www.cchtestingcenter.com** to complete your Quizzer online.

METHOD OF PAYMENT:

☐ Check Enclosed   ☐ Visa   ☐ Master Card   ☐ AmEx

☐ Discover   ☐ CCH Account* _____

Card No. _____ Exp. Date _____

Signature _____

* Must provide CCH account number for this payment option

EXPRESS GRADING: Please fax my Course results to me by 5:00 p.m. the business day following your receipt of this Answer Sheet. By checking this box I authorize CCH to charge $19.00 for this service.

☐ Express Grading $19.00   Fax No. _____

●.CCH
a Wolters Kluwer business

Mail or fax to:
CCH Continuing Education Department
4025 W. Peterson Ave.
Chicago, IL 60646-6085
1-800-248-3248
Fax: 773-866-3084

TOP FEDERAL TAX ISSUES FOR 2010 CPE COURSE   (0796-3)

Module 1: Answer Sheet

Please answer the Multiple Choice questions by indicating the appropriate letter next to the corresponding number. Please answer the True/False questions by marking "T" or "F" next to the corresponding number.

1. ___	9. ___	17. ___	24. ___
2. ___	10. ___	18. ___	25. ___
3. ___	11. ___	19. ___	26. ___
4. ___	12. ___	20. ___	27. ___
5. ___	13. ___	21. ___	28. ___
6. ___	14 ___	22. ___	29. ___
7. ___	15 ___	23. ___	30. ___
8. ___	16. ___		

Please complete the Evaluation Form (located after the Module 3 Answer Sheet) and return it with this Quizzer Answer Sheet to CCH at the address on the previous page. Thank you.

TOP FEDERAL TAX ISSUES FOR 2010 CPE COURSE   0795-3)

Module 2: Answer Sheet

NAME _____

COMPANY NAME _____

STREET _____

CITY, STATE, & ZIP CODE _____

BUSINESS PHONE NUMBER _____

E-MAIL ADDRESS _____

DATE OF COMPLETION _____

CFP REGISTRANT ID (for Certified Financial Planners) _____

CRTP ID (for CTEC Credit only) _____ (CTEC Course # 1075-CE-7953)

On the next page, please answer the Multiple Choice questions by indicating the appropriate letter next to the corresponding number. Please answer the True/False questions by marking "T" or "F" next to the corresponding number.

A $72.00 processing fee wil be charged for each user submitting Module 2 for grading.

Please remove both pages of the Answer Sheet from this book and return them with your completed Evaluation Form to CCH at the address below. You may also fax your Answer Sheet to CCH at 773-866-3084.

You may also go to **www.cchtestingcenter.com** to complete your Quizzer online.

METHOD OF PAYMENT:

☐ Check Enclosed   ☐ Visa   ☐ Master Card   ☐ AmEx

☐ Discover   ☐ CCH Account* _____

Card No. _____ Exp. Date _____

Signature _____

* Must provide CCH account number for this payment option

EXPRESS GRADING: Please fax my Course results to me by 5:00 p.m. the business day following your receipt of this Answer Sheet. By checking this box I authorize CCH to charge $19.00 for this service.

☐ Express Grading $19.00   Fax No. _____

⊙.CCH
a Wolters Kluwer business

Mall or fax to:
CCH Continuing Education Department
4025 W. Peterson Ave.
Chicago, IL 60646-6085
1-800-248-3248
Fax: 773-866-3084

TOP FEDERAL TAX ISSUES FOR 2010 CPE COURSE   (0795-3)

Module 2: Answer Sheet

Please answer the Multiple Choice questions by indicating the appropriate letter next to the corresponding number. Please answer the True/False questions by marking "T" or "F" next to the corresponding number.

31. ___	39. ___	47. ___	54. ___
32. ___	40. ___	48. ___	55. ___
33. ___	41. ___	49. ___	56. ___
34. ___	42. ___	50. ___	57. ___
35. ___	43. ___	51. ___	58. ___
36. ___	44. ___	52. ___	59. ___
37. ___	45. ___	53. ___	60. ___
38. ___	46. ___		

Please complete the Evaluation Form (located after the Module 3 Answer Sheet) and return it with this Quizzer Answer Sheet to CCH at the address on the previous page. Thank you.

TOP FEDERAL TAX ISSUES FOR 2010 CPE COURSE   (0794-3)

Module 3: Answer Sheet

NAME _____

COMPANY NAME _____

STREET _____

CITY, STATE, & ZIP CODE _____

BUSINESS PHONE NUMBER _____

E-MAIL ADDRESS _____

DATE OF COMPLETION _____

CFP REGISTRANT ID (for Certified Financial Planners) _____

CRTP ID (for CTEC Credit only) _____ (CTEC Course # 1075-CE-7943)

On the next page, please answer the Multiple Choice questions by indicating the appropriate letter next to the corresponding number. Please answer the True/False questions by marking "T" or "F" next to the corresponding number.

A $84.00 processing fee wil be charged for each user submitting Module 3 for grading.

Please remove both pages of the Answer Sheet from this book and return them with your completed Evaluation Form to CCH at the address below. You may also fax your Answer Sheet to CCH at 773-866-3084.

You may also go to **www.cchtestingcenter.com** to complete your Quizzer online.

METHOD OF PAYMENT:

☐ Check Enclosed   ☐ Visa   ☐ Master Card   ☐ AmEx
☐ Discover   ☐ CCH Account* _____

Card No. _____ Exp. Date _____

Signature _____

* Must provide CCH account number for this payment option

EXPRESS GRADING: Please fax my Course results to me by 5:00 p.m. the business day following your receipt of this Answer Sheet. By checking this box I authorize CCH to charge $19.00 for this service.

☐ Express Grading $19.00   Fax No. _____

●.CCH
a Wolters Kluwer business

Mail or fax to:
CCH Continuing Education Department
4025 W. Peterson Ave.
Chicago, IL 60646-6085
1-800-248-3248
Fax: 773-866-3084

TOP FEDERAL TAX ISSUES FOR 2010 CPE COURSE   (0794-3)

Module 3: Answer Sheet

Please answer the Multiple Choice questions by indicating the appropriate letter next to the corresponding number. Please answer the True/False questions by marking "T" or "F" next to the corresponding number.

61. ___	70. ___	79. ___	88. ___
62. ___	71. ___	80. ___	89. ___
63. ___	72. ___	81. ___	90. ___
64. ___	73. ___	82. ___	91. ___
65. ___	74. ___	83. ___	92. ___
66. ___	75. ___	84. ___	93. ___
67. ___	76. ___	85. ___	94. ___
68. ___	77. ___	86. ___	95. ___
69. ___	78. ___	87. ___	

Please complete the Evaluation Form (located after the Module 3 Answer Sheet) and return it with this Quizzer Answer Sheet to CCH at the address on the previous page. Thank you.

TOP FEDERAL TAX ISSUES FOR 2010 CPE COURSE   (0977-2)

Evaluation Form

Please take a few moments to fill out and mail or fax this evaluation to CCH so that we can better provide you with the type of self-study programs you want and need. Thank you.

About This Program

1. Please circle the number that best reflects the extent of your agreement with the following statements:

	Strongly Agree				Strongly Disagree
a. The Course objectives were met.	5	4	3	2	1
b. This Course was comprehensive and organized.	5	4	3	2	1
c. The content was current and technically accurate.	5	4	3	2	1
d. This Course was timely and relevant.	5	4	3	2	1
e. The prerequisite requirements were appropriate.	5	4	3	2	1
f. This Course was a valuable learning experience.	5	4	3	2	1
g. The Course completion time was appropriate.	5	4	3	2	1

2. This Course was most valuable to me because of:

_____ Continuing Education credit   _____ Convenience of format
_____ Relevance to my practice/   _____ Timeliness of subject matter
     employment   _____ Reputation of author
_____ Price
_____ Other (please specify) _____

3. How long did it take to complete this Course? (Please include the total time spent reading or studying reference materials and completing CPE Quizzer).

Module 1 _____   Module 2 _____   Module 3 _____

4. What do you consider to be the strong points of this Course?

5. What improvements can we make to this Course?

TOP FEDERAL TAX ISSUES FOR 2010 CPE COURSE   (0977-2)
Evaluation Form *cont'd*

General Interests

1. Preferred method of self-study instruction:
   _____ Text _____ Audio _____ Computer-based/Multimedia _____ Video

2. What specific topics would you like CCH to develop as self-study CPE programs? _____
   _____
   _____
   _____

3. Please list other topics of interest to you _____
   _____
   _____

About You

1. Your profession:

   _____ CPA   _____ Enrolled Agent
   _____ Attorney   _____ Tax Preparer
   _____ Financial Planner _____ Other (please specify)
                           _____

2. Your employment:

   _____ Self-employed   _____ Public Accounting Firm
   _____ Service Industry _____ Non-Service Industry
   _____ Banking/Finance   _____ Government
   _____ Education   _____ Other _____

3. Size of firm/corporation:

   _____ 1 _____ 2-5 _____ 6-10 _____ 11-20 _____ 21-50 _____ 51+

4. Your Name _____
   _Firm/Company Name _____
   Address _____
   City, State, Zip Code _____
   E-mail Address _____

THANK YOU FOR TAKING THE TIME TO COMPLETE THIS SURVEY!

NOTES

NOTES

NOTES

NOTES

NOTES

NOTES

NOTES

NOTES

NOTES

NOTES

NOTES

NOTES

NOTES